EXPERT APPROACHES
TO SPORT PSYCHOLOGY

EXPERT APPROACHES *to* SPORT PSYCHOLOGY

Applied Theories of Performance Excellence

MARK W. AOYAGI

&

ARTUR POCZWARDOWSKI

Editors

UNIVERSITY OF DENVER

Fitness Information Technology
a Division of the International Center
for Performance Excellence
West Virginia University
262 Coliseum, WVU-CPASS
PO Box 6116
Morgantown, WV 26506-6116

Copyright © 2012, West Virginia University

All rights reserved.

Reproduction or use of any portion of this publication by any mechanical, electronic, or other means is prohibited without written permission of the publisher.

Library of Congress Card Catalog Number: 2012941260

ISBN: 978-1-935412-36-6

Cover Design: Bellerophon Productions
Cover Image: Courtesy of Yienkeat. Image from BigStockPhoto.com
Production Editor: Jennifer Bowman
Copyeditor: Jennifer Bowman
Typesetter: Craig Hines
Proofreader: Rachel Tibbs
Indexer: Rachel Tibbs
Printed by: Publishers' Graphics

10 9 8 7 6 5 4 3 2 1

Fitness Information Technology
A Division of the International Center for Performance Excellence
West Virginia University
262 Coliseum, WVU–CPASS
PO Box 6116
Morgantown, WV 26506–6116

800.477.4348 (toll free)
304.293.6888 (phone)
304.293.6658 (fax)
Email: fitcustomerservice@mail.wvu.edu
Website: www.fitinfotech.com

Table of Contents

List of Figures and Tables

Dedication

MA: This book is dedicated to my sport psychology mentors: Rick McGuire and Keith Henschen; and my close friends and colleagues Artur Poczwardowski and Steve Portenga. Without you this book would not have been possible. A sincere thank you to all of the chapter authors who graciously contributed so much of their time to make this work what it is. And to my family: Staci, Mom, and Dad—you are responsible for my ability to reach anything close to performance excellence.

AP: I dedicate my work and growth I have experienced while adding to Mark's vision on this book to my professional and life mentors: Keith Henschen and Jim Barott. All of the chapter authors and to Bruce Ogilvie: thank you for leading the field with your insight, art, science, and personality, all of which inspire so many applied sport psychologists. Thanks so very much, Mark, you have made this project so fulfilling and fun to contribute to. And to my Family: the joy of being together shines through my passion for work and excellence.

Preface

Mark W. Aoyagi and Artur Poczwardowski

University of Denver

In many significant ways, the practice of applied sport psychology that focuses on performance excellence has progressed more rapidly than educational institutions in their curriculum prescriptions and scientific study in its capture of effective sport psychology theory. While this progress has benefited the field, it is due almost entirely to the individual efforts of the innovative few who have earned international acclaim and publicity for their work. There have been several articles and chapters dedicated to recording the history of sport psychology and its significant founders, organizations, research, and academic training (e.g., Cox, 2007; Wiggins, 1984; Williams & Straub, 2010). However, there has not been a similar cataloguing for applied sport psychology and its practitioners. *Expert Approaches to Sport Psychology* attempts to fill this gap by preserving the ecologically valid conceptual frameworks and theories developed specifically to explain and understand performance excellence. In so doing, current and future practitioners will benefit from the accumulated wisdom of the greatest sport psychology minds.

Expert Approaches to Sport Psychology will be entering the sport psychology literature at a critical junction for three reasons: 1) with the notable exception of Bruce Ogilvie, all of the list of possible authors we accumulated were still capable of writing their own chapters, 2) many of the practitioners represented are beginning to exit the dedicated service delivery phase of their careers and transition to a more reflective period while still maintaining practices, and 3) correspondingly, the field is simultaneously at a period of transition and a period of stagnation. The transition is represented by the metaphorical passing of the torch from many of the practitioners represented in *Expert Approaches to Sport Psychology* to younger generations seeking to continue to advance the profession. The stagnation can best be represented by an article entitled "Future directions in psychological skills training" by Vealey. The article was first published in 1988 and then was republished in

2007. While Vealey may have had extraordinary powers of perception in 1988, it would be difficult to classify the republishing of the article 20 years later—with the same title—as representing anything other than stagnation in the field.

We believe this seeming stagnation is due to the lack of overarching theories attempting to understand and explain performance excellence. Certainly there have been tremendous advances in the science and practice of sport psychology in the intervening years between Vealey's (1988; 2007) articles, yet these advances have occurred primarily in terms of interventions, techniques, and methods (see Aoyagi & Poczwardowski, in press; and Poczwardowski, Sherman, & Ravizza, 2004 for a more thorough explanation of the different levels of professional philosophy). *Expert Approaches to Sport Psychology* seeks to turn our attention back to higher levels of abstraction, identified as theoretical paradigm by Poczwardowski et al. (2004), to gain a more complete understanding of the mental and emotional processes necessary to facilitate performance excellence.

Historically, sport psychology models have either been atheoretical or have relied upon theories of personality developed in psychology for the purpose of understanding psychological dysfunction/pathology to explain performance. *Expert Approaches to Sport Psychology* will be the first attempt to collect and document the preeminent practitioners' implicit theories of performance excellence and explicate them in an organized and unified manner. As these theories will now be available for scientific scrutiny, we anticipate an exciting period of growth and validation for both the discipline and profession of sport psychology—specifically, the empirical exploration of theories of performance excellence and the provision of greater structure, meaning, and utility to models, methods, and techniques, respectively.

One of the most daunting challenges in editing *Expert Approaches to Sport Psychology* was determining who to invite to contribute. This was too crucial a task to rely solely upon our own judgments, and thus we are grateful to our colleagues and many of the chapter authors with whom we consulted. Ultimately, our criteria involved the following: a) Ericsson's (Ericsson, Krampe, & Tesch-Römer, 1993) guidelines of 10 years and 10,000 hours for attainment of expertise; b) a significant portion of career spent practicing sport psychology; c) meaningful contributions to the profession through books, articles, or conference presentations; and d) international recognition as preeminent practitioners. We openly acknowledge that there were biases in this process, with two of the most obvious being toward individuals with whom we trained, and individuals in English speaking countries and particularly in North America. The seeming underrepresentation of women consultants reflects the gender composition of the delimited sample. With help from our colleagues, we did our best to mitigate these biases, but they were present nonetheless and should be considered by the readers.

Expert Approaches to Sport Psychology provides these distinguished practitioners of sport psychology an opportunity to reflect on their years of applied work in relation to four specific areas:

1. Autobiographical sketch and how their life experiences influenced their philosophies,
2. Theory of performance excellence,
3. Theory of performance breakdowns, and
4. Consulting process.

In consolidating and recording this knowledge, we, the beneficiaries of this collective wisdom, are afforded a single volume bringing together valuable and essential understandings typically disseminated through oral accounts, such as conference presentations and university classes conducted by these prominent consultants. While emphasizing the importance of the consultant "voice" (Sparkes, 2002), this book is a first step toward documenting the structured and pre-contemplated "stories" of emerging theories of performance behavior with attention to descriptive detail. Such detailed descriptions typically precede the more abstract explanatory narratives of formal theories that are tested in basic and applied research (Brodbeck, 1963).

The first section of each chapter is an autobiographical sketch including the author's background, training, and significant experiences that influenced his/her unique approach to the practice of sport psychology. Not only will this section give readers a more intimate connection with the authors, but it is also essential to provide a greater contextual understanding of how and why the authors' approaches developed.

The next two sections of each chapter are the heart and soul of *Expert Approaches to Sport Psychology*. In them, the authors share their theories of performance excellence and performance breakdowns that have been developed over countless hours of direct observation, scientific study, and practical application. Included are descriptions of the psychological, emotional, and behavioral skills and conditions that facilitate performance excellence, as well as the common issues that prevent people from attaining it. These consultants' experiential understandings will complement and add to approaches such as resonance (Newburg, Kimiecik, Durand-Bush, & Doell, 2002) and flow (Jackson & Csikszentmihalyi, 1999) to further our understanding of conditions facilitating optimal performance, yet not necessarily captured only by optimal psychological states.

The fourth section of each chapter is a description of the typical consulting processes utilized by the practitioners. Interested readers will gain an understanding of the practicalities of productive working relationships, what is addressed in consultation (e.g., sport performance, interpersonal relationships, quality of life), and techniques used to facilitate the client's understanding, growth, and performance. This section is the pragmatic companion to the consultants' theories, and articulates how they go about implementing their theories in consultation.

Each chapter concludes with a self-reflective account of the unique aspects of the author's consulting style, a representative case study that illustrates the author's approach, and a recommended readings list for further exploration of the books and articles that were influential in the development of their perspectives. The intent here is for readers to get a genuine feel for the authors' work and to gain additional insights into their practices. Consistent with this notion, our editing prioritized authenticity of each author's voice over attempts to standardize the volume as a whole. Certainly some approaches and practices will resonate more with a given reader than others, and when this is the case the reader will have additional resources to delve into.

We believe there are many benefits to be gained by this detailed exploration of the works of our preeminent practitioners, but perhaps most important is a first step toward creating comprehensive, functional theories of performance excellence. A quick perusal of sport psychology textbooks reveals a largely intervention-based approach to the teaching and understanding of sport psychology (e.g., Andersen, 2000; Williams, 2010). In other words, aspiring practitioners are taught the canon of sport psychology skills (Andersen, 2009) in a piecemeal approach (the "what"), but little is written about conceptualizing the "who," "when," "why," and "how" of utilizing (or not) these techniques. In order for such conceptualizing to occur, we are in need of overarching theories of performance excellence to guide and structure our models, methods, and techniques.

The atheoretical, intervention-based approach is in stark contrast to one of sport psychology's parent disciplines, psychology, where graduate students have drilled into them the necessity of grounding conceptualizations and interventions in an accepted theoretical framework. *Expert Approaches to Sport Psychology* will provide ecologically valid theories allowing for synthesis and integration into overarching frameworks that can then be scientifically studied and empirically tested. Thus, it is our hope that this text will not only preserve the legacies of these practitioners, but also further their dedicated efforts in advancing the field.

As a final note prior to our esteemed chapter authors, the words of historian Will Durant (2002) in his chapter entitled "A Shameless Worship of Heroes" seem apt:

> I say *shameless*, for I know how unfashionable it is now to acknowledge in life or history any genius loftier than ourselves. Our democratic dogma has leveled not only all voters but all leaders; we delight to show that living geniuses are only mediocrities, and that dead ones are myths. (p. 5)

Readers of *Expert Approaches to Sport Psychology* will hopefully be able to avoid the tempting, but ultimately fruitless, desire to bring these preeminent practitioners down to our level; and rather will delight in the genius of their work whether we agree with it or not. This is not to argue against subjecting the ideas presented to rigorous examination as was communicated in the preceding paragraphs, but it is to say that there is inspiration in each of the authors' work which may not be easily quantified or empirically captured. Thus, *Expert Approaches to Sport Psychology* will serve two equally important missions: a) preserving the applied legacies of the authors in their own words, which will guide and inspire current and future practitioners, and b) presenting enough descriptive detail for deriving hypotheses, which will allow for the authors' theories to be scientifically studied. We hope you enjoy the journey as much as we did.

References

Andersen, M. B. (Ed.) (2000). *Doing sport psychology*. Champaign, IL: Human Kinetics.

Andersen, M. B. (2009). The "canon" of psychological skills training for enhancing performance. In K. F. Hays (Ed.), *Performance psychology in action* (pp. 11–34). Washington, DC: American Psychological Association.

Aoyagi, M. W., & Poczwardowski, A. (in press). Models of sport psychology practice and delivery: A review. In S. D. Mellalieu & S. Hanton (Eds.), *Professional practice in sport psychology: A review*. London, UK: Routledge.

Brodbeck, M. (1963). Logic and scientific method in research on teaching. In N. L. Gage (Ed.), *Handbook of research in teaching* (pp. 44–93). New York, NY: Rand-McNally.

Cox, R. H. (2007). *Sport psychology: Concepts and applications* (6th ed.). New York, NY: McGraw-Hill.

Durant, W. (2002). *The greatest minds and ideas of all time*. New York, NY: Simon & Schuster.

Ericsson, K. A., Krampe, R. T., & Tesch-Römer, C. (1993). The role of deliberate practice in the acquisition of expert performance. *Psychological Review, 100*(3), 363–406.

Jackson, S. A., & Csikszentmihalyi, M. (1999). *Flow in sports.* Champaign, IL: Human Kinetics.

Newburg, D., Kimiecik, J., Durand-Bush, N., & Doell, K. (2002). The role of resonance in performance excellence and life engagement. *Journal of Applied Sport Psychology, 14,* 249–267.

Poczwardowski, A., Sherman, C. P., & Ravizza, K. (2004). Professional philosophy in the sport psychology service delivery: Building on theory and practice. *The Sport Psychologist, 18,* 445–463.

Sparkes, A. C. (2002). *Telling tales in sport and physical activity: A qualitative journey.* Champaign, IL: Human Kinetics.

Wiggins, D. K. (1984). The history of sport psychology in North America. In J. M. Silva & R. S. Weinberg (Eds.), *Psychological foundations of sport* (pp. 9–22). Champaign, IL: Human Kinetics.

Williams, J. M. (Ed.) (2010). *Applied sport psychology: Personal growth to peak performance* (6th ed.). New York, NY: McGraw-Hill.

Williams, J. M., & Straub, W. F. (2010). Sport psychology: Past, present, future. In J. M. Williams (Ed.), *Applied sport psychology: Personal growth to peak performance* (6th ed.) (pp. 1–17). New York, NY: McGraw-Hill.

Dr. Gloria Balague

UNIVERSITY OF ILLINOIS AT CHICAGO

Dr. Gloria Balague is a clinical assistant professor in the Psychology Department of the University of Illinois at Chicago. She is a native of Barcelona, Spain, and has been a consultant for US Track and Field since 1989. Gloria has accompanied the team to Olympic and World Championships and continues her involvement both at the elite level as well as in the Coaches' Education Program. Besides track and field, Gloria has worked with USA Gymnastics and USA Field Hockey.

Dr. Balague is co-founder, with Dr. Hellison, of the TPSR-Alliance (Teaching Personal and Social Responsibility through Sport), and is invested in finding a feasible model of competitive sport for children that preserves and enhances the educational values of sport and physical activity. She has authored numerous articles and chapters in sport psychology and has been keynote speaker at the International Olympic Congress (Australia, 2000), the European Conference in Sport Psychology (Denmark, 2003), and the Latin American Congress of Sport Psychology (Chile, 2006). She is the current president of APA Division 47.

AUTOBIOGRAPHICAL SKETCH

When I think about my background, both personally and professionally, I think in terms of a "before" and an "after": before I left Spain or came to the US, and after. Leaving my country and adjusting to a new place was definitely a difficult thing, but I believe it helped me understand transitions better, and that turned out to be very helpful.

I grew up in a family that valued practicing sports and academics. My father was one of the first sport medicine physicians in Spain, and he held the same expectations for me as he did for my brothers. I studied psychology, but at that time it did not yet distinguish specialties, so I studied a bit of everything. During my schooling in Spain, I sought a practicum site and ended up at the National Sports Medicine Center, associated to the Olympic Training Center where I stayed until I came to the US.

At the National Sports Medicine Center, I had daily contact with swimming, track and field, and modern pentathlon athletes and their coaches. Other athletes, such as those from the alpine skiing team and several members of the mountain climbing team preparing for expeditions to Mount Everest, would come to the Center twice yearly and be evaluated. Psychology was a routine part of the evaluation and it included measures of coordination, speed, reaction time, depth perception, and concentration along with the then standard personality instruments such as the 16PF. Team sports were also given a *Sociogram* to measure group structure and communication patterns. I did not know very much at the start, but I learned a lot there.

From that position, I transitioned to running the Social Sciences Department at the first College of Physical Education. Until then, PE was not a college degree and it was segregated by gender. At the same time, I met the national swimming coach who would soon become my husband and got to see the stress of a coach's position from the inside! I was vice dean of the college when I left Spain, and after a few months I had the status of graduate student at the University of Illinois, Chicago (UIC). A PhD in clinical and social psychology was my choice because I could not imagine trying to understand the individual without the context of the group or environment. Sport psychology was then close to becoming a casualty of the clinical training demands, besides the fact that no one at UIC had any interest in it. For my dissertation I decided to pursue my original passion again, and that choice felt like a real conscious commitment to sport psychology. Afterward I worked for several years at Cook County Hospital and it seemed easy to stay in the health psychology/clinical field, but I was determined to continue with sport psychology and performed work "on the side."

Serendipity worked its way to me when I attended a sport psychology conference in Washington, DC. I was placed in a group discussing the case of a hurdler. I had previously worked with hurdlers and their coaches in Spain, so I actively participated in the discussion. As it turned out, the head of sports medicine for USA Track & Field was sitting in that group and invited me to collaborate with them. In 1990, I traveled with the junior track and field team and afterward was tagged for accompanying the team to the 1992 Olympic Games to be held in my home town of Barcelona.

I have also worked with other national teams such as rhythmic gymnastics and women's field hockey. At UIC I started, also quite accidentally, to work with the baseball team and that provided a different experience, not only because of the age and level of the players, but because of the chance to have a long term relationship with a program. I enjoy that work immensely! I feel that working with coaches is a more effective way to use our resources, and I have learned to have an enormous amount of respect for them.

Recently, I have become very involved with youth sports as a result of my work with Don Hellison (www.TPSR-alliance.org). Through our collaboration I am convinced that our profession can be very effective if we can help demonstrate that coaching young athletes to be responsible, to set goals for themselves, and to be independent thinkers and good teammates, will ultimately result in better citizens and thus better performers, even at the elite level. Looking toward the future, we have a lot of ground to cover.

THEORY OF PERFORMANCE EXCELLENCE

Years ago, I would have said that performance excellence is achieved by those athletes who possess the following characteristics:

HIGH DEGREE OF SELF-AWARENESS. They are able to describe what they are doing, both from a physical as well as from a psychological perspective. They can, in general, describe what thoughts were in their minds at a certain time, are aware of their emotional reactions and can also sense where their body is in space, discriminating between what they wanted to do and what they actually did.

MOTIVATION TO ACHEIVE. The demands of high level performance require that athletes be really motivated to achieve success. Just loving the sport may not be enough because we see athletes who love to train but do not have a great desire to succeed, and it is harder for those athletes to reach performance excellence. Of course, here we are defining from the outside what performance excellence is. The individual definition of the term remains a very important point that we, as sport psychologists, cannot ignore or we run the risk of imposing our definition and thus setting the goals for the athlete. I would define motivation to achieve as the commitment to pursue athletic excellence, and the willingness to put forth the effort and to prioritize that goal over other (also likeable) options.

CONFIDENCE. An athlete who decides to pursue excellence, by definition, has some degree of belief that he or she is capable of it. The resilience of that belief is the base of confidence. Successful athletes are able to tolerate periods of time without results if they know or trust that they are on the right path. It is the sum of the two types of beliefs described by Nideffer (1985): faith (belief in the absence of results) and confidence (belief based in the results achieved) that will result in the most resilient and consistent athlete.

FLEXIBILITY. High levels of confidence allow an athlete to tolerate slow progress or lack of immediate results. A very motivated and confident athlete can also deal with the ambiguity and uncertainty inherent in major competitions such as weather delays, international differences in the interpretation of rules, opponent or lane assignments viewed as unfavorable, etc. The opposite extreme of the continuum, rigidity, allows the athlete to perform only when the conditions are right, which encompasses an uncontrollable set of events.

DISCIPLINE. I consider it a behavioral expression of motivation. Athletes who say they want to perform at their highest level, but do not do the things they need to do to get to that level, have competing motivations (social or personal) that interfere. Discipline alone can be a double-edged sword: Some athletes are extremely disciplined because that is what is required of them or because that is what is expected of them (coach, parents, etc.); thus, in neither case would it be an expression of intrinsic motivation.

All of the previously mentioned characteristics can be bettered in some way when working with an athlete who wants to improve them. There are going to be great interpersonal differences, but success is often achieved by different combinations of these qualities so that, for example, one athlete with less self-awareness can make up for it with more motivation and a better work ethic. Motivation must exist within the athlete, but even motivated athletes can learn ways to stay on track and better direct and use their efforts. Sometimes extrinsic motivation, when it is very powerful, has great intrinsic implications and can function as well as intrinsic motivation. We have seen examples of this in athletes of certain countries or economic situations where athletic success is one of the main ways for the athlete and his or her family to achieve a better socio-economic status and have learning and travel options not otherwise available to them. Once the situation changes, these rewards lose their motivating power, which is one of the issues noticed by some very successful foreign coaches. When they tried to replicate a method that worked in a certain socio-political environment with US athletes, they had very different results, with people leaving or refusing to comply, and generally failing to achieve performance excellence.

Some of the specific issues, such as flexibility, are particularly susceptible to practice and should be included as part of the training regimen. Coaches should work these issues into their practices (e.g., long or short warm-ups, delays, position changes, sun in your eyes). This is also an effective area of collaboration between sport psychologists and coaches.

Confidence is a more complex variable and it must be balanced with a sense of challenge. Some special cases are the early excellent performers—young athletes who are better, physically and technically, than their counterparts. These gifted athletes grow up believing that success means beating everyone else by a lot with minimal effort, and they can get caught in the trap of not taking the opponent seriously. The other risk is that, once they start facing competition of the same quality as their own, these athletes may re-examine their self appraisal and believe that they are not as good as they once thought, lose confidence, and abandon competition for the wrong reasons. Teams who face a lesser caliber opponent are also at risk of underperforming if they perceive they do not need to use all of their skills; high confidence and low sense of challenge often combine to mean low effort, and in sport that is always a dangerous proposition. So the task for the coach and for the sport psychologist is to highlight an individual (or team) goal that is challenging, controllable, and then review the skills the athlete or team has to meet that challenge, protecting confidence but ensuring effort.

Finally, if we are talking about consistent performance excellence, I believe there is a need for some form of balance in the athlete. Good support, interpersonal relationships, and a sense of coherence between values and behaviors are needed, or like Loehr and Schwartz (2003) indicated, to maintain good performance a balance between the demands and the physical, emotional and spiritual energy is necessary. When that happens, there is a level of overall trust that allows the athlete to remain in the present and perform.

As I said earlier, this would have been my response a few years ago, but I now feel a need to qualify this answer.

THE CASE OF YOUNGER ATHLETES. I have seen younger athletes, usually in sports such as gymnastics or figure skating, who perform at an optimal level in competition until about age 12 (age limits are always relative in psychology). After that point, some of them develop fears and anxieties that were not present early on. Part of it is, of course, due to the physical changes and maturation that come with adolescence and the modification of some perceptual/motor sensations. But the main problem, I believe, is associated with the development of abstract thinking. Instead of just performing the well learned skill in an "automatic" mode, these athletes now start thinking about the performance, about its consequences (usually only in the negative, such as the possibility of injury or the possibility of failure) and try to impose a level of control that interferes with performance. So, in a way, it seems like this form of self-awareness is not productive. I believe that it is not exactly the self-awareness per se that interferes, but the fact that fear of failure and perfectionistic tendencies may be emerging. Early on, it is hard to clearly determine the issue, and it is developmentally appropriate to learn to think about one's performance, but that should be accompanied with learning the consequences of different types of thinking, and learning to choose the right type of thoughts. Often, frustrated coaches and parents say phrases such as "Do not think so much," which is not very helpful to the athlete. Instead they should help the young athlete to "think right." During the earlier years, when athletes are performing well, the ability to stay in the present appears to be one of the central skills.

THE CASE OF THE CONCRETE, NON-REFLECTIVE ATHLETE. I have worked with some athletes who are not very prone to self-reflection, who do not verbalize their feelings well and who do not pay close attention to their thoughts or moods. Early on, I tried to change the way these athletes worked, as you can imagine, with little success. Some of them performed at a consistently high level and that made me pay closer attention to their style.

Many athletes have excellent intuition, even if they cannot always clearly verbalize it. They "know" when to change strategy and do not like complex verbal prescriptions, which tend to dominate my interventions (and perhaps sport psychology in general). Perhaps at the risk of simplifying this too much, I would talk of a right brain (as opposed to left brain) dominance. These athletes recognize temporal patterns and spatial sequences but are not very good at translating them into verbal, sequential descriptions. What I have done with these athletes is, depending on their level of experience, try to simplify the process so they only focus on a few recognizable elements and free up their attention for using their perceptual and sensory skills. Images and sensations are the preferred foci of attention, and verbal reminders, if used at all, are more associated with such sensations (smooth, go hard, or even see red). In my experience, too much prescription backfires with these athletes, probably because I suggest strategies more appropriate to my perceptual style, which does not match theirs.

I was first alerted to this when an athlete on a national team asked for my help with his insomnia due to jet lag. As is standard for my procedure, I made a relaxation tape and gave it to him. The next day the athlete came and said that there was "too much talking" on the tape and that he found it distracting rather than relaxing. So after talking to him I made a new one, with few words repeated rhythmically and some soothing music. That worked well for him. Afterward, I paid more attention to how athletes described their events and their reactions, listening to whether my questions made sense to them right away or not, so I could adapt my interventions to their style.

I want to clarify that a concrete style by no means implies lower intelligence. It is just a different style of processing and expressing themselves; these athletes may appear to lack self-awareness, but this is not exactly the case.

PERFORMANCE EXCELLENCE IN TEAMS. Finding consistent performance excellence patterns in teams is much harder than in individual sports, and I remain intrigued by the rapidly changing conditions in teams that make our work much more challenging. What I have seen is that teams that perform very well are not necessarily the ones with the most individual talent. As a matter of fact, higher levels of individual talent tend to result in more individualistic behavior and lower level team performance. Just as with individual athletes, performance excellence starts in practice, and the following are the characteristics I would list as best describing successful teams: (a) Strong work ethic that also keeps alive the fun and enjoyment. These athletes work very hard and train with intensity but enjoy the process; (b) Good interpersonal relationships among teammates, on and off the field. Teams must enjoy being with and supporting one another. The team is an important entity and athletes care about it almost as much as they care about their individual performances; (c) Trust. These teams trust themselves, their teammates and their coaches. There are always disagreements with coaches, but there must exist a strong element of trust in the process for the team to perform at a high level; (d) Competitiveness or love of competition. Some teams "train" very well together, but successful teams love to compete, are energized by competition, and are not afraid of failure.

How do we get all of these characteristics together in a team? The main issue has to do with leadership within the team, and that relates both to recruiting as well as to the culture of the team. It is important for team coaches to select not just an individual with athletic talent, but also one with exceptional interpersonal qualities and values. Part of our job should be to work with coaches to develop the list of desirable traits and ways of assessing their presence or absence. Team culture also has the power to influence team dynamics by reinforcing the style that characterizes the team and helping athletes who do not fit in to move out to other teams (what Collins [2001] calls "getting off the bus"). When there is a sense of identity within the team, older athletes help the new ones develop the right approach, and that speeds up the process. For that to occur the athletes have to feel invested, feel pride in their team and believe they have a say in it, which is, of course, an issue that relies heavily on the coaching system. Finally, there is also an element of luck or uncontrollability that makes some combinations of players work great and helps them to reach excellence, while others just remain mediocre.

Even in individual sports, the impact of the team culture is major and should be addressed when looking at performance excellence. The younger the athlete, the more important the group influence is likely to be, but the impact is felt even at the elite level.

THEORY OF PERFORMANCE BREAKDOWNS

The same way that many pathways, or combinations of traits and skills, lead to performance excellence, many pathways lead to performance breakdowns.

DOING THE WORK. We have to start with athletes completing the necessary amount of work, since there is no substitute for quality practices. In the same way, confidence is mainly based on the work done, so when athletes know they have not put in the necessary effort (sometimes because of injuries, etc.) or believe the training they have done was not sufficient (they do not trust the athletic system), that undermines their confidence in a very powerful way and their performance suffers. Similar to this issue are changes in coaching that do not allow for a good enough transition phase before results are expected. Too often I have seen athletes switch to train with a renowned coach the year of the Olympic Games, without giving themselves enough time to develop a good communication system with the new coach or to absorb the new technique, etc., and it results in a decrease in performance. For post-collegiate athletes, there is an added environmental difficulty in that training conditions are sometimes substandard: There is often no "training group," and athletes have to train alone or without any one capable of pushing them. Some athletes try to coach themselves; and that is often a very difficult task because coaching oneself interferes with the ability to just perform and engages the analytic, judgmental perspective.

EXCESSIVE PRESSURE. Assuming that work has been done, the next most common source of performance breakdowns is excessive pressure. When the athlete switches from an "I CAN" to an "I HAVE TO" attitude, the result is likely to be a switch to a more "controlled" type of performance, often having as a main goal the avoidance of mistakes, which is very different from the mindset of trust and achieving performance excellence.

Excessive pressure sometimes occurs as a characterological issue: Some athletes are perfectionists and always look for the total absence of mistakes, which is not the path to performance excellence. These athletes tend to do well when there is no pressure or a reason that would explain a lower level of achievement, such as an illness, injury, etc., but the more they want to succeed, the worse they often perform.

Some of these athletes translate good practices and good performance in training into pressure, as in, "I have no excuse to perform badly." Once they are aware of the fact that they are doing well, they assume that everyone's expectations for them are of success and soon switch to the over-controlling mode. Other examples of excessive pressure are attendance of scouts to practice, parents present during an event, and players who are not starters and are given a chance to start. In these instances, the dominant thought of the athlete is some version of "I have to perform well, or else."

LACK OF SELF-AWARENESS OF SELF-CONTROL. Some of the most frustrating settings have to do with athletes who are unable to describe what happened because they do not know. A common example is athletes who are low in self-awareness not being able to accurately convey what happened when they experienced success or failure. In many instances the issue is really a lack of experience or practice at self-regulation. For example, some athletes know that they often doubt their ability to perform and fear making mistakes. A common assignment would be to help them focus on what they can do or what they did well during their last practice. If athletes tell themselves that this is what they want to do before the competition, they may report this. But wanting to do it is very different from doing it, and the intensity of their emotional response at the competition obscures everything else and many cannot remember or report what actually happened. Sometimes videotaping the athletes at the actual warm-up and competition and watching the video with them helps to start the process of awareness.

LACK OF EMOTIONAL REGULATION. Unexpected or unprepared emotions are one of the main issues that often underlie performance breakdowns. Getting angry at an official's call, unexpectedly being ahead of a "superior" opponent, or celebrating a good performance too much or too soon are all unexpected emotional reactions that an athlete cannot regulate in the moment. The emotion does not have to be negative; it just has to be the wrong focus for the moment to interfere.

MOTIVATIONAL ISSUES. I have also seen a number of motivational issues negatively impact performance when they interfere with the right focus and intensity of competition. A prime example is athletes who are angry or resentful towards their coaches or athletic system. They become conflicted with the desire to perform well and the feeling that the coach or system does not deserve the success and enjoyment that their success would give them. I have seen this especially in athletes who have an intense coach/athlete relationship like those in gymnastics or figure skating. Other motivational issues that I've seen emerge are from interviews with elite female athletes who had children: Some of them felt very ambivalent about pursuing athletic achievement when that meant separation from their children for extended periods of time.

Performance Breakdowns in Teams

Some of the issues seen in the individual athlete section would result in performance breakdowns of a team, but there are also specific issues that are unique to a team's performance breakdown.

PREPARATION PHASE TOO LONG OR INADEQUATE. Some national teams, composed of elite players from all over the country, sometimes underperform in major competitions, such as the Olympic Games, because of their pre-competition preparation. For example, one national team had moved to the city where the Olympic Games would be held a full year before the competition. Being moved out of their familiar environment and knowing only each other made for many difficult interpersonal situations, which eroded the team's chemistry and transferred negatively to the field of play. Training camps before a major competition can be helpful, but they can also be damaging if they do not allow for individual ways of managing pressure.

LACK OF ROLE CLARITY OR CONTRADICTORY GOALS. Effective team performance requires the synchronization of players having to fulfill different and complementary roles. Teams in which role clarity is lacking may get disorganized and end up having sub-par performances. Sometimes coaches describe this as a lack of leadership on the team, or it is sometimes a consequence of players having individual goals that do not match the team's goal. I have often seen teams with many talented individual players underperform for that reason. One of the most successful US Track and Field teams was one that lacked the "superstars" in a major international competition, but where the staff and the athletes had a common goal of supporting everyone else and performing to the best of their abilities. This made for one of the most enjoyable trips!

CONSULTING PROCESS

I have had good, bad, and very bad entrances. Some of these entrances have not necessarily translated into equally good or bad consulting outcomes, but they initially made my consulting experience easier or harder.

VERY BAD ENTRANCES. One constant throughout the consulting process has been when the individual requesting my services is not the one who will use them. I do not necessarily mean athletes mandated by a coach to consult with me. I mean Federation X asking that I work with a team and coach and they (a) do not know anything about the situation (bad) or (b) they do not want any part of it (very bad). My first trip with the Junior US Track team started with everyone gathering in Miami's airport. As we introduced each other the head coach made a public statement indicating that his team did not need me, that he had no use for me and that I was there over his protests. I acknowledged him just by nodding (what could I really say?) and made myself useful as one more staff member, assuming that his attitude had to do with his perception of a psychologist's work and how I would potentially interfere with the team. The trip gave us many chances to interact and we ended up having a great working relationship, but if he had been a coach in a different setting he may have never given me the opportunity to perform my work.

On another occasion, I was asked to consult with a national team two years prior to the Olympic Games. The federation requested my services and I, wiser at that point, asked about the opinion of the head coach. The answer was unclear, and I agreed only to meet the team and coaches and then we would jointly decide about the viability of the option. The head coach interviewed me and she was positive enough about the situation. The team, on the other hand, was not interested. The captains asked to meet with me and I understood their hostility: They felt their previous sport psychologists had revealed much of what they thought would be confidential to the head coach and to the federation. I assured them that I would not do that, but also stated my understanding of their reticence, since they only had my word and no real reason to trust me. The long questioning session ended with an agreement on both our parts to try and see if we could work together and to revisit the issue after one month. I made it very clear at all times that I had not signed any contract and that I was not sure I could accept the assignment either.

The whole first four or five sessions were very slow in terms of productivity because of the reticence of the team. There were times that I believe several of the team members were never really engaged. Perhaps it would have happened anyway, but I felt the manner in which the consultation was initiated had a lot to do with it. In the end, the lack of communication and trust between the federation and the team should have been a loud message to me. I loved working with the team, but the national office had other goals in mind, and I ended up resigning after one year upon recognizing the setting as an example of what I have labeled as a "toxic environment." Learning the lesson that sometimes one has to decline a job assignment has been very helpful for me.

BAD ENTRANCES. Most of my bad entrances have had to do with a lack of clear communication, usually on my part. Whenever I have made too many assumptions, or failed to clarify goals and specify expectations, I have ended up having to work extra to re-direct the situation or to clarify issues.

Once, a figure skating coach wanted me to work with several of his athletes. I agreed to go to the skating rink and meet with everyone. I was expected to conduct the sessions there every week, but I did not think the setting was adequate. We tried the sessions there for a few weeks, but I had to change the location because it was not effective. In the end, few athletes made the switch to my office, and, again, the initial mix-up had something to do with it.

Another bad entrance had to do with a coach who wanted me to work with his team and listed a number of general goals such as "help the team manage their emotional reactions." I made the assumption that the goal meant the same for him as it did for me. Eventually I came to realize that he did not want to deal with any emotional issues from any of the team members, and thus my work became ineffective.

GOOD ENTRANCES. Of course the best entrances have been those where I took the time to clarify things and was clear to myself that I needed to know whether that job or consulting situation was the right one for me. With that I mean I did not go to just get a job, I went to see if it was a job that would be best suited for my skills. When I have centered on that issue I in turn have asked better questions, been more myself and the job has always worked better. Clearly the chance to talk directly with the individual who is going to use the services is a major benefit, but the communication with the hiring personnel is equally important.

In retrospect, and perhaps related to the comment I made above about making sure that the task was right for me, I realize that in good job starts I have been wary to not promise too much and to ask very specific questions about the goals they have for consultation. Sometimes people ask for results that I cannot guarantee. On occasion, I have said directly that I could not "make sure they win more games" but that I felt confident that I could help improve the player's communication or confidence; that is restating the goal to what I could do and under what conditions (i.e., specifying the information that I will and will not be able to share) and clarifying what I would not be able to do.

Just like the entrance process is important, the first sessions are also very important in setting the tone of the relationship. I always try to do a few basic things in my initial sessions: I spell out the confidentiality issues and their limits. When I work with young athletes and their families I typically ask the parents to come in for the first 10 minutes, so I can state the confidentiality issues that apply to them. Sometimes parents have a hard time understanding confidentiality agreements, and even though they pay for the session, they cannot find out what their son or daughter told me if he or she is 12 years of age or above. Of course, I will often encourage young athletes to communicate with their parents, but it cannot be just because the parents want to know about their child's session.

I tend to ask open questions in my initial sessions and frame it in such a way that the athlete informs me what information he or she thinks will be most useful in our session. I use a pie chart often to convey the fact that the individual as a whole matters, not just the athlete. If the athlete feels that other issues may be relevant to the session, I encourage him or her to discuss it with me.

When consulting with athletes who live far away, such as some of the track and field athletes, I will often ask them to fill out a questionnaire as a way of helping me get some background information and generate hypotheses more quickly. In the past, I have used Nideffer's TAIS; I like it very much and the athletes find the feedback very helpful. Recently, I have been using a web-based tool that I helped develop (TESKAL.com); it is a good way to gather initial information about the athlete as well as specific follow-up during the season. In any case, I do not do the same for every athlete because for some the questionnaires are a communication barrier, so I will not use them if they are not going to be helpful for our session.

I try to end every session with a joint summary of the main points covered and an agreement of what the athlete is going to do between sessions. I strongly believe that practice in between sessions is as important as, or more important than what we talk about in the office. I usually schedule about three sessions a month at the beginning of the consultation process and after that, I like to space out the sessions to give the athlete a chance to practice and see what needs refining. I also want to make sure that I do not convey the message that the athlete needs to talk to me before important competitions. Occasionally, parents or coaches want to schedule sessions before a major competition, but that is not necessarily helpful and conveys a lack of confidence in the athlete.

Sport performance is usually the stated reason for consultation. I make clear in my initial meetings that things outside sport are also part of the picture, so I inquire about school, family, or relationships, but I respect the goals set by the athlete. I also ask for a description of the coach or coaches, their coaching style, and relationship with the athlete. Depending on the age of the athlete I emphasize different areas. In general I always want to know: Why do the athletes do their sport and what would happen if they decided to stop? What would they miss? Who else would have a reaction? Sometimes I also ask about the achievements they hope to accomplish in their sport. There is another area that I emphasize initially in the session, and that is an assessment of where the athlete is in the process of change. Exploring the motivation for actual change, versus a wish to be different or for things to be different, has saved some frustration for both my clients and myself. It goes back to the issue of "I would like to change" as opposed to "I'm committed to do what I have to do to change." I follow Prochaska, Norcross, and DiClemente's (1994) model and draw a line, labeling the extremes 0 and 100 in terms of commitment to making changes, and ask that the athletes place themselves on the scale. It often sparks a fruitful discussion about the ambivalence towards change. After clarifying the actual motivation for change, the next thing I evaluate is the degree of confidence in being able to change. These two aspects have to be clarified before trying to teach or implement any intervention.

I have a cognitive-behavioral (CBT) orientation, so I look for ways in which the athletes perceive the situation, how they anticipate consequences and what the perceived main threats are. I also use elements from other frameworks: More and more I find myself spending time talking with the athlete about how memories and thoughts are just that—thoughts and images, not facts. Thoughts and images only have the power we give them in the current moment. I like to use examples and metaphors from the *Acceptance and Commitment framework*, such as the story that illustrates that fear should be acknowledged and respected but not obeyed. Fear is powerless as long as one does NOT succumb to it. Understanding that emotions do not determine the behavior allows us to do our jobs; we may feel angry but we do not have to "act" angry; we may be afraid but we can still perform our tasks.

Some athletes learn cognitive restructuring skills and can use them in a nonstressful situation. Very often they do not recognize that their stress level is rising, but this is a consequence of the indiscriminate use of "think positive," in that the athletes start to feel stressed but tell themselves that it's OK and plow ahead without addressing the change in conditions until it's too late. The role of emotions in performance is under developed in most CBT interventions. As a result, I spend more time on it now in my consultations.

The message society sends today to our field is that unpleasant emotions should not be tolerated: We have to fight that belief. I tell athletes that feelings are like smells: Some are pleasant and some are unpleasant but smells are not dangerous and always pass. In the same way, an unpleasant emotion can be tolerated and does not need to be "escaped from" right away. Using emotions for information is a message I often repeat and look for in activities that will increase awareness of what information the emotion is providing.

Throughout my work I have found that athletes are not very aware of all the emotions they experience. Exploring the function that emotions serve is often very helpful in a session. A common problem for athletes is difficulty controlling negative emotions, mainly anger, after a failure or bad performance. When given alternative ways of acknowledging the emotion and letting go of it, many athletes report that they cannot do it. As we reconstruct the situation, athletes frequently realize the exact moment that they do not want to stop the negative feeling. When exploring the function of different emotions, it is clear that after a poor performance many athletes realize that they are frustrated. Letting go of the negative emotion feels like they are letting themselves off the hook, and for many athletes it is also important to show their coaches or teammates how upset they are at their bad performance. Standard self statements such as "it does not matter" are too far from the actual feeling the athlete experiences in that situation. The best way to show their team how much they care about their performance is to refocus and play well, and this is something that takes awareness, choice and practice. I have also found that the notion of being focused on process goals is a hard one for an athlete to master, so I spend some time having the athletes set daily practice goals focused on recognizing emotions and modulating their intensity.

In the same way, I encourage athletes to keep track of improvements and positive emotions, such as keeping a journal of improvements. I have them tell the coach at the end of practice three things that they feel they could have done better. This is a hard exercise for perfectionist athletes, but once it makes sense to them, they understand the reasoning behind it and find it helpful for shoring up their confidence. The key here is for athletes to understand that perfectionism may have helped them get to their current performance level, but it is also going to keep them there. Most of the athletes have been told they should stop being so hard on themselves, but if they attribute their success or a good part of it to this trait, it makes sense that they do not want to change it. So many times, I talk about it with athletes and have them consider what it would be like to be less of a perfectionist. I encourage them to bring well-thought-out answers to the next session before we agree on any change strategies. No intervention will work if the athlete believes that having the trait is helpful.

During my sessions, I combine images associated with the feelings felt by athletes in different situations. Time and again athletes feel stronger when they have negative emotions—when they are angry and argue, or throw things—but if they think about the emotion and can associate it with an image of useless activity (i.e., a hamster running in a wheel) it may be easier to start changing it. We will also need an image associated with the appropriate reaction, such as seeing the behavioral response under control as a sign of strength (a cheetah staying very still until ready to pounce), rather than seeing it as a sign of weakness.

UNIQUE FEATURES

I'm not sure I have any unique features, but I will talk about some of the things I have been doing in recent years.

COACH-ATHLETE SESSIONS. I have worked with a number of coach-athlete pairs in the last few years, particularly in intensive coaching sports such as figure skating or gymnastics. The athlete has to agree to include the coach, and I ask in an individual session if that would be OK. During our sessions, we address specific practice and competition issues, and I have found that extremely helpful for the athlete. We identify goals for the season, working backward from the most important competition all the way to the current practices. In every session I ask the athlete first how their practices went, and then I ask for the coach's view. It may be opinions of how the athlete is handling difficulty with a move or a jump, or about his or her performance in a recent competition. The main part of the session is usually spent talking about what the athlete is going to do differently and how the coach is going to help the process. I like to make sure that the athlete is in control of the session, sets the goals, and decides the pace. With some pairs we meet about once a month; with others we have been meeting for a couple of years. If needed, we set individual sessions without the coach, but for the most part the sessions with the coach and athlete have been the bulk of the intervention. Of course, you need a coach who is psychologically minded and who will be able to sit in the session and not control it. Not every coach is able to do this, and not every athlete has a good enough relationship and trust with the coach, so I do not advocate this as a blanket intervention.

WATCHING TAPES TOGETHER. When athletes report on a competition performance it is sometimes hard to get a specific picture of what happened, and whenever possible I like to watch video of the performance with the athlete. I use these sessions for many things: from understanding the athlete's evaluation criteria, to seeing the emotion shown in competition, to helping the athlete identify his or her emotions.

TALKING TO YOUR "INNER COACH." For athletes who are very critical of themselves, I encourage a discussion of the impact that this kind of behavior has on their performance. I ask, "If you had a coach who talked to you the way you talk to yourself, how would you react?" Often they acknowledge that they would lose confidence or think of quitting. I point out that they are their own coach and I encourage a "conversation" with that internal coach, in a similar way to the *empty chair* technique in emotion-focused therapy, to identify the elements that are present and to learn to respond to it with the part that is the confident, supportive athlete.

LONG-TERM CONSULTING RELATIONSHIPS. I have enjoyed some consulting relationships that have lasted for several years. As I think about it, I realize how much the style and content of our work together has changed as these athletes grow in age and in knowledge. More and more the focus is holistic and in some cases existential. With that I mean that issues related to overall life mission and values take more of a center stage, and that for the most part, specific performance goals must be connected to these larger issues.

The relationship is fully collaborative and the athletes take a stronger role in leading the sessions. Sometimes we may not talk at all about specific sport questions, but what we talk about still relates to their performance, attitude, or perception of the sport.

References

Buckingham, M., & Coffman, C. (1999). *First, break all the rules: What the world's greatest managers do differently.* New York, NY: Simon & Schuster.

Collins, J. (2001). *Good to great.* Harper Collins.

Hayes, S., & Strosahl, K. (2004). *A practical guide to acceptance and commitment therapy.* Springer.

Loehr, J., & Schwartz, T. (2003). *The power of full engagement.* New York, NY: Free Press.

Nideffer, R. M. (1985) *Athletes guide to mental training.* Champaign, IL: Human Kinetics.

Prochaska, J., Norcross, J., & DiClemente, C. (1994). *Changing for good.* Avon Books.

Recommended Readings

Bob Nideffer and Bruce Ogilvie had a great influence early on in my career and their writings and expertise have been invaluable.

My Utopia group: Ralph Vernacchia, Rick McGuire, Keith Henschen, Rich Gordin, Jim Reardon, Ken Ravizza.

The following books (and the ones cited in the references) are ones I use over and over:

Bull, S. J., Albinson, J. G., & Shambrook, C. J. (1996). *The mental game plan.* Sports Dynamics.

Cook, D. *Golf's sacred journey.* (e-book)

Dweck, C. (2006). *Mindset.* Random House.

Mahoney, M. (2003). *Constructive psychotherapy.* Guilford Press.

Vealey, R. (2005). *Coaching for the inner edge.* Fitness Information Technology.

2

Dr. Jim Bauman

UNIVERSITY OF VIRGINIA

Dr. Jim Bauman is a full-time sport psychologist within the Athletic Department at the University of Virginia. Prior to this position, he was the sport psychologist in the Athletic Department at the University of Washington (2009–2011). Here, similar to his current position at UVA, he developed a full-service sport psychology program for the athletic department. From 1999–2009, he was a senior sport psychologist at the United States Olympic Committee. In that position, he provided clinical, counseling, life, and specific sport performance programs and services to both summer and winter game athletes. During that time frame, he worked with athletes and coaches at the 2000 Sydney, 2002 Salt Lake City, 2004 Athens, 2006 Torino, and 2008 Beijing Olympic Games, as well as multiple Olympic trials, World University Games, Pan American Games, World Cups, and World Championships. He has been the consulting sport psychologist for USA Swimming since 2004 and is continuing to work with swimmers preparing for the London Olympics in 2012. He also created and developed a working relationship between the Olympic Training Center and the Navy Special Warfare Center in San Diego (Navy SEALs). From 1993–1999, he was the sport psychologist in the Athletic Department at Washington State University. Dr. Bauman has an undergraduate degree in pre-physical therapy, a master's degree in education, and he received his doctorate in counseling psychology at Washington State University. He is a licensed psychologist in Washington, California, and Virginia.

AUTOBIOGRAPHICAL SKETCH

Long before I found my passion in sport psychology and after completing my undergraduate degree, I spent more than twenty years in other careers that included active military duty, forensic psychology, construction (building/remodeling), and financial planning. All of those experiences provided me with a unique set of experiences and knowledge that have subsequently helped me in my work with athletes, coaches, and sport organizations.

Although I didn't know it at the time, my first experience with "sport psychology" was when I played high school football in the mid-1960s. Before every Friday-night game, our team would lie down on a dark gymnasium floor and were told to imagine playing our best game. Most of us really just got an extra 20 minutes of sleep! After the "visualization session," our coach would bring us into the locker room and read letters to us that he had received from teammates who had graduated the previous year. They were part of a much larger group of young men who had either been drafted or enlisted in the military, and most were sent to Vietnam. We thought this was our coach's way of "motivating" us, if we heard how tough it was for them in a war zone, how they missed being safely back home playing football, or how they were encouraging us to appreciate being safely in school and to have a great season.

Sadly, in war, families lose sons, brothers, daughters, sisters, fathers, mothers, and best friends. Two of our teammates, who had been sending us letters, were killed in Vietnam in the fall of 1966, less than four months after their graduation from high school. Between football weekends that season, we had a double military funeral service in the same gymnasium and on the same floor that we had shared with these teammates the previous year. However, this year, they were lying in caskets, instead of with us in the pre-game darkness imagining playing our best game. No one anticipated, at that time, that our images and perspectives about what is important in life would forever change as we continued our pre-game visualization sessions for the remainder of that football season. We never slept through those sessions again. Coach continued to read letters from other teammates who were in Vietnam, but with deeper and different emotions than we had seen before. Like him, from that day forward, we all seemed different in our pre-game preparation. Later in life, I realized that by reading us the letters, he was really teaching us about appreciating life and it wasn't really an attempt to motivate us at all. That insight helped me understand that "winning" is important, but less important than the life and death challenges we all face off the field. Life has a much bigger picture than sport.

Over those incredibly formative years, most of us lived through the Vietnam War and the devastation that followed. We experienced the violence associated with the civil rights movement and the tragic assassinations of President John F. Kennedy, Martin Luther King Jr., and Bobby Kennedy. These were times when the greatest power on earth, the United States, was caught up in a sense of confusion, frustration, mistrust, chaos, anger, and fear. Through music, an "invasion" of emerging musicians from the United Kingdom (The Beatles, The Rolling Stones, The Kinks, and others) and homegrown musicians (Jimi Hendrix, Bob Dylan, Joan Baez, Janis Joplin, Crosby-Stills-Nash & Young, and others) described a world and a nation in turmoil and promoted a movement of "revolution and change." Part of the "revolution" included widespread use and abuse of a growing variety of illicit drugs that swept across the nation and around the world. To this day, music and substance use/abuse continue to be woven into the fabric of what is happening in our social system, including sport.

My first Olympic Games experience was the Munich Games in 1972. I was in the military and had been assigned to a missile battery north of Munich and on the East German border. East and West Germany were divided at that time. Tickets to the Games were limited, but I fortunately won tickets in a lottery that was being conducted in Germany. I actually arrived in Munich the day that the Palestinian-sponsored Black September terrorists stormed the Olympic Village and held the Israeli athletes and coaches hostage. From less than 100 meters away, I witnessed that infamous event. I watched, with athletes from around the world, the surreal terroristic act upon Olympic participants. It was the first violation of a long-held human understanding that during the Olympic Games, ancient and modern, all warring empires and nations granted all participants safe passage to and from the games, as well as during the games. As an American, I watched that event and those Games with no idea that twenty years later, I would be working with Olympic athletes competing at the 1992 Olympic Games.

As I think about helping others—and this is important—it has become increasingly necessary for me to reflect upon, know, understand, and appreciate how the people, events, and my life experiences have directly contributed to the very foundation of my personal and professional philosophy. Although I will talk more, later in the chapter, about how I "do the business of sport psychology," it is essential that I convey the significance of these earlier experiences.

I am now in my 23rd year in the field of sport psychology. I began in 1989, while completing a doctorate in psychology at Washington State University and concurrently providing part-time sport counseling services in the athletic department. After finishing the doctoral program, I subsequently worked in full-time sport psychology positions at Washington State University (seven years), the United States Olympic Committee (10 years), the University of Washington (two years), and the University of Virginia (one year). I steadfastly believe that the business of providing quality sport psychology services requires a broad range of experience and competencies in sport science, psychology, and life. After more than 22 years of practicing sport psychology, 12 years of formal education (undergraduate degree in pre-physical therapy, masters in education, doctorate in psychology), and licensure as a psychologist, I've got a good start!

THEORY OF PERFORMANCE EXCELLENCE

Although I have been exclusively practicing sport psychology for a long time, I feel rather hesitant to label my perspective about performance excellence a theory. I don't really know, I guess, how long one has to be immersed in a field to become qualified to claim ownership to a theory. Anders Ericsson's research (1994) supports the idea that 10 years or 10,000 hours of deliberate practice is necessary to become an expert. If that prevails, I guess I've qualified!

In that spirit of improving performance, I would suggest there are two major components, neither of which one can simply assume is present. The first component is an experienced and qualified teacher. Coyle (2009) has found that in order to teach the requisite skills that are necessary for performers to become elite, "master coaches" are required. In sport, this would include teachers of the physical skills (coaches) and the mental skills (sport psychologists) that are associated with the sport. As a teacher of human performance, one must have a theoretical understanding of human software (the brain and how it functions), human hardware (anatomy, physiology, motor movement, and how these function), the context of the activity where performance is occurring, how this context seems to change over time, and a willingness to continually expand one's own knowledge base.

The second component is a talented and coachable athlete. An athlete must have the minimal genetic physical and mental talent potential that is required by the sport and the level of competition where that athlete competes. Equally important, the athlete must be ready and able to learn, willing to train, and remain healthy over a fairly significant period of time. As previously noted (Ericsson & Charness, 1994), about 10,000 hours or 10 years of deliberate practice is necessary to attain an expert level of performance. By their definition of deliberate practice, simply "being in the business" does not qualify as deliberate practice. That goes for athletes, coaches, and sport psychologists. There are many individuals who claim years of experience as a sport psychologist, but most of that time is spent in a faculty or part-time position. All of my years of experience have been as a full-time professional practicing applied sport psychology on a daily basis. There continues to be ongoing dialogue with regard to what deliberate practice might entail. However, there doesn't seem to be much disagreement that expert performance takes a long time to achieve. In sum, without a good teacher (in this case a sport psychologist) or without a good student (athlete), performance will either suffer, be compromised, or not reach its full potential.

There has been a fairly long-standing discussion about what a sport psychologist actually does. A division exists between individuals trained primarily in sport sciences, individuals trained primarily in psychology, and those trained in both. More recent attention has been given to the legal and ethical implications of using the word "psychologist" and that attention is beginning to clarify, for practitioners and athletes, the actual qualifications and competencies of the providers. Clearly, nearly all states require individuals to be licensed in the respective state that they provide psychological services. State laws also delineate services that are specifically provided by a psychologist, including anyone who practices sport psychology.

My undergraduate training is in sport science (pre-physical therapy) and my graduate degrees are in education (MEd) and psychology (PhD). Therefore, my theoretical basis for practicing sport psychology stems from sport science, educational, and psychological disciplines. My tenure in the business of sport psychology has, without question, reinforced my belief that training and licensure in psychology are prerequisites for providing quality sport psychology services. Well over 90% of the athletes with whom I've worked (collegiate, professional, and Olympic) initially presented with clinical, counseling, and/or life situations that they felt adversely affected their athletic performance. Without my graduate academic coursework in psychology, supervised clinical/counseling training, and licensure in psychology, I would not have been prepared or qualified to identify or provide the psychological services in response to help athletes eliminate or at least reduce the effects of these clinical, counseling, or life circumstances. Once these issues are cleared, I then begin working on the mental skills and strategies that would further enhance an athlete's performance. Even after the mental health issues have been addressed, many of the same principles are utilized in working with the subsequent and specific sport performance issues. There is a clear interrelationship between both psychological issues and specific sport-related mental strategies in athletic performance. There is also a clear message and direction emerging in terms of who is legally and ethically competent to deliver either or both of these important variables in sport performance. Later in this chapter, I will more specifically address the sport mental skills and strategies (*High Performance Blueprint*) that enhance athletic performance.

The *foundation* of my applied sport psychology work is grounded in my life experiences and careers previous to my work in sport psychology. The more formal and academic *framework* of my sport psychology work originates in psychological theory and research. Specifically, my master's degree was Adlerian (Alfred Adler). This approach emphasizes increasing social interest, modifying self-destructive behaviors, and solving problems rather than amplifying them. Adler believed that family dynamics, current life styles, and early childhood experiences are key areas of inquiry. During my nine years in forensic psychology, I utilized this therapeutic model in a group therapy format for felony offenders in legal offender units in psychiatric hospitals. My doctoral training included Rogerian training (Carl Rogers), a humanistic approach dealing with the development of one's self-concept and cognitive therapy (Aaron Beck), that assumes humans are logical beings and make choices based upon what makes the most sense to them. Cognitive therapy focuses on overcoming individual issues by identifying, challenging, and changing dysfunctional thinking, emotional responses, and self-defeating behaviors. My training in cognitive therapy was more specifically in Cognitive Behavioral Therapy (Donald Meichenbaum) and Rational Emotive Behavioral Therapy (Albert Ellis). Both focus on how life adversities can "derail" us and how we might construct a somewhat self-destructive reality about that adversity through expressed language, behaviors, and particularly in beliefs about ourselves, others, and the world around us. Cognitive therapy is a therapeutic process whereby these self-defeating or dysfunctional thoughts are shifted to a more realistic and constructive belief system. Once that occurs, subsequent cognitive, emotional, and behavioral changes result in a much more productive outcome, in and out of sport. Although I still employ some Adlerian and Rogerian techniques, I have moved more toward the cognitive approaches in my clinical/counseling/performance work with athletes.

We are all in the business of teaching or selling ideas, regardless of whether we are providing psychological services or specific sport performance interventions. I am convinced that nearly everything I've heard, learned about, and believe with regard to life and self-improvement has either been said by our early philosophers, written about in the scriptures, or taught to me by those whom I would recognize as my mentors. Much of what many claim to be their own is merely a new packaging of ideas already expressed by others. However, over a long period of time, I have distilled that collective knowledge and personal experience into the *domains* that I believe comprise what is necessary to improve human performance, in and out of sport.

During my work in the construction business, all of our projects were guided by blueprints that specifically detailed the work to be done. For example, blueprints provided specifications for the dimensions of the house, as well as detailed information about how all of the subcontractor work would be applied (plumbing, electrical, insulation, interior walls, flooring, cabinetry, etc.). All of what was necessary to build a home from start to finish was clearly outlined in the blueprints. Similarly, in an effort to create a system of progressively helping to build performance, rather than houses, I have created a *High Performance Blueprint* for athletes.

A prerequisite for performance is talent. Talent is a genetic potential or capacity to do just about anything. Talent can range from having very little apparent potential to having very high levels of potential. We have yet to become good at developing a metric for quantifying talent potential and, therefore, talent is currently measured by the level of skills that an athlete can develop over time. The more genetic potential that a performer possesses, the faster he or she seems to learn the skills associated with a particular talent area (e.g., music, athletics, math, language, science, etc.). For illustration purposes, talent potential could be conceptualized as being similar to various sized containers. Imagine a set of empty glasses that might range in size from 2 ounces to 20 ounces, each with a different capacity to hold liquids. The bigger the glass, the more it can hold. Similar to the varying capacities of these glasses, I see athletes with varying capacities to "develop and hone their skills." The bigger the capacity (talent), the more one has for any given skill set, and the higher the potential for one's skill and competitive level. Every competitive level requires a certain skill level. Therefore, in order to achieve the necessary skill level, there must be a requisite capacity (talent) available to develop that level of skill. I'll talk more about talent later in the chapter.

Using the construction of a custom home as a metaphor, there are specific and necessary subcontractors who are involved in transforming an empty real estate lot into a beautiful custom home. If, for example, the electrician and electrical work are left out of the blueprint, the owners will be extremely disappointed with having an amazing home with no electrical capabilities! Similarly, there are necessary subcontractors (people and their work) who transform a beginner athlete into an elite performer. If any of the domains are left out, the athlete may look like an amazing athlete, but the final product will fall short of what was planned or envisioned.

The *High Performance Blueprint* is a system that requires participation of a number of supporting people. Each domain has clear "subcontractors" who specialize in that domain and who must cooperatively coordinate their efforts with the others involved. Cooperation, timing, and planning are necessary for subcontractors who build custom homes, and the same is required for building an elite athlete.

The *High Performance Blueprint* is composed of 10 specific and necessary *domains*. These domains have been developed over the last 15 years, and are as necessary to athletic performance as subcontractors are to finishing a custom home. These domain descriptions are written in second person, as if the reader were the athlete. The people who are primarily involved in assisting an athlete in each area are in parentheses, following each domain. I will talk more about how these people work together in the consulting section of this chapter. Following each domain is a listing and/or description of subareas associated with that particular domain. In many cases, the descriptors are general, in order for this blueprint to apply to all sports and at all levels of competition. Again, using a construction blueprint as a metaphor, if "Health" (#3 domain) were associated with the electrical part of the plan, it would describe the types of wire being used, how much wire was necessary, how many electrical outlets, how many switches, wiring to appliances, etc. Therefore, in the "Health" domain, health is broken down into smaller areas of sleep, rest, nutrition, etc. It is not enough to simply say sleep, rest or nutrition. For example, the plan would require more specificity with regard to how much, when, what, and special needs for each topic. As you can see, this approach is initially time consuming, but so is building a custom home. Once you have built a house or two, those that follow are less difficult to build, but the quality improves with experience.

The High Performance Domains

(1) Talent (Mom and Dad genes). As previously discussed, talent is a genetic potential or capacity to do anything. Progressively higher levels of competition require higher levels of "hardware potential" (anatomy, physiology, motor speed/coordination, etc.), higher levels of "software potential" (cognitive processing speed, memory storage, memory retrieval, intelligence, intuitiveness, etc.), and an "operating system," which is the ability to effectively combine "hardware" and "software" potentials into skills, and then

skills into performance. You must be near, match, or exceed the talent potential necessary for the competitive level at which you are competing. If you aren't, it could be that your talent/skills could better be matched with a different talent area. I never discourage individuals from continuing to work toward their potential, because, as noted before, talent potential is difficult to measure and we have not yet ruled out performance issues that are outside of the athlete's control (e.g., environment, poor coaching, geographical location, funding, etc.).

Although I never discourage an athlete from continuing, there are times when "wanting it more than anything" just isn't enough. Wanting it is a necessary ingredient, but by itself, it isn't enough. My adage is, "I don't care how bad a rooster might want to lay an egg, it just isn't going to happen!" In sum, talent is the basic ingredient for performance excellence. With great coaching and deliberate practice, skill development within that talent potential is the measure of how high that performance level can go.

(2) Game plan/Business plan (athlete, coach, and psychologist). These are your aspirations, visions, and the strategies to achieve them. This section clearly describes what you are going to do. A helpful guidebook for developing a business plan is *Creating a Business Plan: Pocket Mentor* (HBS, 2007). Others routinely label these as goals, but plans are much more adaptable and inclusive than one-statement goals. Game and business plans are used interchangeably to emphasize the business part of the game of sport. Business plans carry a more deliberate message that compares athletes to entrepreneurs. Sport is a business and so is sport participation; therefore, you will want to view your athletic participation as a business. Defining your success, or how you measure profitability, changes with each level of competition. Since your definition of success changes over time, it is important to always have a clear and current picture of what your definition means, including metrics for measuring your success. Beyond the overriding vision about where you are aspiring to go, game and business plans must also include how to get there. Domains 3–10 provide structure to how you get there.

(3) Health (athlete, coach, health providers, nutritionist, and psychologists). This area includes, but is not limited to, rest, sleep, recovery, fueling for sport (nutrition and hydration), illness (acute or chronic), medications, menstrual cycle, cognitive resilience, emotional resilience, physiological resilience, pain thresholds, speed of recovery from injuries, an ability to perform under a variety of environmental factors, and many more.

(4) Physiology/Strength & conditioning (athlete, coach, physiologist, and strength & conditioning coach). This includes weights, resistance, training

devices, and activities to develop sport specific muscle strength, endurance, flexibility, speed, quickness, explosiveness, physical recovery, power, and more.

(5) Sport skills (biomechanics), tactics, and rules of the game (athlete, coach, and biomechanist). These include maintaining/improving/applying mastered skills based upon the application of the biomechanics and physics of your sport; increasing your inventory of mastered skills; improving upon mastered skills; improving or managing necessary skills that are not yet mastered; love for and pursuit of precision; transitions from training to competition; muscular-skeletal efficiency; application of force; high speed video technology; knowing the rules associated with your sport (read the rule book); learning and knowing your sport tactics; becoming a student and teacher of your sport, and more.

(6) Pre- and post-performance routines and willingness to take risks (athlete, coach, and sport psychologist). These are specific pre-training and pre-competition routines (physical and mental warm-up), not rituals or superstitions. Implementing post-training and post-competition routines (physical and mental cool-downs) that develop and evolve with meaningful relevance to your sport performance. Continuously train toward improving performance comfort levels and once you get comfortable, it is time to create a new sense of discomfort by requiring higher levels of performance expectations. You must prepare to take risks (physical and mental) that are on the edge of current perspectives of your perceived performance abilities and skill levels. Finally, it is necessary to create a sense of adaptation and problem solving. In business, you are either part of the problem or part of the solution. Be solution oriented.

(7) Distraction management (athlete, coach, and sport psychologist). This area includes effectively identifying and managing sport, non-sport, internal, and external distractions; knowing the difference between real, perceived, and self-amplified pressures; becoming increasingly more proficient at applying pre-competition routines, the game plan, and post-competition routines as strategies to stay in the game and to minimize distractions.

(8) Equipment (athlete, coach, and equipment personnel). Your equipment is the "tools of your trade" that are matched to your skills and competitive level. It is your responsibility to be sure that your equipment is operationally maintained and present for use. I have witnessed athletes who have not been successful at Olympic Trials, Olympic Games, and World Championships because their equipment was not ready for competition! Prepare a

"battle bag" that has all you need to compete. Whenever possible and when you travel to competitions, carry on those equipment items that would be difficult to replace, just in case they were to get lost in shipped baggage.

(9) Personal life (athlete, sport psychologist, spiritual, and other significant people in the life of the athlete). In any business, including sport, your personal life can directly affect your performance (good or bad). Managing your personal life and life circumstances is necessary. These can include issues involving relationships, family, friends, financial, moving, travel, media, and much more.

(10) Athletic perspective (athlete, coach, sport psychologist, spiritual, and other significant people in the life of an athlete). This domain begins with asking the question "Why do I participate in this sport?" The answer to that question can and does change over time. However, some of the initial reasons for participating in athletics often get systematically eliminated over the course of a career. In the beginning, sport participation is fun, until it later turns to work, and still later a business. The key is to maintain a degree of fun, enjoyment and a sense of personal worth for all it takes to continue to be competitive at increasingly higher levels. Having a *healthy perspective* becomes the inner spark that fuels the flame of maintaining and clarifying a constructive view of the "big picture" in sport and life.

Perspective provides a clear understanding of where you are on the competitive continuum; transitioning from one performance level to the next; understanding who you are in the life process; learning and understanding what components make up your identity; developing and applying the capacity to relate to others; becoming increasingly more independent, responsible and accountable for yourself, your needs, your direction, and quality and quantity of your evolving, forward movement in sport and life. Perspective is an ongoing awareness and pursuit of life balance, contributing to improving the community and society, and doing this in the most simplistic manner possible. Perspective is the glue that holds the house together.

All of these domains have examples of important items within them. Realize that depending upon the sport and the individual, there will be more items in each domain than are noted above. That said, the *High Performance Blueprint* provides a structure to begin the building process.

One last, but equally important, piece to building a custom home or a custom athlete is the paperwork. Every successful business must have an accounting of how the business is doing. Therefore, an accounting or journaling of progress is paramount. Journaling is the bookwork for your business of being an athlete. It is your personal record of what you are doing, where you are going, and whether or not you are on track. The structure for journaling is outlined in the domains previously noted. The items in each of the domains serve as a checklist of items to track. It is important to document what is present when you are successful and what is missing when you aren't. Journaling is not necessary every day. Document those training and competitive days that are either far above your average performance or far below your average performance. These relative extremes will be more productive in streamlining your blueprint than an endless narrative form of documentation that you do daily.

Athletes with whom I work put together 3-ring binders, or electronic versions of a 3-ring binder, to build their "business book," with each of the domains serving as a chapter in the book. As you gather more data or information about your performance, simply put that data or information in the corresponding domain section. This organizes an otherwise difficult to manage and growing amount of paperwork that can simply turn into a hassle for you; if you stop doing the bookwork, you run the risk of losing track of your business and your progress.

Before I conclude this section, one of the issues in the blueprint needs additional attention. A dream house begins with a vision or dream (the plan) and is then transferred to paper in the form of a blueprint. Athletes also start with a vision or dream. And even though the *High Performance Blueprint* documents the process, it is imperative to be able to clearly describe the dream. Game/business plans regularly outline some level of success. Describing success has taken many forms, but the most consistent definition in sport is to win. In sport, it seems that because winning (being profitable) is the main stakeholder in success, a great performance without winning is often not seen as being successful. Athletes have described to me competitions where they have won, but felt they had a terrible performance. They didn't really feel successful in their own mind, even though the sport definition of success had been met and they were publicly praised. On other occasions, athletes have described great performances (personal best), but they didn't win. They actually felt successful, but because they didn't win, they didn't get the recognition from the sport world.

We know that both winning and feeling successful can, and do, occur at the same time. I am suggesting that winning is not the only measure of success. Instead, I am suggesting that consistent and progressive improvement over time is real progress and success. Winning will happen when the emphasis is placed on getting better. If athletes maintain a clear perspective about why they are engaged in sport and continually clarify their vision of how they define success, they will move toward feeling successful and being profitable (winning). Clearly, I have seen an increasing number of athletes perform at their best when they focus on their job, rather than on the results.

Being profitable is necessary for any business. According to Collins and Porras (1994), "Profitability (winning) is a necessary condition for existence and a means to more important ends, but it is not the end in itself for visionary companies. Profit is like oxygen, food, water, and blood for the body; they are not the *point* of life, but without them, there is no life" (p. 55). In sport, winning is a necessary condition, but it is not the point of sport. The point of sport is to help athletes move toward their dreams of being the greatest at what they do, without extinguishing those dreams with a flood of messages about winning.

Collins and Porras (1994) address what it takes to create a business that stands the test of time, and this is directly applicable to the business of sport. In business and in sport, the need to be profitable (money and winning) seems to traditionally take center stage. However, Collins and Porras convincingly illustrate why the most successful and resilient corporations in history are successful and remain successful. Although not losing sight of the need to be profitable, they focus on the very reason they exist in the first place (their ideology). Those corporations that maintain a steady eye on *why they are in business*, are the ones that remain profitable through good and bad economic times. Athletic performance is no different. Great teams and giant visionary corporations use the same formula to stand the test of time. Focusing on the job and why we do it, rather than the outcome, results in profitable businesses.

THEORY OF PERFORMANCE BREAKDOWNS

Performance breakdowns (i.e., choking, panic, slumps) seem to happen, in varying degrees, at nearly every level of competition and probably in all sports. The consequences of these performance breakdowns also vary, depending upon what is at stake. Performance breakdowns during regular season competition may have a much different outcome than during playoffs, qualifying for the next level of competition, national championships, world championships, Olympic Games, or professional championships. Much has been written about a multitude of mental skills associated with high performance. My experience, rather than theory, has demonstrated that great performances really come down to keeping things very simple with a few basic mental strategies and tactics.

Key strategies for high performers include: (1) maintaining a clear and healthy perspective about sport, (2) deliberate training, (3) staying healthy, and (4) having a viable and somewhat adaptable plan that includes preparing to compete, a plan for competing, and a commitment to sticking with the plan. Once the overriding strategies are developed, then the mental tactics associated with those strategies can be developed to stay on track. These mental tactics include: (1) an ability to envision the outcome (imagery), (2) monitoring and adjusting self-talk (solution oriented), (3) being mentally pliable as opposed to mentally tough, and (4) managing physiological and psychological energy.

How do athletes get off track? If they lose their perspective, varying too much from their plan or failing to have a plan, failing to self-monitor during competition, and/or failing to remain mentally pliable, their performance results will predictably be below what they are capable of demonstrating. Athletes devote a tremendous amount of time to preparing their hardware (below the chin) for competition. However, until recently, there has been little time devoted to improving the software (above the chin). Amazingly, the most important regulator to performance, the brain, has typically been left out of the formula.

CONSULTING PROCESS

In the Theory of Performance Excellence section of this chapter, I referred to how the implementation of the *High Performance Blueprint* required a team effort. The best way to describe the consulting process that I utilize would be to use the metaphor of a NASCAR pit crew. Imagine that the athlete is the driver and the coach is the crew chief. In NASCAR races, the other service people who are allowed to go over the wall to assist the driver during a pit stop are restricted by NASCAR rules: The crew is limited to seven people. They are the jack man, front tire carrier, front tire changer, rear tire carrier, rear tire changer, gasman, and the gas catcher. Each is assigned a specific role, but all are experts in their role, and they are familiar with the roles of the other pit crewmembers.

The "pit crew" that we wrap around an athlete in an intercollegiate environment would include assistance coaches, sport psychologist, athletic medicine, nutritionist, strength & conditioning, academics, life skills, and compliance personnel. During my Olympic experience, academics and compliance were replaced with physiologists and bio-mechanists. In sum, it is important to understand, work with, and consult with the other pit crew members that have direct contact with the athlete.

In order to generally understand the other members' roles, it requires that you learn a little about areas outside of your own expertise, but those that are still relevant to helping an athlete. Gaining that additional knowledge is only to assist in the team approach and by no means implies that minimal knowledge warrants providing any of the other services being delivered by the other trained professionals. In addition, and from a more clinical perspective, it is equally important to have and utilize a reliable clinical group of colleagues with whom to consult when more complex clinical, counseling, or ethical issues arise.

UNIQUE FEATURES

Over the past 20 years, there seems to have been an increasing number of sport psychology related publications, all of which have been impressive. However, it seems that much of what I have read lately has generally been the same message, just packaged differently. Therefore, I have redirected my attention toward three other non-sport but fascinatingly relevant areas.

First, I have focused on research involving brain physiology, military special operations (US Navy SEALs), and survival under the harshest of conditions. As a professional organization, we must move toward being able to identify and quantify what happens in the brains of elite performers who consistently perform at high levels under the most challenging of conditions. In order to move in that direction, I fully support a movement toward neuropsychology and researching of special performance populations (e.g., high level sport, high level endurance sport, special military operations, and personnel dealing with crisis situations) and I believe this is the future of sport psychology. Although we continue to learn more, a great deal is known about our anatomy and the physiology of motor learning, motor movement, and what is happening in the body during elite sport performance. However, what is occurring psychologically and neuropsychologically continues to leave many important questions unanswered. In fact, we are just now beginning to understand what questions to ask!

Second, over the years, I have had the unfortunate experience of having to deal with multiple incidents involving athletes who have suffered life changing injuries and loss of life associated with sport participation. Dealing with the issues surrounding permanent injury and loss of life is not an area in which I particularly wanted to become proficient. However, because tragedy is a part of sport and life, it has required that I develop skills in this very difficult area. Tragedy affects the athlete, family, friends, teammates, coaches, and entire sport organizations. It is during these times that consulting with other professionals is paramount.

And third, it is necessary that we become more proficient in marketing principles as we vend our sport psychology services to prospective athletes, coaches, and sport organizations. We all go through the rigors of our professional training, but I am not aware of any graduate psychology curriculums that include classes in marketing. We are obviously in the business of selling our ideas to athletes, yet most of us have never been exposed to the principles of retail! We can have the best products available, but if we can't sell them, they just sit on the shelf. There is a myriad of great resources to assist in developing your marketing skills.

I think the most unique feature of my work is my style of interacting with athletes and coaches. I spend a lot of time with them and in their world. My "office" includes fields, pools, tracks, lakes, rinks, mountain slopes, beaches, hospitals, weight rooms, and an array of other locations where athletes and coaches can be found. I've worked with athletes on and in the water, in all weather conditions (rain, sun, snow, hot, freezing, daylight, darkness), throughout the year (weekdays, weekends, holidays, and days off), and with lots of notice or no notice at all. I have learned their languages and their challenges. I've seen them start sport and end it. I've seen female athletes become moms and male athletes become dads. I've been around long enough now to see sons and daughters of previous athletes begin their athletic careers. From that ongoing involvement, I have developed hundreds of worksheets, exercises, metaphors, and stories that help move athletes through the process of facing a problem, resolving the problem, and becoming more proficient in sport and life as a result of that experience.

CASE STUDY

Earlier, I mentioned the importance of strategies and tactics. One of the tactics noted was having a plan. To illustrate the importance of having a "tactical plan," I am reminded of a situation that occurred at the 2008 Beijing Olympic Games. One of the sports that I worked with at those games was track and field, which was contested in the Beijing National Sport Stadium. The national stadium was also known as the "Bird's Nest" due to its unique architectural design that actually resembled a bird's nest. While watching the track and field events from the athlete and coach section of the "Bird's Nest," an athlete who had just finished the preliminary qualification found her way back to our section and sat right behind me. Although I did not know this athlete, we began to discuss her situation and qualifying performance. She told me that she had qualified first in the preliminary rounds of her event and was going to the finals in that event in two days. She also mentioned that she had a high level of nervousness and anxiety about making the finals, even though her qualifying mark was more than a meter beyond what the other competitor marks had been. She further disclosed that she had not prepared a plan for the finals, thinking she probably would not perform well enough to make the finals.

I inquired about the plan that got her through the season, Olympic Trials, and now leading all competitors going into the finals. She pulled out a crumpled up piece of paper that had three simple objectives (be quick, stay low, and have fun). This was a plan that she and her coach had devised several months earlier. Until I suggested it, she did not understand that this was her plan for the finals. It had been successful to this point and she needed to stick to it for the finals. She expressed immediate relief, now understanding that although being in the finals was something special, she didn't have to have a special plan or do something special to be successful; just use the plan that got her there.

Two days later, she had a gold medal performance by sticking to the plan. As she jogged around the track, in the "Bird's Nest" with the American flag draped around her shoulders, she visually found me in the stands, held up that same crumpled-up paper that had the plan written on it and smiled. I could read her lips saying "thank you, I followed the plan!" About two weeks later, I received an autographed picture of her with her gold medal and a note that simply said "thanks for the plan!"

This situation is a typical encounter at competitions. Athletes often get derailed and don't know how to get back on track. Had I worked with this athlete prior to the Olympic Games, we would have had her blueprint and domains outlined, practiced, and ready to go for this event. Initially, it seemed obvious that her perceived lack of a game plan was the presenting issue. But, in conversation, I still needed to eliminate the other domains to ensure I was dealing with all of the issues. In our conversation, I ruled out health issues, physiological issues, technical issues, performance routines, personal issues, and equipment problems. The three areas that surfaced were (1) her thinking she had *no plan* for the finals, (2) becoming *distracted* by that worry, and (3) then *losing her perspective* about how she could perform in the finals. The root problem was her believing that she had no plan. Once that was resolved, she was no longer distracted by that misbelief, and her perspective switched from destructive to optimistically constructive. This case is a good example of how I use the domains of the blueprint to help athletes create their own independent performance programs through a systematic process of identifying performance problems, finding the solutions, and developing reliable routines to keep them on track.

At the end of this chapter, I have included a recommended reading list.

These books and articles, as well as the authors themselves, have added a great deal of perspective to how I do the business of sport psychology and maintain healthy personal perspective. I hope I have been able to do the same for you with this chapter.

References
Collins, J., & Porras, J. (1994). *Built to last: Successful habits of visionary companies*. Harper Business.

Coyle, D. (2009). *The talent code: Greatest isn't born, it's grown, here's how*. Bantam.

Creating a business plan: Pocket mentor. (2007). Harvard Business School Press.

Ericsson, K., & Charness, N. (1994). Expert performance: Its structure and acquisition. *American Psychologist, 49*(8), 725–747.

Recommended Readings
Buckingham, M., & Coffman, C. (1999). *First break all the rules: What the world's greatest managers do differently*. Simon and Schuster.

DeBecker, G. (1997). *The gift of fear*. Delta.

Frankl, V. (1959). *Man's search for meaning*. Beacon Press.

Gladwell, M. (2002). *The tipping point*. Back Bay Books.

Godin, S. (2001). *Unleashing the antivirus*. Hyperion.

Godin, S. (2005). *All marketers are liars*. Portfolio.

Hillenbrand, L. (2010). *Unbroken*. Random House.

Jackson, S., & Csikszentmihalyi, M. (1999). *Flow in sports*. Human Kinetics.

Kouzes, J., & Posner, B. (2010). *The truth about leadership*. Jossy Boss.

Huizenga, R. (1978). *You're okay, it's just a bruise*. St. Martin's Griffin.

LeDoux, J. (1996). *The emotional brain*. Simon & Schuster.

LeDouz, J. (2002). *Synaptic self*. Penguin.

McDougall, C. (2009). *Born to run: A hidden tribe, superathletes, and the greatest race the world has never seen*. Alfred A. Knopf Publishing.

Morgan, N. (2003). *Working the room: How to move people to action through audience-centered speaking*. Harvard Business School Press.

Morgan, N. (2009). *Trust me: Four steps to authenticity and charisma*. Jossy Boss.

Starkes, J., & Ericcson, A. (Eds.). (2003). *Expert performance in sports*. Human Kinetics.

Stengel, R., 2009. *Mandela's way*. Crown.

Wooden, J., & Tobin, J. (1988). *They call me coach*. Contemporary Books.

3

Dr. Rich Gordin

UTAH STATE UNIVERSITY

Rich Gordin is a professor at Utah State University. He has been at the university for 30 years. He is a professor in the Department of Health, Physical Education and Recreation and is an adjunct professor in the Department of Psychology. He was the department's graduate coordinator for 15 years. Dr. Gordin has published 80 articles and book chapters and has made 350 professional presentations at state, regional, national and international conferences. He has been a sport psychology consultant for numerous athletic teams, including teams at his university, USA Gymnastics, USA Track & Field, US Ski and Snowboard Association and for several professionals on the PGA Tour. He is the former chair of the certification committee of the Association of Applied Sport Psychology (AASP). He is listed on the sport psychology registry of the US Olympic Committee for the 2008–2012 quadrennium. He is also listed as a member of the USA Gymnastics Athlete Wellness Program National Referral Network for 2008–2012, and is listed on the USA Swimming Sports Medicine Directory for this quadrennium. He was the sport psychologist for the USA Women's Gymnastics Team in Seoul in 1988 and a sport psychology consultant for the USA Track and Field team for the 2004 Olympic Games in Athens. He recently served as the sport psychologist for the USA Nordic Combined Ski Team in Vancouver in 2010. During spring semester 2010, Dr. Gordin was a visiting professor at Jagiellonian University in Krakow, Poland and has also consulted in the business world for Bank of America, ING, The Hartford, Transamerica Retirement Services, Nationwide, and Pioneer Investments.

AUTOBIOGRAPHICAL SKETCH

I grew up surrounded by athletics. My father was a coach at a university and later an athletic director at a small liberal arts institution. Our family consisted of my mother, father and two brothers. Both of my brothers were athletes but not interested in the same sports as I. The influence on me growing up around coaches was long lasting. When my father associated with his colleagues, I would tag along and listen to the coaches talk. I watched their behaviors and I visited many locker rooms. This exposure instilled the culture of sport in me.

I started to play organized sports when I was very young, and played football, baseball, and basketball and was also on the age group swimming team in the summer months. During high school I continued to play sport, specializing in football. I also played basketball and participated in track and field. Every season was a different sport for me. I learned to be self-reliant, but also a team player. This upbringing had a major effect on my career choice, as I never considered any other profession but teaching and coaching. If it is possible to be born to coach, I guess this was the case.

Other experiences that influenced my interest in sport were family outings to sporting events, such as attending games and activities, and my early experience as a lifeguard. I enrolled in lifeguard training at 14 years old—the earliest you could possibly certify. My first job was teaching swim lessons to young children. I learned a work ethic and from a very early age was proud to earn my own spending money. I enjoyed the sense of autonomy that accompanied hard work and sacrifice. I learned that nothing comes to you for free in life and that persistence and continued effort are essential ingredients to success. I have never since accomplished anything in my life worth much without some sense of sacrifice put forth in order to achieve the goals I set for myself.

I was recruited to play major college football after a successful high school career, but chose to attend a small liberal arts university instead. I felt then that being a well-rounded individual was more important than only concentrating on one sport in college. I played college football and studied physical education and coaching. I also was a high school teacher and coach for a few years. My experiences as a coach convinced me early on that there was a mental side to sport that was untrained in athletics, at least in a formal way. In the 1950s and '60s, Ohio was considered the cradle of coaching. As a child I met and conversed with Woody Hayes, Fred Taylor, and other personal friends of my dad. I would even get to hang out in the locker rooms of many of these bastions of sport. When I remember these early exposures with fondness, it is no wonder I developed a locker room mentality. When my dad would compete in golf, for instance, I would caddy for him. If he went to a bowling league, I went along. I was able to bond with my dad and see competitive athletics up close and personal. I believe now that my competitive nature was developed and nurtured in these early experiences.

My formal education consisted of more exposure to sport. I attended The Ohio State University for a graduate degree and studied with the best scholars of the day in physical education. I also obtained great exposure to applied sport psychology by attending The University of Utah in the late '70s. There I met a young and upcoming pioneer in applied sport psychology named Keith Henschen. Keith and I had, and still have, a very special relationship. It is not so much mentor/student as collegial in nature. In fact, many in our field will be surprised to know that Keith was my major professor at Utah.

At the time, the field of applied sport psychology was still in its infancy and Keith and I were able to explore, discuss and develop together. I was able to obtain a position with the university women's gymnastics team in the late '70s to supply my services. It was perfect timing as Greg Marsden, the head coach, was also a student in sport psychology at Utah and was very interested in employing the services of a consultant for his team. Keith and I then became established in the gymnastics world at the national level. I will never forget going to the national championships for the first time knowing no one and coming away with a job as a consultant for the US Gymnastics Federation. This resulted in my first appointment to an Olympic Games in Seoul in 1988. This also happened to coincide with the first ever official sport psychologist being sent by the USOC to an Olympic Games when Shane Murphy was sent as an official delegate to these games. These experiences have influenced my style tremendously.

I am not sure how to name my style but will settle for "Humanistic Sport Psychology." I believe that if you can gain the trust of all involved in the consulting relationship including coaches, trainers, physical therapists as well as, of course, the athletes, then you have a chance to help the organization. I believe my experiences have instilled in me a respect for the consulting relationship. As stated earlier, I am a team player. I am one of many who might help in some small way develop a healthy, lifelong relationship in any consulting experience.

THEORY OF PERFORMANCE EXCELLENCE

When addressing performance excellence it is critical to begin from a solid base. I include in this base determination, drive, discipline, and desire for excellence. This is an intrinsically driven need to perform at an optimal level. In my opinion, if an athlete does not have a high level of intrinsic motivation, then the task of becoming great is possible but less likely to occur. After assessing and ensuring a solid base, I teach the following mental skills: focus and refocusing, poise under pressure, and mental toughness.

The ability of an athlete to focus has been studied in sport psychology for many years. Unfortunately there are no formulas for teaching this ability in every case. All great athletes with whom I have had the privilege to work within the past 35 years give maximum effort, *but no more*. They focus only on what they can control *and no more*. These extraordinary athletes couldn't care less how they compare to others at participation time. They try to get the competition to react to their actions rather than reacting to the competition. They are extremely aware of the conservation of energy for times when they must flip the switch. Distractions are considered not only a normal part of the contest but also an expected part of it. These extraordinary people even find it amusing and curious when the competition begins to unravel. Interestingly, some athletes describe their best performances occurred at "easy speed." That is, the athlete's perception was giving a little less than 100% or trusting more and trying less. In order to be able to trust your training, the athlete must be advised and encouraged to have quality practices of both mental skills and physical skills.

The ability to refocus is a critical skill to master. Jack Nicklaus, considered to be the greatest golfer of all time, was known to have extreme, highly developed concentration power. Sport is an arena where very little can be controlled externally. Yet, many poor performers try to control the uncontrollable aspects of their environment. The best performers are very clear and decisive about control. They spend almost all their time on the things that are in their control. Very little energy is expended on other aspects of the contest. These extraordinary athletes also perform in a state of total acceptance. That is, very little emotion is expended on either good or poor breaks in the game. If you spend time emitting unnecessary anger or joy then the next play will pass you by before you can react. I once asked Gustav Weder, a two-time gold medalist for Switzerland in the two-man bobsled, how he reacted to such fast conditions on the track. He laughed and told me that if he waited to react he would be in trouble. He said he must anticipate rather than react.

The next skill to be learned is poise under pressure. Great athletes learn to change the pressure to challenges or change the "p's" to "c's." They have the ability to monitor their activation levels and adjust them as if they were set to a thermostat. This comes with the ability to learn to activate or deactivate upon command. There are many ways to teach these skills, and I will discuss these later in the section named *Consulting Processes*. However, this ability can be learned and regulated. Originally taught in the Eastern Bloc countries, (e.g., Russia and East Germany) my early contact with these procedures was extremely influential upon my way of doing sport psychology. I learned rather early in my consulting career that athletes do not like to practice progressive relaxation but rather prefer to practice mind-to-muscle techniques. Conservation of physical and emotional energy is a prerequisite to a great performance of any kind. Also, when one is in a poised state, the focusing abilities are maximized.

The final skill to be enhanced and developed is mental toughness. Although very difficult to define, it is easily recognizable. The mentally tough athlete is resilient, has an ability to recover quickly from setbacks, has high self-confidence, healthy self-esteem, and considers himself a fighter rather than a victim when adversity strikes. Another part of mental toughness that is often not mentioned in the sport psychology literature is decisiveness. On the day of a competition, I never ask an athlete a question. By asking any question you might plant a seed of doubt that serves no purpose other than to confuse the athlete. For instance, even the commonly polite conversational piece of, "How do you feel today?" could plant the idea that perhaps I do not feel as well as I could or, even worse, should feel. I only make declarative statements in a decisive and forthright manner. In this way, athletes will sense an utter confidence that will transfer to their decision making process.

These skills that I have discussed are all associated with maximum performance. However, the development of these skills does not ensure maximum performances as there are many factors in an athletic contest that might influence the outcome (poor officiating, luck, weather conditions, time of day, etc.). However, if I can help an athlete achieve some competencies in these skills and become adroit in their usage then I can increase the probability of a more consistent performance on the athlete's part.

Emotional management is an often-neglected part of the mental skills training. In my opinion, it is essential to a great performance. As an example, worry is the most natural and spontaneous emotion imaginable. We all worry from time to time, including athletes. My job is not to rid athletes of worry but to help them manage it. Fear is also natural. To be fearless is associated with poor performance in my experience. The ability to deal with worry and fear and accept these emotions as a normal part of competing is a valuable skill to teach. I do this by telling the athlete that worry is normal and to not fight it but use it to perform better. Anger is another emotion that can stimulate good performance if used appropriately. I have seen some very angry athletes place themselves right into contention. Whereas perhaps a more laid-back approach was ineffective, the athlete sensed a need to press and created just the right level of anger and urgency that was needed to bring their level of effort to a higher level.

I will end this section by describing a Psychological Mastery/Performance Loop (see Figure 3.1) that Jim Reardon and I created many years ago for throwing in track and field. We have received much positive reinforcement from coaches and athletes concerning the applicability of this model. If athletes can integrate this type of pre-performance and during-performance routine, it increases their chance of competing well. I think most athletes have well-developed physical routines but not as well developed mental routines. The loop begins before the performance in the physical and psychological warm-up phase. I like to teach visual or kinesthetic warm up imagery. Imagery is best done in real time while moving. At the same time athletes should narrow their focus to internal cues and positive self-talk like "I've done this thousands of times before," "Just like in practice," "Let's go!!" or other such phrases. At the same time it is important to teach triggers for positive breathing techniques that come naturally as part of the routine. As athletes begin to perform they should sharpen their focus internally and get "the eyes on a target." These types of triggers are taught through "inner mental training" which takes place in a 16-week program that I have been teaching since learning it from Lars-Eric Unestahl 35 years ago.

These routines are learned and automated by using cues. The routines, not rituals, can be used without forcing anything and are conditioned to occur automatically. During performance this frees the athlete to truly trust one's self and one's training. I teach athletes to not force anything extra, just do what you do and trust what you have trained for. After each throw or performance a quick non-emotional evaluation with positive and corrective feedback is self-given, followed by a refocus back to the next trial. Breathing control is essential in this phase. Also, positive "now" self-talk is a must with some type of coping imagery if needed. This loop has been essential in

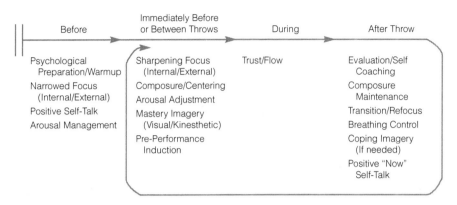

Figure 3.1. **Psychological Mastery Continuum/Performance Loop.**

my work for 35 years and can be taught and automated so it becomes a natural part of each athlete's performance.

Finally, I spend a lot of time on balance in the life of the athlete. It takes time to clear one's plate to optimize performance. An athlete must eat well, rest, recover, rejuvenate and balance. If one's life is in order off the court, the chances of good performance on the court go up. I spend time talking about social support, competencies in areas other than sport, and making sure to eliminate the sports-only identification. If you allow athletes to associate their self-worth totally on athletic performance, this is a recipe for disillusionment and disappointment.

THEORY OF PERFORMANCE BREAKDOWNS

I will address this part of the chapter just as I addressed the *Performance Excellence* section with a model developed by Jim Reardon and me and written in 1992 (see Figure 3.2). There are many errors associated with poor performance, including: over trying and over importance, fear of rejection, fear of change, fear of the unknown, fear of success, fear of failure, distractions (both internal and external), routine disruption, over coaching, over thinking, and confidence issues, just to name a few.

The concept of over trying is an interesting one to dissect. When we first enter organized sport we are taught to "try harder." In fact, this is an attribution that gives one a chance to get better when performance is poor. However, this instruction often backfires by giving the illusion that trying harder will result in success. Unfortunately many athletes that I have been associated with during my career believe this myth: "Hard work always pays divi-

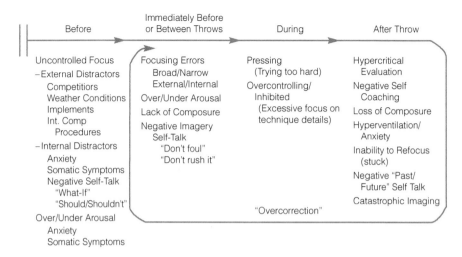

Figure 3.2. **Psychological Breakdown Continuum/Performance Loop.**

dends" is their creed or motto. This may be true in practice but not in competition. In fact, it is the antithesis of advice I give to my clients. Along with this concept is the "big game syndrome." Over importance of athletic contests is the coach's weapon. "This is the most important game of your life" has been uttered many times in locker rooms. My response is what about the other games? Aren't they important? I think the most important game is the one you're currently playing. I get athletes to give the same amount of effort in all games. This way the effort applied becomes the dominant and consistent habit.

Fears of all kind are stoppers of great performance. I do not recommend the absence of fear but the mastery of it. Fear of rejection, the greatest of all human fears, thrives in doubt, comparison, critical and sometimes destructive self-talk, and moreover has ruined many careers of promising athletes. Also, fear of change (either technique or coaches), fear of the unknown (doing something outside your realm of consciousness), and fear of success are equally disruptive. Rather than deal with each one of these separately, I will give my philosophy for dealing with all of these fears: Recognize and conquer them. An athlete must realize that all athletes have fears. The great ones deal with them and do not hide from them.

I will address this issue in my case study later in this chapter but for now let me say that all fears are embedded in the amygdala. Since we can't perform brain surgery, I advocate another type of surgery—the surgery to correct bad thinking about fear. Fear is a natural part of life and sport. I teach my athletes to recognize theirs and to make a change in perception about what it is that is feared. For example, if you do not perform well today, what will be the consequences? Will your life end? Will your family dislike you? Usually the answer is no and the point is made to the understanding of the client/athlete. I heard a great athlete say once "sometimes it's how you do it and sometimes it's how you view it." Isn't that so true? Thinking does not hurt us in competition but poor thinking or ineffective thinking could.

Distraction is another factor in performance errors. The more I continue to consult in applied sport psychology, the more I am convinced that the inability to focus and refocus is the major cause of poor performance. Distraction can occur because of internal factors (anxiety, somatic symptoms, negative self-talk) or external factors (other competitors, weather, poor officiating). These types of distractions disrupt the best routines of athletes and put them into a panic state. It is very difficult for the athlete to recover once this occurs. The game will not stop and the athlete must regain his or her composure and focus very quickly. It reminds me of some research conducted a few years ago with soccer. It was discovered that immediately after a goal in soccer, the probability of another goal being scored quickly after the first increased significantly. This was due to the inability of the goalkeeper to refocus. I try to teach the athlete to come back to the present immediately, if not sooner. Also, over coaching can cause disruption in routine because if an athlete is ready to play, then no more coaching is necessary at that time. Sometimes what you don't say to an athlete immediately pregame is more important than what you do say.

Finally, confidence is a big issue in performance errors. If a coach shows lack of confidence in an athlete close to competition, the athlete will recognize this immediately with negative effects. Anyone around the athlete should exude confidence or get out of the room. Athletes are in charge of their own performance at this point and it is time to let them compete. If they haven't done their homework prior to this time it is like trying to pull an "all nighter" to get a better grade on an exam. It is an illusion.

CONSULTING PROCESS

My consulting process is described as eclectic. I prefer not to label my style, as I use whatever method works well. However, my preference is to initially establish rapport with the athlete and/or organization. The first meeting with an organization is devoted to establishing the terms and types of service that I will provide based upon its needs. I make sure that everyone is aware that my client is always the athlete. This does not mean that all others in the organization are out of bounds regarding a relationship with me. As I established earlier, it is imperative that I have an association with all of the team in order to be an effective consultant. However, some of the information that will remain private regarding confidentiality has to be identified up front in the consulting relationship. Also, if the athlete is a minor, it is my practice to meet initially with the athlete, and one or both parents, to establish guidelines of our working relationship. Moreover, I have always found it very helpful to hear the parents' views regarding the situation, as they invariably are part of the situation.

In my initial assessment of each athlete, I can determine a desire or lack thereof almost immediately. If this desire is missing, my task of helping the athlete achieve performance excellence becomes extremely difficult. In fact, one of our first discussions must be addressing the question, "Why are you playing this sport?" Of course, there are many motives for participation but usually the initial one is to have fun. The athlete who lacks desire is probably not having any fun anymore due to many possible factors such as lack of success, high performance expectations, etc. Perhaps there are coach/athlete communication issues, parent/athlete communication concerns, reoccurring injury problems, perceived "failure," self-sabotage or many other possibilities. These issues must be identified and addressed in order to clear the path to excellence. To this end, I use a variety of methods to help athletes. Typically, the skills I teach are: focusing, confidence building, composure skills, imagery, self-talk awareness, affirmations, and commitment. However, one skill or technique that I have used for 35 years is hypnosis. I will discuss this further in the next section.

UNIQUE FEATURES

As I stated in the previous section, I do not believe I possess something so unique from all other colleagues; however, I believe there are two aspects that might distinguish me from my colleagues: my use of stories to connect with athletes, and my use of hypnosis. I often use stories to help athletes understand their particular situation in a more *indirect* way. I can be very direct and didactic at times, but my general style is to use metaphors and stories to do my work. In fact, one day I plan on writing a book with the stories that I have accumulated in my 35 years of consulting: that is, if I can remember them. Sometimes, after using this storytelling method, I have forgotten the story because it was not about me but about how athletes could use this story to help themselves perform or think well in any situation.

As for hypnosis, many practitioners do not discuss it in our field. I became acquainted with its usefulness while a graduate student. I attended several conferences and made several presentations regarding the use of hypnosis in sport. Lars-Eric Unestahl was my mentor in this area. He had written a classic book on hypnosis in 1975 and he visited Utah in the late '70s when we became lifelong friends and colleagues. Lars-Eric is one of the most creative minds in our field and has been a big influence on my approach to teaching mental training as a developmental model rather than a medical model.

My use of hypnosis involves allowing the athlete to use self-hypnosis to enter a trancelike state in preparation for competition as well as during competition. Sometimes the athletes I have coached are actually in trance state while performing. Many people call this flow or peak performance state, but I have always used the term "ideal performing state" (IPS) based on Unestahl's early terminology. I teach the athlete in many different ways to use "triggers" that have been hypnotically conditioned so that while performing the athlete does not have to do anything special to induce this state other than utilizing the conditioned triggers. If you ever watch Tiger Woods as he stands and waits to hit a shot you will see him trigger this state with a very slow and deliberate blink of his eyes. Very few would recognize this, as it is something very subtle.

The other uses of hypnosis that I have found noteworthy and useful are to explore previous performance in a more intense in vivo state for increased development of awareness. For instance, it is much more powerful to enter a trance state and relive a previous performance than to merely recall it verbally by description. The information is more rich and valuable to obtain in this fashion. Other than this particular use of hypnosis, I believe my consulting process is rather like most of the other authors of this book.

CASE STUDY

I believe this story, a true case study, will illustrate my consulting methods very well. I was once on a trip with a junior national team to a world championship in track and field. I was with a group of young athletes between the ages of 17–19, in a foreign country, and some of these athletes had never been out of the United States before. I was acquainted with most of them from junior camps, where I had been with them in training situations with their coaches in either Colorado Springs or Chula Vista. Thus, the athletes and coaching staff knew me well and trusted me.

On the day before Raymond's first competition, I was contacted by the head coach, a former Olympian and gold medalist, with an urgent request. He asked me "Would you please talk to Raymond?" I inquired about his request and he stated that the athlete was going to withdraw from the competition. According to the coach, he had developed blisters on both his big toes because he had worn a new pair of shoes to training that day. I immediately called the team's athletic trainer at the hotel and inquired as to the seriousness of Raymond's condition. The trainer informed me that he indeed had blisters on his toes and was distraught about his situation. I asked the trainer if Raymond ran in this upcoming race and competed as scheduled whether any further damage could be inflicted. The trainer assured me that no further damage would occur if he ran the race.

I then called Raymond and asked him to meet me in my room at the hotel and he gladly came to see me. We discussed the situation for a few minutes and I found out that he was in extreme pain because of his injury. We discussed injury in general for a while and how he usually reacted to it and he stated that any time he was injured in his entire athletic career, he would withdraw or not compete. I asked him if he thought he could control the pain and he said he didn't know if he could. I asked him on a scale of 1–10 what was the pain in his toes feeling like: He said "10." I asked him if he wanted to lower this pain level and he was curious about doing so. I used a hypnotic trance to allow him to dial his pain to a 3–4 on the scale. After the trance state he told me he was amazed at how much better his toes felt. I asked if he thought he could do that technique on his own tomorrow and he said yes. I asked him how long it takes him to run 400 meters and he said "About 45 seconds." I replied, "You can take anything for 45 seconds can't you?" He said at a 3–4 on the pain scale of course he could. I also pointed out the benefit that he could initiate this procedure in the call area just prior to the race so that while the other competitors were becoming more and more nervous, he would become more ready to perform.

The next day, I approached the coach and said all he had to do was make sure Raymond made it to the call area in time and all would be fine. As a special caveat to this case study, the trainer did not know what I had done, but he cut the leather off the top of Raymond's new shoes just for special effect and comfort. It was fantastic. Raymond ran the race and won a silver medal. The next day he was a member of the World Championship 4 × 400-relay gold medalist team. I saw Raymond many times over the years as he advanced into becoming a world-class 400-meter runner, and we would always have a good laugh over his "new shoes." The moral of this story is you have to think creatively and on your feet in our field. There is no time to consult the textbook in such important circumstances and you must completely trust your own methods to do so.

Recommended Readings

Bloom, B. S. (1985). *Developing talent in young people.* New York, NY: Ballantine.

Csikszentmihalyi, M. (1990). *Flow: The psychology of optimal experience.* New York, NY: Harper & Row.

Hanin, Y. (1980). A study of anxiety in sports. In W. F. Straub (Ed.), *Sport psychology: An analysis of athlete behavior* (pp. 236–249). Ithaca, NY: Mouvement Publications.

Hemery, D. (1986). *The pursuit of sporting excellence: A study of sports highest achievers.* Champaign, IL: Human Kinetics.

Johnson, M. (1996). *Slaying the dragon.* New York, NY: Regan Books.

Nideffer, R. M. (1976). Test of attentional and interpersonal style. *Journal of Personality and Social Psychology, 34,* 394–404.

Ogilvie, B. C., & Tutko, T. (1966). *Problem athletes and how to handle them.* London: Pelham.

Orlick, T. (1986). *In pursuit of excellence.* Champaign, IL: Human Kinetics.

Ravizza, K. (1988). Gaining entry with athletic personnel for season-long consulting. *The Sport Psychologist, 2,* 243–254.

Ravizza, K., & Hanson, T. (1995). *Heads up baseball: Playing the game one pitch at a time.* Indianapolis, IN: Masters Press.

Seligman, M. (1991). *Learned optimism.* New York, NY: Knopf.

Snyder, C. R. (1994). *The psychology of hope: You can get there from here.* New York, NY: Free Press.

Thompson, M. A., Vernacchia, R. A., & Moore, W. E. (1998). *Case studies in applied sport psychology: An educational approach.* Dubuque, IA: Kendall Hunt Publishing.

Tuckman, B. (1965). Developmental sequence in small groups. *Psychological Bulletin, 3,* 364–389.

Unestahl, L-E. (1983). *Inner mental training.* Orebro, Sweden: Veje.

Unestahl, L-E. (1983). *The mental aspects of gymnastics.* Orebro, Sweden: Veje.

Vanek, M., & Cratty, B. (1970). *Psychology and the superior athlete.* London: The Macmillan Company.

Vernacchia, R. A., McGuire, R. T., & Cook, D. L. (1992). *Coaching mental excellence: It does matter whether you win or lose.* Dubuque, IA: William C. Brown and Benchmark.

Williams, J. M. (1986). *Applied sport psychology: Personal growth to peak performance.* Mountain View, CA: Mayfield Publishing Company.

Postscript

I would like to dedicate this chapter to my colleagues in Krakow. I wrote most of it while on sabbatical in Poland during the spring of 2010. I would especially like to recognize: Aleksandra Tokarz, Jan Blecharz, and Malgorzata Siekanska who acted as wonderful hosts and colleagues during my experience in Poland.

4

Dr. Peter Haberl

UNITED STATES OLYMPIC COMMITTEE

Peter Haberl, EdD, works as a senior sport psychologist for the US Olympic Committee at the Olympic Training Center in Colorado Springs, Colorado. Born in Austria, he received his undergraduate degree in sports science from the University of Vienna, Austria, and earned a master's degree in counseling and his EdD in counseling psychology at Boston University. He is a licensed psychologist in Colorado. Before joining the USOC in 1998, Peter served as the sport psychology consultant for the 1998 US Women's Ice Hockey Olympic Team. In his 12 + years at the USOC, Peter has worked with a variety of sports and National Governing Bodies (NGBs), and provided sport psychology services at the Nagano, Sydney, Salt Lake City, Athens, Torino and Beijing Olympic Games, as well as the Torino Paralympic Games and numerous world championships. In his applied work, Peter has a specific focus on mindfulness-based interventions and cognitive-behavioral treatments with both individual and team sport athletes. Prior to becoming a sport psychologist, Peter earned a living as a professional hockey player in his native Austria. Peter and his wife, Corinne, reside in Colorado Springs with their two children.

AUTOBIOGRAPHICAL SKETCH

My personal journey of working the Olympic Games started in 1998, in Nagano, Japan, while I was enrolled in graduate school, in counseling psychology, at Boston University. Four years prior, my advisor at BU, Dr. Len Zaichkowsky, had arranged an applied internship with Coach Ben Smith and his Northeastern University Men's Hockey Program. Ice hockey proved an ideal internship fit, given my educational background in sport science with an emphasis in sport psychology, along with a 10-year career as a professional hockey player in my native Austria. Then, in 1996, when Coach Smith became the head coach of the US Women's National Team I had the good fortune of continuing my internship with this remarkable group of women, working with them for two years and then eventually joining them in Nagano during the Olympic Winter Games. Turco (1999) has written a detailed account of the journey of the 1998 Women's Team to the Gold medal so there is no need to go into further depth here; suffice it to say that it significantly impacted my professional career and continues to do so. The 1998 Olympic Games experience led to successfully applying for the highly coveted two-year fellowship position in the sport psychology department at the USOC in Colorado Springs. After the fellowship I was hired full time by the USOC, where I have now been for 12 exciting years.

Looking back at 1998, I can't believe how fortunate I was to have the opportunity to work with the Olympic Team and I feel deeply grateful to Coach Smith. Now, more than 12 years later, it amazes me how much my knowledge has grown, how little I really knew, and how much my work has evolved. Much of this evolution was influenced by the experience of working in the competitive cauldron of six Olympic Games. The Games are a living laboratory of human performance, and each Games experience has shaped and refined my approach—now it is best described as mindfulness based sport psychology with a heavy dose of CBT. Hopefully, 10 years from now, I will look back at today the same way.

TOWARD A THEORY OF PERFORMANCE EXCELLENCE AT THE OLYMPIC GAMES

There are three questions that I consider essential in my theory of performance excellence at the Olympic Games:

1. What is on the mind of the athlete prior to and during performance at the Games?

2. Can the athlete put the mind where it needs to be to perform at the Games?
3. Why is doing this sport important to the athlete?

Performance at the Olympic Games is a puzzle—a very complicated puzzle. As a sport psychologist, I am concerned with one particular piece of this puzzle: the mind of the athlete. Specifically, I am concerned with the mind's ability to pay attention to the task at hand and the mind's tendency to wander away from the task. Addressing the three questions above helps me navigate the puzzle pieces of the athlete's mind. Let me use an example from the recent Vancouver Winter Olympic Games to illustrate my point and show how the trained mind of an athlete works effectively at the Games in my opinion.

It's February 13, 2010. It is the day after the opening ceremonies at the Vancouver Olympic Games and the first day on which medals will be awarded. The first event is women's freestyle moguls skiing. After the first run in finals (the competitors have two runs), the Canadian Jen Heil, the Torino Gold medalist and Canada's hope for its first Olympic Gold medal on home soil, sits in second place, in between the two Americans, Hannah Kearney, who is in first place, and Heather McPhee, who is in third place. Heather McPhee, going first out of the last three, in her first Olympic final, crashes on her second jump and falls out of the medal standings. After McPhee's crash eliminates her from the podium, Jen Heil puts down a solid run and sits in first place. Hannah Kearney has to wait for Heil's score before she can take her turn. Moments later she can hear the roar of the crowd, suggesting that Heil is in first place. So this is a quintessential sport psychology moment. The quality of your performance will determine the color of the medal or no medal at all. You are so close to your dream goal, you can almost taste it. The commentator on TV, 1998 Olympic Gold medalist Johnny Mosley, utters the phrase: "Pressure at its max! Will she feel pressure?" As she waits for the score, as she waits for her own turn, there is plenty of time to think, there is plenty of time to think the wrong thoughts, and it is almost impossible not to think. What was she thinking at this point? Was she thinking "play it safe, settle for silver, avoid McPhee's fate, or go for gold"? What was going through her mind?[1] The next day on NBC, correspondent Bob Costas asked her exactly this question. She answered:

I came here to win the gold medal. I had consciously thought about how your skiing would change if you would ski for a silver medal and it would have been easy to just give it to Jen, she is an unbelievable competitor, she is on her home turf. But I had made up my mind days before, that that was not going to happen. So I heard the roar of the crowd, I heard her score and I skied the best I possibly could.

Then she describes her run, starting with her first jump:

> . . . Back layout, I did a thousand of those onto the water this summer, as soon as I landed that, I felt like all I needed to do was go, and here is where I am not thinking (skiing the moguls), that is just my instincts taking over, those are my strengths, the turns, I remember thinking about keeping my hands out in front of me. And here it is, I messed up this Heli (the second jump) in the first run, so I popped as hard (voice inflection rising) as I could and when you land, there it is, just like pure adrenaline.[2]

Now why is "what is going through your mind?" the key question from a sport psychology perspective? Four years earlier, Hannah Kearney was the reigning World Champion going into the Torino Games; a 19-year old favored to win the gold medal. Yet, after a botched qualifying run, she failed to make finals, not even making the top 20. She left Torino, feeling like she had let everybody down, including her coach, family, and her country.

I assume much changed in those four years in between the two Olympic Games. Once all the physical training is done, it is the mind that determines how well the athlete executes. It is the mind of the athlete that enables and facilitates performance, and it is the mind of the athlete that disables and debilitates performance. In order to perform well, in order to execute the well-learned skills when the medals are on the line, the mind's attention needs to be on the task at hand, and not on the outcome. However, at the Games, this is easier said than done. At times, for athletes in the Olympic Games, it seems like the mind wants to do anything but stay on the task at hand. The mind wants to wander to the outcome, to the implications of winning, or not winning, a medal. And the moment the mind of the athlete does this, attention is no longer fully on the task at hand, and performance will suffer. This is why I want to know what is on the minds of my athletes. This is also why I think it is important for the athletes to get very good at understanding how their minds work. Judging from a distance, simply based on her performance and the description of her performance in this interview with Bob Costas, Hannah Kearney seems to have mastered this skill at the Olympic Games in Vancouver. She was mindful rather than mindless. She understood that as the favorite going into the final run, thoughts might arise in her mind—thoughts about perhaps settling for less than gold, or about playing it safe. She understood that these thoughts, if bought into, could have led to a conservative, defensive approach on the second run. She understood that she didn't want to ski for second place. She was very clear about what her outcome goal was. Her goal was the gold medal. She also was very clear on where she wanted her attention to be, after making the decision to go for it. Then she succeeded at bringing her full attention to the act of skiing: to skiing the moguls, to executing the jumps. All thoughts about gold medals vanished from her mind and she was completely absorbed on the task at hand and focused on skiing. Her training numbers gave her confidence in the first jump, then as she stated: "thinking stops and instinct takes over." This means all her attention is focused on the present moment execution, there is no cortical real-estate left to judge the performance or worry about the outcome. She reminds herself to focus on her hands as an appropriate attentional cue, and she *"pops"* her second jump, again, using an appropriate attentional cue.

In this interview, it is clear that Hannah Kearney is in charge of her mind. She knows how her mind works, and she knows how to work with her mind. She is able to aim her attention, to sustain her attention, to regain it, if necessary, and not lose herself in her own story of failing four years ago, or of skiing for silver. Hannah Kearney is focused on the present moment, all the while aware of what is on her mind. She is mindful. Bishop et al. (2004) defined mindfulness from a western psychological perspective as the self-regulation of attention, consisting of aiming attention, sustaining attention, regaining attention, and inhibiting "elaborate processing."

For performance to happen at the highest level, the self-regulation of attention is the crucial mental skill. If you want to regulate your attention, the first order of business is knowing where your mind is at. Knowing where your mind is at addresses the metacognitive skill of awareness. Knowing where to put your attention addresses the skill of concentration. Awareness and concentration are essential elements of mindfulness and are cultivated through mindfulness practice. Hannah Kearney may have never heard about mindfulness, yet I strongly assume that she has practiced awareness and concentration (and thus, informally practiced mindfulness). For me, mindfulness, and its component skills of awareness and concentration, is the foundational skill of performance. Thus, my theory of performance at the Olympic Games comes down to knowing where your mind is at, and being able to put your mind where you want it to be, namely on the process of performance.

The German neuroscientist Arne Dietrich (2003, 2004) proposed a very helpful neuroscience theory to explain what happens when athletes are performing at their best. As Csikszentmihalyi, (1990) put it, "athletes are in flow, athletes are in the zone, when there is a "merging of action and awareness." Dietrich says athletes enter a state of *transient hypofrontality* during performance excellence (and also during altered states such as meditation and hypnosis), meaning there is reduced activity in the frontal cortex with the exception of the attention network during times of optimal physical performances. As a result, while attention is fully engaged on the task at hand, the self-critical, judgmental, or worrying voice that so often disrupts performance by interrupting well learned movement patterns is silent. The moment the mind does this during performance, attention is no longer focused on the task. So during transient hypofrontality all the relevant brain resources are dedicated to attention and movement at the expense of commentary, judgment, evaluation, or desire. Dietrich's theory of transient hypofrontality and Csikszentmihalyi's theory of flow are some of the theoretical underpinnings of my understanding of elite performance at the Games.

While the aspirational goal is to be in flow at the Games, the reality of the matter is that this is very difficult. The mind likes to wander, and suspending the pre-frontal cortex from a steady stream of commentary and advice is difficult in the Olympic environment. It is very difficult to avoid "elaborate processing." It is very difficult not to get lost and sidetracked in our minds, in our own story about what should unfold, in the mind's tendency to provide commentary, analysis, and judgments. Mindfulness allows us to catch the wandering mind, and bring attention back to the task at hand.

Mindfulness is a 2500-year old Buddhist idea (Gunaratana, 2002). It has received considerable attention in western psychology in the last 30 years with all kinds of fascinating research findings (i.e., Brown et al., 2007; Davidson et al., 2003; Jha et al., 2007; Lazar et al., 2005). And various authors in sport psychology have also introduced it to our field (e,g., Gardner & Moore, 2006; Parent, 2002). Over the last 10 years, it has become the key skill that I focus on in my own work with Olympic athletes and why my approach to sport psychology is best described as mindfulness-based sport psychology. Such sport psychology staples as imagery, goal-setting, self-talk, pre-performance routine, relaxation, or activation, all still matter. However, I view them through the lens of mindfulness. For example, goals fulfill a motivational and attentional function. Outcome goals, such as Kearney's goal of winning the gold medal, provide motivation for the athlete to engage in years of training and sacrifice and nurture belief. The outcome goal of winning is what perhaps helped Kearney to engage in the hard training and sacrifice of comfort that is necessary to become an Olympic Champion. The outcome goal helped her execute those thousand jumps into the pond in the summer, which then fueled her confidence and belief in her ability to execute, which in turn allowed her to attend to the execution, rather than attend to worrying about executing. The outcome goal helped her to overrule the thought of skiing safe, and settling for the silver medal. Saying the outcome doesn't matter is foolish in my opinion. The outcome matters to the athletes, it matters to the opponents, and because it matters it provides energy.

Yet at the Games, right before and during performance, more often than not, the outcome goal has the potential to be tremendously distracting for athletes, simply because it interferes with the goal of staying in the present moment. After all, the outcome is something happening in the future, and it is uncertain. Uncertainty will often produce worrying thoughts, and a mind that is focused on the future is not present for the here and now. What matters in the moment of performance is focusing attention on performance, and this focus is captured in the process goal(s). Process goals have an attentional function. Kearney's ability to let go of any outcome-based thoughts and fully refocus on the task at hand is what made the difference in the end. To borrow a term from the Buddhist psychology literature, she was able to balance the two efforts, the effort to get somewhere (the gold medal) with the effort to be fully present (Carroll, 2004). Hannah Kearney's process goal of "keeping her hands in front" served the function of being a relevant anchor of attention, and the goal of winning the gold medal provided motivation, belief, and a willingness to risk failure.

Here we can see how Kearney mastered two key questions in my theory of performance. She knows what is on her mind, she knows where she wants to put her mind and she has cultivated the ability to do so. Hannah Kearney was skillful at being mindful. She skillfully worked with awareness and attention. While mindfulness is a set of skills and techniques, it is also a way of being (Kabat-Zinn, 2005). And again, I think Kearney embodies this way of being, as an aspect of mindfulness, quite well in the process addressing the third question in my theory of performance—why is doing the sport important for you? Earlier, I raised the question: Did she experience pressure in the quintessential moment? In a radio interview on National Public Radio (NPR) after her victory she provided this insightful answer (Goldman, 2010):

> I am pretty sure—Pressure is just a made up thing. There is no such thing as pressure. I remind myself sometimes that I am skiing because I love to ski. I am not skiing for air time on NBC, I am not skiing for the fans at the bottom. I am skiing because that this is what I want to be doing.

The dictionary defines pressure as a "constraining influence on the will or the mind." Of course that begs the question "what is this constraining influence?" And the answer is it is the mind itself. Again, this is an example of how Kearney understands how the mind works and how to work with her mind. She neutralizes the potential experience of pressure, the constraining influence on the will or the mind by the mind, by tapping into her intrinsic motivation, and by reminding herself of her love for skiing, her love for simply being present, without any thoughts about future rewards or fame. She proactively addresses why skiing is important for her, and she answers this question by calling forth the intrinsic value of the activity itself. And in this sense, in my mind, she embodies mindfulness as a way of being.

In the end, when it comes to a theory of performance, it can't just be about winning and losing at the Olympic Games. Experiencing failure is part and parcel of the athletic experience. As baseball shows so well, hitting 3 out of 10 pitches is very good, but there is still failure and room for improvement. So having the ability to be present in this moment, to be fully here, irrespective of how it will go, is also part and parcel of mindfulness. Mindfulness does not guarantee you a better chance for a gold medal, but it does offer a structured way of training your mind to being fully present, and to respond skillfully to whatever arises. To conclude this section on my personal theory of performance excellence at the Games, it comes down to being present, to bringing yourself to the table, and fully immersing yourself in the process of performing, irrespective of the outcome, thus, successfully balancing the "two efforts." All of this starts with such questions as "Where is my mind right now?" "Can I put my mind where it needs to be?" and "Why is doing this activity important for me?"[3]

THEORY OF PERFORMANCE BREAKDOWNS

Simply put, as follows from the above theory of performance excellence, when the mind's attention wanders away from the task-at-hand and the athlete is not aware of this wandering mind, then performance at the Olympic Games will break down. Unfortunately, the mind wanders easily at the Games because so much is riding on the athlete's performance. The opportunity to medal at the Games not only comes once every four years, it might never happen again for some. As one prominent winter Olympian, Chad Hedrick, put it, the "five rings can make or break you." Thus, it is this predominance of the value of success at the Games in the mind of the athlete and the mind of the public that can make performing at the Games such a challenge. The failure to succeed at the Olympic Games, and the fear thereof, can weigh heavily on the mind of the athlete.

Here is an example, again from the women's moguls competition on that first day of the Games, that shows us how quickly the mind can get in its own way: Shannon Bahrke, Olympic silver medalist from Salt Lake City, was in 6th place after the first run of finals. In an interview ("Bahrke," 2010) after the Games she spoke about how she experienced 6th place and her feelings of disappointment and despair before the second run:

> I burst into tears. You don't win a medal after qualifying sixth in moguls skiing. It's really, really hard to do that. I just remember looking at my coaches and being devastated. I sat down with my fiancé and we just had a moment of breakdown.

At this point in time, Bahrke's mind is flooded with negative emotions (sadness, disappointment, a loss of hope and optimism) and defeatist thoughts ("you don't win a medal after qualifying in sixth"). Clearly, this mindset won't be helpful for the second run of finals. Most likely, she did not choose to have any of these thoughts and emotions. These thoughts and emotions possibly arose in the mind automatically after the 6th place finish. Her mind quickly paints a defeatist picture of what just happened ('elaborate processing' so to speak). Her mind, in this moment, is not in the right place or in the present: it is in the future. Her own thinking has become an internal distraction and a barrier to performance. If Bahrke continues to believe her own thoughts and goes on ruminating about her predicament, she will not be in a position to compete for a medal. She will fail to generate the right focus and the right intensity for the second run. Fortunately, Shannon Bahrke seemed to have time in between those two runs to let go of predicting the future and ruminating about her predicament:

> Finally I thought, 'It's not over, I can do this. I have worked so hard these last four years, and overcome two knee surgeries. I am good enough to be on that podium.' When I stood in the gate, I knew that I could do it and I put down one of the best runs that I've had. From so low to so high in such a short amount of time really was a little crazy.

Shannon's mind took her on a roller coaster ride. She successfully let go of the automatic belief that she can't make it onto the podium and she let go of predicting a negative future. She stopped believing her own automatic thoughts, replacing them with a newfound determination and intentionality. This change in her mindset may have freed her up to refocus again on the task at hand and find the intensity to "put down one of the best runs" of her career. Shannon Bahrke jumped all the way to third place, finishing her Olympic career on a definite high note, as was evident by her ebullient celebration of Hannah Kearney's gold medal run.

We think we can control our thoughts, yet research (e.g., Wegner, 1994) and the experience at the Games paints a different picture. Thoughts come and go (as do emotions) without us really having much, if any, conscious control over that. With formal mindfulness practice, such as mindful sitting, we can easily test and experience this assumption on our own. Sitting quietly, attempting to keep our attention on our breathing, we notice how quickly we have a serious case of 'monkey mind.' The mind indeed can be like a monkey in the trees, the monkey jumping from branch to branch, similar to the mind jumping from one random thought to the next. Here I am focusing on breathing, and before I know it, my mind jumps to the last competition, the next competition, the argument with the coach, the teammate I don't like, the bad review from the *Sports Illustrated* reporter, the fact that I haven't done my taxes yet, and so forth. In short, my mind can be all over the place and can be a barrier to performance. I believe mindfulness training, with its emphasis on non-judgmental awareness and concentration, provides an antidote to the mind's tendency to create such performance barriers.

CONSULTING PROCESS

My colleague Sean McCann has written an important article outlining our service philosophy at the USOC (McCann, 2008). For us, everything in the psychological life of the athlete is a performance issue; everything in the life of the athlete can impact performance. Thus, we do not make a distinction between clinical and educational services. To address the psychological piece of the performance puzzle, I basically offer four pillars of service. In this section I want to address what I do in the consulting process, how I do it, and how I know what I am doing makes a difference.

The first pillar is a straightforward education piece. Educating athletes about sport psychology and the psychology of the Olympic Games can be delivered in group talks but also in individual sessions and through educational materials such as DVDs, books, journal articles, and weekly emails. The second pillar is the individual work with the athletes. Here the focus can range from straightforward mental skills work, to a host of life issues that can potentially impact performance. The third pillar deals with team building work, when you work with an intact team or team sport to make a contribution to being a cohesive unit going into the Games. And lastly, there is also a practice pillar, where the focus is on the practice of regular mental skills with the athletes.

In my mind, each pillar is important in order to provide effective sport psychology. In the world I work in, the athletes and coaches get evaluated all the time, and so should my work. I go to some lengths in regularly assessing the effectiveness of each pillar as much as practically possible, and this feedback allows me to continue to improve in my work. I gather feedback and evaluations both formally and informally. Formally, at the end of an Olympic quadrennium, or at the end of a season, I use a modified version of the Consultant Evaluation Form (CEF) (Partington & Orlick, 1987). The CEF consists of a mixture of qualitative and quantitative questions, covering consultant characteristics (trust, positivity, flexibility, etc.), an overall effectiveness rating, general recommendations and I have added questions such as what should I stop, start, and continue doing.

There are a number of ways of addressing the question of effectiveness of the service delivery in a setting like the Olympic Games, ranging from medals won, skills developed, behaviors that changed, mindset in competition, and psychological well-being. One way to address the question of effectiveness is simply to ask the athletes. I work with multiple teams and athletes at the Games. Each team's service provision is quite unique, ranging from regularly traveling with teams prior to the Games to no travel at all, from being present for each competition to not being there for some of the competitions, from working with the teams before specific games to only working with the team prior to the start of the Olympic Games, and from dealing with unexpected crisis situations to ongoing individual and team consultations. The athletes' quantitative rating of effectiveness on the CEF along with their qualitative feedback provides me with a certain reassurance that a flexible and individualized approach with multiple teams, to a large extent, met the needs of the coaches, teams and athletes.

I also address effectiveness at the end of a seminar or workshop with a team using a quantitative rating of satisfaction scale (from 1 to 5, 5 being highly satisfied) and three qualitative questions to get feedback from the participants (What did you like best? What did you like least? What did you take away from the presentation?). Presentations can be one-offs or they can be part of a multi-year program with a particular sport in preparation for the Olympic Games. It goes without saying that the goal is to provide a useful, sport-specific, engaging, memorable and satisfying presentation. For such presentations, I use a combination of didactic and experiential approaches laced with stories and strive for a high satisfaction rating. Sometimes I present to Olympic sports with whom I am less familiar and the challenge lies in presenting the material in such a way that it "fits" the respective sport. The qualitative feedback gives me an idea of how successful I was in presenting the material in an engaging and understandable fashion, applicable to their sport. One such example:

I liked how Peter presented himself and the material. In a discussion of mindfulness, listening to a calm well organized presenter reinforced the specific points of the presentation. I really enjoyed how the presentation was specific to *our* sport as opposed to a general overview of sports psychology. I really liked how Peter got us involved in the presentation from the beginning with the meditation exercise. The two hours went by quickly—like a good movie when you are thoroughly engaged you don't notice the time. Very effective, well organized, sport specific presentation. (personal communication, September 20, 2010)

Upon entering the field, public speaking certainly wasn't a strong suit of mine, so feedback like the example above has been rewarding in providing reinforcement for deliberately cultivating these skills over the years.

One of the most enjoyable aspects of my work is the one-on-one relationship with the athletes. Here again, I try to assess my performance so to speak, either formerly through the end of year evaluations as well as after an initial meeting in the early stages of the relationship, and also informally through athlete comments. The information gathered after an initial meeting helps me to triangulate my own sense of the quality of the relationship, perceived satisfaction with the session, and willingness to engage in mental practice.

The quality of the consulting relationship is perhaps undervalued when it comes to addressing performance barriers. Being attuned to the world of the athlete, showing empathy and gaining the athlete's trust opens the doors for all further interventions. Along with formal feedback, a rich source of insight and understanding with regards to the effectiveness of the relationship and the interventions applied is informal feedback, provided by the athletes themselves without me asking for it. The quote below provides a rich example of the perceived effectiveness of the consulting relationship. In trying to qualify for the Olympic Team in the last month before team selection, the athlete's performance began to deteriorate. The focus of the athlete moved away from the task at hand. More and more the athlete became lost in worrying thoughts about not making the team. The thinking mind had become an obstacle to performance. The consultation happened over the phone, as I was traveling in Europe with another team during this time. Here is what the athlete wrote after implementing the intervention suggestions:

I took your advice, wrote down the reasons I love (names sport) and almost ran out of paper. I started the match and had one of the best . . . games of my career. I got every (play) in and gradually became confident enough to be more aggressive and challenge the (opposing player). I feel so much better mentally. The thing that I liked best about our conversation was the point that I do NOT have a position to LOSE in this team . . . I have to have the fighting spirit every day. I'm ready to compete, and I'm smiling again. This is going to be a really hard month, but I have nothing to lose and everything to gain. Thank you so much Peter for taking time out of your day in EUROPE to talk with me. I appreciate that more than I can vocalize. (personal communication, 2004)

The feedback tells me the athlete understood and successfully implemented the various intervention strategies successfully. A combination of mindfulness and CBT techniques allowed the athlete to become aware of and see through the illusions of the thinking mind. The athlete succeeded in coming back to a predominately intrinsic motivation, which, combined with the understanding of how the mind became an obstacle, allowed the athlete to focus on the proper attentional cues and focus attention back onto the task at hand. It is also an example of how the strength of the prior relationship allowed for an effective consultation across two continents using the telephone. The quote also provides a glimpse of how truly rewarding this type of work is and how it has become a calling, rather than a job.

Becoming a unified group is important for Olympic success (Gould et al., 1998) and thus is one of the pillars of service provision. It is a most fascinating pillar and a tremendous challenge to get right at the right time. It is everyone's responsibility, from the head coach to the athlete and the support staff, and I greatly enjoy making a small contribution to it in my work with teams. To work on team issues, I utilize a lot of interactive, experiential games:

I really loved all of the games. They were very innovative, and fun, and so unlike other team building stuff. At first, I thought it would be like other psychologist sessions we'd had that I thought were kind of hokey. But all of the "silly-ass" games translated perfectly to our sport. We learned a lot about our team and ourselves through those activities. I believe that Peter was a catalyst in the success that our team had this summer. (personal communication, 2008)

As the quote indicates, the games come across well with the athletes. The games engage the athletes in an active way, getting them out of their chairs (and sometimes out of their comfort zone). They serve as a metaphor and an ideal jumping off point to discuss team dynamics or individual mental skills. The games allow me to tap into the competitive and playful nature of the athletes and experientially address my teaching points. For example, one of my favorite games is a modified version of a group juggling game. Here is roughly how it goes: The athletes stand in a circle. With one soft throwable object (e.g., a foam ball) we establish a pattern of passing and receiving with every athlete becoming part of the pattern. Once this pattern is established, we add more objects, such as rubber chickens and rubber fish (particularly the squeaky kind). Then I have the group set a performance goal of how quickly they can pass all the objects through the passing pattern and how many mistakes they will make. Inevitably, on the first try, athletes will make mistakes, and confusion, pandemonium and lots of laughter almost always break out while concentration breaks down. After this first try, we might spend some time discussing distractions, goals, and strategies to improve and reduce errors. Then, after a couple more tries, I offer my Olympic Games modification of this activity. I ask the athletes if they are ready to try the Olympic version of this game. Then I switch the soft throwables with a carton of eggs (using a mixture of real, uncooked and fake ceramic eggs). Immediately thoughts explode: "You have got to be kidding me," "Are they real?" and "We are not going to do this with real eggs, are we?" Along with the thoughts come a host of emotional reactions, ranging from surprise to anxiety. Then, for dramatic purposes, I hand out paper towels, asking the athletes to tuck the towels in their waistband, just in case they drop and crack the eggs. Often, once we start the round with the eggs, the group gets very quiet, and the giggling and laughter stops. Focus becomes more intentional and more intense, and, perhaps not surprisingly, the athletes often do better in their performance.

Irrespective of whether or not performance improves, the experiential component of the modified version of the game lends itself for a rich and relevant debrief that can go in a number of ways as it relates to performance at the Olympic Games. We can discuss focus, losing focus, regaining focus, process goals, outcome goals, willingness to fail, fear of failure, handling mistakes, fear of disappointing teammates, resilience, distractions and so forth. The ripple effect of a well-placed debrief question can take the learning from this activity in many directions. Of course, a key mindfulness perspective learned from this activity for athletes at the Olympic Games is how quickly thinking (and emotions) happens in the mind; particularly how quickly thinking happens when there is a real consequence to the activity, and how quickly thinking can undermine learned performance. Nobody wants the egg to drop on their shirts, just like nobody likes to screw up and make mistakes in front of a world audience at the Olympic Games. Such a "silly ass" game provides me with a vehicle to address the key questions in my theory of performance. The athletes will gain first-hand experience of mindfulness and mindlessness. The games and activities are also an excellent tool to work on team cohesion issues. Rather than being talked at, the activities provide a stage for talking with each other and in the process begin to solve obstacles to team cohesion.

UNIQUE FEATURES

Mindfulness is a practice and a skill. It needs to be practiced and not just talked about. Practice can be done formally, through such activities as mindful sitting, mindful walking, mindful eating, or informally. Informal practice can happen every time the athlete engages in the practice of the respective sport. Daniel Siegel (2010) defines practice (any practice) as the intentional focus of attention. So every time an athlete practices his or her sport, the athlete can practice intentionally focusing attention on the task at hand, noticing when the mind wanders and intentionally bringing it back.

To think we can talk about mindfulness and then apply it when it matters most at the Games is probably wishful thinking. Mindfulness is a trainable skill, a skill that requires hard work, diligence, intentionality and commitment. As Jon Kabat-Zinn (1994, p. 111) puts it so well, mindfulness "practice is the slow, disciplined work of digging trenches." I find this aspect of mindfulness, this absence of being a silver bullet, very appealing and completely in line with all the hard work that awaits Olympic Champions. Here is an example from an Olympic Gold medalist who diligently practiced mindfulness (daily) and then applied it during the Games:

> I used a lot of things at the Olympics to stay mentally focused. I worked on meditation beforehand, and at first I started out with five minutes and I was opening my eyes and I was like "are we done yet" because it was just so hard to sit there and breathe and relax and allow all the thoughts of expectations of the Olympics to come in and pass through me and not really judge them or worry about them. Later I got to the point where I could sit for 30 minutes and really relax and deep breathe and focus and I really used that at the Olympics ("Psyched," 2000).

One of the challenges in my work now is figuring out how to use the science of psychology to communicate this practice aspect to my athletes and how to help them find the motivation to practice "digging trenches." To this end, I hold weekly group practice sessions for resident athletes at the Olympic Training Center and send out a short weekly email framed around performance and mindfulness.

CASE STUDY

In August 2008, at the Olympic Summer Games in Beijing, I received a phone call from one of the coaches with whom I have the privilege to work. I have worked with this particular team for a number of years now. I believe we have an excellent working relationship, strong levels of trust, both with the coaching staff and the team. I've traveled with the team to a number of international competitions; they are used to having me present at major competitions.

> Coach: "Peter, I want you to talk to the guys during our team meeting before the quarterfinal game. Do you have time this evening?"
>
> Peter: "Yes, I can make that work. What do you want me to talk about?
>
> Coach: "Talk about being present. I want them to fully focus on this game and not get trapped by looking ahead. We have the ideal quarterfinal opponent, but we both know there is danger in that."
>
> Peter: "OK, that sounds good. I can certainly address that. How much time do I have?"
>
> Coach: "10–15 minutes, then we will go over our game plan. Will that work?"
>
> Peter: "Yes, I will work with that, short and sweet."
>
> Coach: "We will be up in the dorms, in the common room."
>
> Peter: "Thanks, I will see you then." (personal communication, 2008)

Knowing the meeting space is helpful. As I addressed above, in my team sessions, often I use activity-based learning to address the key points in a fun, enjoyable and unexpected way. In order to do this, I often need space for the athletes to be able to move. This particular team is composed of athletes with rather broad shoulders, so I know with this set-up, moving around will be a challenge, if not impossible.

Based on knowing the topic and knowing the limitations of the setting, how will I get the message of "staying present" across? The quarterfinal is a unique juncture during the Olympic tournament. During the round robin format, often you can afford to lose a game. Not during the quarterfinal; now it is 'one and done.' Furthermore, if you are the top seed out of your bracket, you assume the role of the favorite, and the expectation is you "should" win. You "should" win can easily lead to a defensive mindset, where you are trying to "protect" something. The underdog, your opponent, often has the easier psychological setup, as the underdog generally comes in with "we have nothing to lose" mentality and thus plays freely without any psychological constraints and without feeling pressured.

Both mindsets, the underdog "we have nothing to lose" and the favorite "we should win" are simply that, constructions of the thinking mind. These thought constructions come up in the mind, but they are not necessarily an accurate description of reality. More often than not, they are an illusion of the thinking mind, an illusion that can disrupt our ability to fully focus on the present moment. So I want to alert the team to the possible presence of such illusions of the mind. I want them to become aware of "what is on your mind" when it comes to the upcoming quarterfinal. Such questions as "How do you think about your opponent?" "Are you glad we got this quarterfinal opponent, rather than the other one?", "Are you, perhaps, already looking ahead to the semi-finals, or to the medal rounds?" and "Do you know how these thoughts will influence you on the field of play?" arise. Once I have raised their awareness to this stew of thoughts that often brews just below conscious awareness, I want to remind them of the importance of making the conscious choice of where they will put their minds, namely on the relevant task specific cues of the game (which in essence is what the coach will talk about in his pre-game talk right after) and to do this throughout the course of the game. Clearly, I want to remind the athletes to be mindful of their own thinking, and to use their awareness of thinking to put attention on the task at hand.

Another consideration is that I don't want to really talk "at" them for 10-15 minutes, because I am preceding the coaches' talk. The coaches will need to talk "at" them, so the shorter I can make my "talk" and the more interactive and unexpected I can make it, the better my message will come across that supports the message of the coach. So I decide to do a brief experiential exercise with the team and let them reflect on the exercise, then tell them a story from the Games of a team in a similar situation to frame the experience and give them a chance to learn from the other team's "failure of being present."

During lunch time, I am over at Beijing Normal University, the "home away from home" for the US athletes. The USOC has rented this university to set up training, living and dining space for the American delegation. The dining facilities are outstanding, and I know I will be able to get my "prop" for the evening session with the team. The "prop" is a bag full of raisins. I've decided to use Jon Kabat-Zinn's (1990) eating meditation exercise for which he uses raisins. The experiential part of the exercise lasts about 10 minutes, all of which is spent eating one or two raisins. You attempt to fully focus on the sensation of eating, using all your senses while at the same time being mindful of any wandering thoughts and emotions arising and distracting this attentional focus. Raisins are ideal, as they are easily transportable and no one on the team is allergic to them. While I have talked to the team about mindfulness before, I haven't used this specific exercise, so it will have an unexpected quality to it.

After some opening remarks, I instruct the team to pretend to be a scientist studying a foreign object. The athletes play along, reporting aloud the various observations from their sensory perceptions (wrinkly, squishy, soft, malleable, etc.). The facial expressions reflect openness, curiosity, maybe consternation, and for some, the question forms "where is he going with this?" The question arises particularly as I ask them to slowly bring the object to their lips, placing it between their lips and then putting it in their mouths, resisting the urge to chew and swallow. Now that the object is no longer sitting between their lips, they can continue to report out again (sweet, explosion of taste, saliva forming, urge to chew, smoothing wrinkles, etc.) and on we go, eventually beginning to chew the objects, and finally swallowing the remaining pieces.

At the end, I ask them what thoughts and emotions they were aware of during the exercise. They share a variety of thoughts and emotions ("I love raisins; I hate raisins; Is he going to make me eat the raisins?; I don't want to eat them; I can't wait to eat them; When can I finally chew them?; I had memories of eating raisins as a child;" etc.). Then I ask them what the task at hand was (focus on "eating—experiencing" the raisin) and if they noticed all the other "stuff" coming up that intrudes or distracts from this focus and what they did to refocus on the task at hand. After a short discussion, I ask them what thoughts and emotions they are aware of with regards to their quarterfinal game and how they think these thoughts and emotions, if unreflected, might impact behavior during the games. The team does a great job expressing their thoughts and emotions, getting them out in the open and out on the table. Now we have awareness of what is on their collective minds. Then I tell a story of an Olympic team who failed to be aware of their preconceived notions about their quarterfinal opponent, which ended up costing them dearly. This then sets the tone for what to pay attention to in the game itself, leading right into the coach's talk.

As an epilogue, the coach asked me to address the team again prior to the semifinal game and the final game. I decided to repeat the raisin exercise on both occasions. I wanted to get at the counterintuitive effect of "we did this exercise during the other meeting" to remind them that this particular raisin is completely new, and completely different then the last one, and thus requires our full attention again. Inevitably, a thought will arise such as "we have done this before," just like a thought might come during a game such as "we have never beaten this team in a medal game." I wanted the athletes to be aware of such thoughts arising in the mind, and not get "sucked into" them, but rather simply recognize the thought and then take control of attention, bringing it back to the present moment. So the repeating of the exercise (with a different story each time) allowed me to emphasize the key

point of focusing on the present moment, while being aware of any distracting thoughts, emotions, memories, or desires arising in the mind about each
particular game.

Of course it is impossible to say how effective an exercise like this is.
Having the coach ask for more, though, may have been a good indication.
An athlete comment in the end of quad evaluations, answered the question
of what the sport psychologist should stop doing by replying: "Stop doing
the raisin exercise every time. That's a joke. Peter should keep doing what
he is doing." Indeed, as long as I get feedback like this, I will keep doing
what I am doing, which means constantly learning and revising and refining
my approach as it is shaped and molded by the fascinating real life laboratory called performance at the Olympic Games.

References

Bahrke: Retired but not slowing down. (2010, July 5). Retrieved from
   http://www.fisfreestyle.com/uk/news/bahrke-retired-but-not-slowing
   -down,120.html.

Bishop, S. R., Lau, M., Shapiro, S., Carlson, L., Anderson, N. D., Car-
   mody, J., et al. (2004). Mindfulness: A proposed operational definition. *Clinical Psychology: Science & Practice, 11*, 230–241.

Brown, K. W., Ryan, R. M., & Creswell, J. D. (2007). Mindfulness: Theoretical foundations and evidence for its salutary effects. *Psychological
   Inquiry, 4*, 211–237.

Carroll, M. (2004). *Awake at work*. Boston, MA: Shambala Publications.

Csikszentmihalyi, M. (1990). *Flow: The psychology of optimal experience*. New York, NY: Harper/Collins.

Davidson, R. J., Kabat-Zinn, J., Schumacher, J., Rosenkranz, M., Muller,
   D., Santorelli, S. F., et al. (2003). Alterations in brain and immune
   function produced by mindfulness meditation. *Psychosomatic Medicine, 65*, 564–570.

Dietrich, A. (2003). Functional neuroanatomy of altered states of consciousness: The transient hypofrontality hypothesis. *Consciousness
   and Cognition, 12*, 231–256.

Dietrich, A. (2004). Neurocognitive mechanisms underlying the experience of flow. *Consciousness and Cognition, 13*, 746–761.

Gardner, F. L., & Moore, Z. E. (2006). *Clinical sport psychology*. Champaign,
   IL: Human Kinetics.

Goldman, T. (2010, February 14). Mogul skiier Hannah Kearney wins
   first US gold. NPR. Retrieved from http://npr.org/templates/story
   /story.php?storyid = 123710221.

Gould, D., Guinan, D., Greenleaf, C., Medbery, R., Strickland, M., Lauer,
   L., et al. (1998). *Positive andengative factors influencing U.S. Olympic
   athlete and coaches: Atlanta Games assessment*. US Olympic Committee Sport Science and Technology Final Grant Report, Colorado
   Springs, Colorado.

Gunaratana, B. H. (2002). *Mindfulness in plain English*. Boston, MA: Wisdom Publications.

Jha, A. P., Krompinger, J., & Baime, M. J. (2007). Mindfulness training modifies subsystems of attention. *Cognitive, Affective, & Behavioral Neuroscience, 7*, 109–119.

Kabat-Zinn, J. (1990). *Full catastrophe living: Using the wisdom of your body and mind to face stress, pain and illness*. New York, NY: Dell.

Kabat-Zinn, J. (1994). *Wherever you go, there you are. Mindfulness meditation in everyday life*. New York, NY: Hyperion.

Kabat-Zinn, J. (2005). *Coming to our senses: Healing ourselves and the world through mindfulness*. New York, NY: Hyperion Press.

Lazar, S. W., Kerr, C., Wasserman, R., et al. (2005). Meditation experience is associated with increased cortical thickness. *Neuroreport, 16*, 1893–1897.

McCann, S. (2008). At the Olympics, everything is a performance issue. *International Journal of Sport and Exercise Psychology, 6*, 267–276.

Parent, J. (2002). *Zen Golf. Mastering the mental game*. New York, NY: Random House.

Psyched at noon. (2000, November). Lecture series presented at the Olympic Training Center.

Partington, J., & Orlick, T. (1987). The sport psychology consultant evaluation form. *The Sport Psychologist, 1*, 309–317.

Siegel, D. J. (2010). *Mindsight. The new science of personal transformation*. New York, NY: Bantam Books.

Turco, M. (1999). *Crashing the net. The U.S. women's Olympic ice hockey team and the road to gold*. New York: Harper Collins.

Wegner, D. M. (1994). Ironic processes of mental control. *Psychological Review, 101*, 34–52.

Endnotes

1. I do not know Hannah Kearney personally and I have never worked with freestyle moguls, yet the description of her experience, and her reply to the question of what was going through her mind provides a vivid example of how I view an ideal performance at the Olympic Games. My interpretations, though, are simply that, my interpretations and perhaps since they are based on media comments should be taken with a grain of salt.

2. This interview can viewed at http://i.nbcolympics.com/video/asset id = 23af87b2-dd9c-4bdc-a944-4f20393ce572.html

3. The quote can be retrieved from http://nbc olympics.com/news-features/news/newsid = 412055.html

5

Dr. Kate F. Hays

THE PERFORMING EDGE, TORONTO, CANADA

Kate F. Hays, PhD, maintains an independent practice, The Performing Edge, in Toronto, Ontario, Canada, with a specialized focus on performance enhancement for athletes, performing artists, and business executives. She earned her master's and doctorate from Boston University in 1971. In New Hampshire following her graduate training, she directed a community mental health center and subsequently developed an individual and group private practice. Her research, writing, teaching, and practice, both in New Hampshire and, since 1997, in Toronto, has been directed toward the mental benefits of physical activity and the application of sport psychology techniques to other performance populations as well as athletes. An independent scholar, Dr. Hays regularly offers tele-consultation group training in sport psychology and performance psychology. She is the author of *Working It Out: Using Exercise in Psychotherapy* (1999); *Move Your Body, Tone Your Mood* (2002); *You're On! Consulting for Peak Performance* (with co-author Charles H. Brown) (2004); and edited *Integrating Exercise, Sports, Movement and Mind: Therapeutic Unity* (1998) as well as *Performance Psychology in Action* (2009). A former president of American

Psychological Association's Division of Exercise and Sport Psychology, she is the recipient of its Bruce Ogilvie Award for Professional Practice.

AUTOBIOGRAPHICAL SKETCH

My life in sport psychology began on a May evening. I was living in New Hampshire and had been in practice as a psychologist for 10 years. Although professionally established, it was a time of personal familial uncertainty. My good friend Anne and I went out for a walk, but the swirling, nipping black flies drove us back. Not ready to return to the house, I did something that a few friends kept talking about: I ran. Well, I jogged to the next telephone pole. And then walked a bit—and jogged another telephone pole length. Until that moment I would have told you that running was the world's stupidest, most boring activity imaginable. I didn't think much about the experience until the next night . . . when the impulse to run struck again. I was a 24-hour convert.

What's relevant is what I learned from that experience. It wasn't that, unbeknownst to them, everyone secretly desires to run. Rather, it was that there probably is some form of physical activity that is deeply satisfying to everyone. It may be perfectly obvious, or we may not know what it is until we bump into it. I also came to understand that a time of crisis is a good time for engaging in new ways of coping. Further, I came to recognize that some forms of exercise for some people can allow for different ways of thinking about things. This knowledge, still fascinating to me, has yet to be fully explained experimentally. And finally, I learned that those thoughts that come during a run are as evanescent as a dream—if one doesn't hold onto them actively and deliberately or write them down, they vanish.

Born in New York City, I attended an elementary and high school that provided both the stability of a small, supportive community and an ethos that extolled exploration and creativity. At the University of New Hampshire, I majored in psychology because it was in the liberal arts college, the coursework seemed effortless to me, and I could take many courses in music history and art history (my other passions).

There was no question in my mind that I would get a doctoral degree, and that took me to Boston University. The highlights of my experience there involved being in the forefront of the community psychology movement, and living in the spirit of "giving psychology away" (Miller, 1969)—the burgeoning of primary prevention in psychology. (Formal coursework, meanwhile, suited me less well: I learned how to do long-term play therapy with young children, under a psychoanalytic model against which I chafed.)

Following graduate school, I returned to New Hampshire for 15 years, directing a community mental health center. There, I wore numerous hats and developed new skills: school consultant, program evaluator, psychotherapist to people of all ages, couples and family therapist. I offered numerous workshops, especially on the value of keeping a personal journal, and learned about and offered psychotherapy to adult survivors of childhood sexual abuse and people with eating disorders. Each new developing interest and skill, although perhaps on the surface seeming random, was in one way or another connected to the preceding one.

Once I started running—and became captivated by that shift in thinking—I immediately tried to find information on that process. I thought of it as "right brain problem solving." Astonishingly, the small city library had a copy of Michael Sachs' *Running as Therapy* (1984), about the only source that I could find to even begin describing the interaction between running and thinking. Contact with Sachs led to an intensive workshop and extensive reading, as I immersed myself in learning about sport psychology. Two areas in particular held appeal: the mental benefits of physical activity and mental skills for optimal athletic performance.

The first AASP (then, AAASP [Association for the Advancement of Applied Sport Psychology]) conference proved to be a pivotal moment: While there, I made the decision to go into private practice. Community mental health had by then changed enough that I thought I'd be in a better position to offer primary prevention on my own; I was also ready to begin exploring what I could do with sport psychology in my practice.

The time I spent in New Hampshire in private practice allowed for a very gradual shift toward working with more athletes (and performing artists—but that's a whole other story). One practice lesson I gradually came to realize, however, was "location, location, location." The rural setting, with its sparse population and lack of collegiate or professional sports teams, was never going to provide more than the occasional athlete client.

That assessment proved accurate and was influential in my decision to move to Toronto in 1997. Since becoming re-licensed there, the vast majority of my clients have been athletes—as well as other performers.

THEORY OF PERFORMANCE EXCELLENCE

In order to describe the psychological, emotional, and behavioral skills necessary for performance excellence, it is first important to define performance excellence and performers. From a cognitive, affective, and behavioral perspective, performers need to be able to function very well in a high-pressure context, perform in front of an actual (or implied) audience at a particular point in time, meet stringent performance standards, cope with extremely high external (and internal) demands and judgments, and be able to manage the consequences of their performance (Hays, 2009).

Competitive sport has a distinct advantage over other performance domains: Optimal physical performance is frequently defined by specific outcomes. The outcome is often used as the defining measure of successful performance.

Necessary Mental Elements for Performance Excellence

The combination of knowledge in the psychology of performance with athletes and interest in performance issues with other types of performers was the impetus to research that colleague Charlie Brown and I conducted (2004). Drawing on the research and practice literature in sport psychology, we interviewed top performers in domains other than sport—performing artists, business executives, and professionals in high-risk occupations—conducting semi-structured interviews with them on key elements in performance. In a satisfyingly circular way, our findings, regarding both the similarities across domains and the issues specific to particular domains, inform the work that I now do with athletes and professionals interested in sport and performance psychology. For performance excellence, we concluded, three elements are necessary. Each component builds on the other in a sequential manner. These elements include foundational aspects, thorough preparation, and the management of the actual performance itself.

The structural undergirding essential to performance— the foundation— is set to some degree by an athlete's basic or innate abilities. While practice can (and does) indeed make "excellent" (if not perfect), the emergence and development of skills will be either easier or more challenging as a function of an athlete's genetic physical and temperamental structure. Another basic attribute will be a coherent "sense of self." This may be expressed through self-confidence, purpose and direction, identity, and self-knowledge. An optimistic attitude and capacity for reframing can be critical. The work of positive psychology helps us recognize both dispositional traits and the ways in which we can influence them (Lyubomirsky, 2007). The final necessary element to (sustained) performance excellence will be a capacity for self-care. Athletes who are "managed" by others—parents, coaches, and team health care professionals—may be able to cede this responsibility for some time; subsequently, however, they will need to learn this necessary aspect for themselves.

The relative balance of innate ability compared with learned skill is of course central to understanding performance excellence, and I am much influenced by the research of K. Anders Ericsson (1996). Building on the foundation, active intentional learning or deliberate practice is critical. Technical knowledge and understanding about how one goes about learning is an important element of the learning process. An athlete needs to appreciate both the differences and similarities between practice and competition: how and where does she or he incorporate the kinds of knowledge and skills that will be necessary for competition, while still continuing to learn and refine the knowledge and skills?

The majority of my practice is devoted to assessing and assisting athletes with mental skills for performance excellence. I've come to think of the "canon" (Andersen, 2000) of mental skills as sport psychology's "Big Five": (a) arousal regulation or activation management, (b) thought management, (c) goal setting, (d) attention management, and (e) imagery. The endlessly fascinating question is some variant of: Which of these skills, expressed in which way, in which order, will be most helpful for this particular client at this particular time? This viewpoint has been described as informed pluralism or technical eclecticism, based on an actuarial rather than theoretical approach to treatment (Norcross, 2003).

What is involved in the "Big Five"? Rather than being technique-driven, the practitioner needs to recognize the functions or issues for which certain techniques may be appropriate. For performance excellence one needs: both some level of somatic and cognitive activation and the ability to assess and manage it; awareness of thought and affect and the capacity to manipulate it; motivation and achievement focus; the ability to focus in systematic ways; the capacity for sensory awareness and the ability to manipulate thoughts, feelings, and behaviors outside of their actual expression, through the imagination.

Because applied sport psychology emerged at approximately the same time as the rise of cognitive behavior therapy (CBT), and because the assumptions and techniques of CBT are concrete enough to be fairly easily learned and applied, there has often been a synchrony between CBT and sport psychology, as if that is the only option for athletes (and sport psychologists) to consider. Cognitive behavioral methods often work well—but others can also address these fundamental performance issues. For example, awareness of thought and affect often gets reduced, in sport psychology, into a set of specific techniques. A broader view recognizes that the issue is not "just" stopping or countering a thought, but more, knowing what the options are for how to handle thoughts. A decision tree begins with the question: Is this a thought that is useful or not? If not, then perhaps one can remove the thought by, for example, "throwing it in the garbage can" or "dumping it in the toilet." On the other hand, the athlete may decide that the thought itself is useful but the issue is one of timing: Deal with the thought right now or examine it at a later point. Postponing the thought may involve the stop thought method, "parking" intrusive thoughts, or creating a specific regularized "worry time" to work on the issue (Borkovec, Robinson, Pruzinsky, & DePree, 1983). Challenging the thought may well involve common CB techniques such as creating thought records or developing an alternative response to a frequent thought or action. Affirmations may serve as counters to negative thoughts or methods of bolstering self-confidence. Some athletes will actually be interested in exploring negative thoughts (though preferably, not just at the moment they are about to deliver the second serve for match point!). Exploration, often through reflection or journal writing, can engage a vast array of methods, whether the athlete addresses the issues symbolically, explores the affective components, or recognizes the historic relevance of these thoughts. A combination method might involve appreciating the affective reaction (empathy) and then moving to more pragmatic solutions (rational cognitions). Using Gestalt techniques, the athlete might engage in a "dialogue" between himself and his sport. Alternatively, paying attention without engagement, (i.e., non-judgmental mindfulness or acceptance [Gardner & Moore, 2007]), may be most appropriate. Finally, the application of positive psychology to athletic populations focuses on athletes' strengths and abilities and is consistent with a mental toughness perspective (Gucciardi & Mallett, 2010; Park, Hays, & Solomon, 2009).

My theory of performance excellence also speaks to the actual performance itself. It is an exquisite irony that the most excellent performance may feel indescribable. Peak performance will often be experienced by the athlete as transformative, a time of "flow" (Csikszentmihalyi, 1990) in which access to verbal description is limited. This is the essence of being in the moment, in the zone, at one with the process. Recognizing the affective and kinesthetic aspects of that performance may be as important as being able to verbalize it (Hanin, 1999).

One final, critical element of performance that is often overlooked is how and when the athlete assesses the performance after it has occurred. The timing, presence or absence of others, medium for assessment, and method of evaluation will have great impact on the athlete's sense of self, motivation, and capacity to learn and grow. For example, I met with Jim, an adolescent hockey player, regarding his hesitant game-day performance style. By Jim's preference, his father, Malcolm, was present for all sessions. Malcolm was an interested, engaged man with aspirations for his son, yet willing to learn how best to support him. We discussed how, when, and where they reviewed Jim's game performance. Jim was able to articulate his own preferences, I shared examples of "positive sandwich" feedback (Smith & Smoll, 2001), and Malcolm eagerly absorbed the information.

Performance excellence is not going to depend on the athlete alone or on his or her intrapsychic process. Instead, it will occur in relation to others, whether those others are teammates, coaches or other ancillary personnel, or organizations and systems within which the athlete functions. An athlete's personal history, often with one's family of origin, will have an impact upon the athlete's functioning as well. Particularly relevant may be the role of athletics and sports in that family (Côté, 1999; Hellstedt, 1995).

The Process of Change

Performance excellence doesn't just happen. People need to learn and grow—to change—whether through self-directed knowledge or the assistance of another. It is therefore important to understand *how* people change. To that end, I have found the transtheoretical model of change (Prochaska, Norcross, & DiClemente, 1995) especially useful both in the way that I direct my work and to help athletes learn about their own process of change. The transtheoretical, or stage, model of change has embedded within it a number of implications, for example: Interventions often founder if one assumes without checking that they are ready to take action (Stage 4 of 5). Lack of action often means that an athlete needs to address prior stages (i.e., precontemplation, contemplation, preparation) and the processes that are involved. Considered within a psychodynamic frame as the client's "resistance," it may be more accurately described as a less than full appreciation of the client's present reality. Also implied in this model is the incremental nature of change: an athlete can keep one "foot" in the known while venturing forth into unknown or unfamiliar territory. Starting small and moving gradually also allows athletes to build confidence and trust in their own process of change. People not only change incrementally; at times, change occurs in a spiral, rather than linear, fashion. One confronts the same issue as at a prior time, but is now in a different emotional (or actual) "place" and thus able to make use of earlier knowledge and experience in a different way.

THEORY OF PERFORMANCE BREAKDOWNS

Not surprisingly, the common issues that prevent people from attaining performance excellence are to some degree the obverse of those that allow for performance excellence. There are some, though, that merit specific commentary.

One of the key elements to performance has to do with the ways in which an athlete manages the stress that is inherent to performance. The process of experiencing stress has been described as "a substantial imbalance between demand and response capability, under conditions where failure to meet that demand has important consequences" (McGrath, 1970, p. 20). Athletes will feel stress, then, when they perceive a high level (or increase) of demand, perceive a low level (or decrease) of support, and/or deem the outcome to be important.

These three variables—demand, supports, weight of outcome—are all ones that can be addressed in a variety of ways by athletes. The most challenging of the variables may be the third: Often, the outcome *does* matter; it's not just a question of perception. The sport psychologist can work with athletes to learn how to control the points at which they will attend to the outcome and ways in which they can temporarily disregard the outcome while focusing on elements within their control.

Athletes are most likely to experience the highest level of stress in relation to performance in the period just before competition. Having a "pre-performance plan" in place—and making use of it—has often been classified as a separate element of the necessary mental skills for performance excellence.

Issues within the "canon" that are most likely to arise include: becoming over-aroused and unable to control that activation; becoming over-aroused in the context of high levels of cognitive tension (as, for example, envisioned in cusp catastrophe theory; Hardy, 1996); being flooded by negative thoughts, feelings, or general "mind chatter;" being unclear about or losing track of one's goals; and becoming distracted and then disconcerted by losing focus and not having a means to regain concentration.

In the process of change, there are also predictable challenges that can result in errors or inadequate learning and knowledge. Athletes can attempt too much change too fast. They may not be ready for some of those changes, may not recognize the past psychological utility or value of the errors that they have made (in psychodynamic-ese: "Defenses are there for a reason"), or may simply become overwhelmed by too many expectations and thus be unable to concentrate fully on any.

Another problem may be an attempt to make changes without full regard for the context in which that change is being undertaken. "To understand a system," social psychologist Kurt Lewin is purported to have commented, "try to change it." For example, there may be a mismatch between coach and athlete—but the athlete needs to work with the coach at hand; parental pressures and ways of doing things may have kept a tidy, albeit dysfunctional, equilibrium; or financial exigencies may determine or impact upon a number of aspects of the athlete's life.

In striving for perfection, athletes berate themselves for errors. Yet paying attention to and learning from their past mistakes or issues can be immensely useful. Basketball player Michael Jordan is famously quoted as saying, "I've missed more than 9000 shots in my career. I've lost almost 300 games. Twenty-six times I've been trusted to take the game winning shot and missed. I've failed over and over and over again in my life. And that is why I succeed."

CONSULTING PROCESS

Particularly in a field that is relatively new, such as sport psychology, the consulting process must also be one that operates within a framework of active ethical responsibility (Hays, 2006). "Positive ethics," as compared with "principle ethics," suggests that ethics is an active engagement (Aoyagi & Portenga, 2010). Ethical awareness can be understood as "a continuous, active process that involves constant questioning and personal responsibility" (Pope & Vasquez, 2011, p. 2).

My philosophy of consultation in sport psychology is grounded in a number of underlying beliefs and assumptions. One is the question of what is efficacious in the work that we do. Within psychology over the past number of years, various "wars" have been waged concerning best treatment practices. Empirically supported treatments (ESTs), based on randomized controlled trials (RCTs) of specific interventions, consider manualized treatments to be the ultimate object, the so-called gold standard. Yet, ESTs actively remove some of the elements most citical to consulting: the practitioner's knowledge and skills and the central importance of the interaction between practitioner and client (Whiston & Sexton, 1993). Instead, I find guidance through the three-pronged definition of evidence-based practice in psychology (EBPP), "the integration of the best available research with clinical expertise in the context of patient characteristics, culture, and preferences" (APA, 2006, p. 273).

The EBPP definition works especially well within my approach to practicing sport psychology: I take into account the extensive research base of sport psychology and I make use of my years of experience with various types and kinds of athletes, and this in turn privileges the athlete in a number of ways. Sports and athletics can be seen as a culture of its own, along with the more obvious socio-demographic characteristics typically considered as "culture." Further, EBPP recognizes the essential relevance of the fit between athlete and practitioner and the practitioner's obligation to appreciate the client's own preferences.

From the time of our first encounter, I involve the client actively in the process of change. I typically offer certain tools for change during the initial session. For example, I may assess the clients' skill in diaphragmatic breathing and then teach them how to engage the diaphragmatic muscles while relaxing their shoulders and minimizing thoracic breathing. I will then write out instructions for practice, so that clients can, over time, incorporate diaphragmatic breathing into their daily and sport life.

I also find that having available a wide array of tools leads to the best fit for this client at this time. When I offer a "smorgasbord" of options, as compared with the One Right Way, clients feel empowered, can experiment, and we can discover the best match for them.

I consider my consulting practice to be broader than "just" working directly with clients. I communicate what I know to colleagues or students (through writing and teaching) or with the general public (through a trade book, my *Psychology Today* blog, and workshops). Not surprisingly, learning by teaching is a way in which I increase my own knowledge in a more profound way. Most recently, this type of learning by teaching, this kind of Eriksonian generativity, has taken expression in tele-consultation groups that I have developed over the past few years (Hays, 2010).

One aspect of good consultation practice is accurate self-knowledge (Brown, 2009). My clinical background keeps me attuned to potential issues of clinical depression or anxiety, as well as less frequently encountered issues, such as relevant family dysfunction, eating disorders, or childhood sexual abuse. At the same time, I am aware of various self-limitations, such as the potential for viewing issues from a psychopathological perspective; overwhelming clients with too much information in the process of wanting to share a variety of options; and the importance of recognizing my own limitations of background, training, knowledge, and interest. I try to handle these issues by such methods as learning about specific sports through reading and observation, as well as recognizing that the client may well be more of an expert on the particular sport than am I. It is also critical to know of other resources and referral options (e.g., coaches, registered dietitians, sports medicine physicians, athletic trainers, or exercise physiologists). Colleagues to whom I can turn, whether for knowledge or review, serve as a very important resource. I make sure to maintain contact with a group of colleagues with whom I consult on a predictable basis, as well as those who I contact for specific suggestions and review. Often, the very process of articulating a concern can help determine what the issues are and methods of handling them.

UNIQUE FEATURES

As may be evident from my earlier description and the case description that follows, certain guiding principles are important to my functioning as a sport psychology consultant. My "Top 10" are listed here—though not in order of importance.

(1) A spirit of collaborative empiricism in consultation. The term "collaborative empiricism" was originally coined by George Kelly, a brilliant and under-appreciated American personality theorist and clinician with whom I had the amazing privilege of studying as an undergraduate. Kelly (Maher, 1969) compared our work as practitioners to that of experimental scientists. Although not engaged on a regular basis in formal experimental research, in fact I consider every encounter—and most moments in it—to be a series of experiments in which hypotheses are formed, tested, and revised. These hypotheses may be directed toward the problem and its solution; hypotheses may concern the most effective manner of relating to the client at any particular moment: Should I be in empathic mode? Educational (and if so, at what level and with what language)? Directive? Self-disclosing?

(2) Even from the beginning, give clients something they can use. Clients participate with us in a variety of ways. I see my task at an initial session as multi-faceted, involving learning about the client and making an empathic connection. In one way or another, clients come to us experiencing some level of distress or dissatisfaction. They are looking for practical solutions to their issues; as well, often, they would like to understand what is occurring. We are the "keepers of hope." If I can give clients some practical information that will begin to address their issues, I am serving a number of purposes simultaneously: I am not only giving them a tool, I am demonstrating that I have understood their concern; that I actually *can* help; and that they can take action on their own behalf that will make a difference for them.

Most often, at some point in that first session, I will teach the client, actively and directly, how to make use of diaphragmatic breathing (Hays, 2009).

The vast majority of athletes who I see come in because of a discrepancy between their skill during practice and their presentation in competition. Typically, this is fueled by an inability to manage levels of arousal effectively. For me, the most fundamental performance skill—as well as a skill valuable in and of itself—is the capacity to regulate tension, most easily and rapidly through diaphragmatic breathing.

(3) Go in the direction the camel is already going. I am a pragmatist, curious about what is going on within the person and interested in finding out what works. The transtheoretical model helps me appreciate that, even though a client is in some distress, he or she may not be at a point where major change can occur. I can assess his or her readiness for change, adapt our work to take that into account, and help him or her move to the next stage without feeling crowded, pushed, or rushed.

As the client begins to make changes, we can notice and celebrate those changes, whether through metaphor, solution-focused "scaling" (Berg & de-Shazer, 1993), or observational accounting. Attending to those changes can help "steer the camel."

(4) You don't have to teach the client everything you know. This phrase, spoken to me by one of my early supervisors, is one that has, obviously, stuck over the years. It is, among other things, the difference between being a bright graduate student who wants, needs, or is expected to show a professor how smart and capable she is, as compared with working collaboratively with a client. I consider myself a translator in a variety of ways: To some degree, I translate from theory or research to practice, so that the client has effective access to knowledge; translation may involve helping clients more completely appreciate what they have learned or how it applies to them; sometimes, translation means helping them understand their own internal workings—the "why" questions. In order to do that, I have to have the widest possible range of knowledge, so that I can be selective from amongst my repertoire.

(5) Interaction of thought, affect, and behavior. In order to enact an integrative model, it is important to be both a generalist and a specialist. I need to have a general understanding of how people function, a model of human behavior. At the same time, I need to learn about the unique elements of a particular person in a particular context at a particular time.

I am curious about the interaction of an athlete's thoughts, feelings, and behaviors, recognizing that change in any one sphere can lead to change in another aspect of being. My awareness of individual differences—the ways in which general principles must be applied at an individual level—influences my preference for working with individuals (including those directly within their sphere) rather than focusing on such abstract concepts as team cohesion or leadership.

(6) Pay attention to culture, context, systems, and domains, in addition to individuals. Although the work that I do is generally with individuals, at times with input or consultation with parents, coaches, or others, it is important that I understand the ways in which this person functions within their particular context. Whether it's in regard to demanding parents, one-method-only coaches, or harassing teammates, I need to appreciate and work with *this* athlete within *this* situation.

(7) Maintain awareness of subtexts and relational factors. I have heard sport psychology colleagues comment that they don't deal with transference, as if it were only a heuristic and as if disregarding it could make it go away or not be relevant. My view, instead, is that transference—and sometimes, counter-transference—happens. I need to maintain awareness of the ways in which I am experienced by my client (as well, of course, as the ways in which I experience this client). Whether I choose to actively work on this awareness with the client, or we discuss it as related to family of origin or cognitive schemas, is a whole other matter.

In a similar vein, practitioners trained in life coaching, careful not to overstep their bounds, avoid "diagnosis," as if focusing only on an athlete's future will erase what may be some very real and active stumbling blocks. Whatever the label—and sometimes, a diagnosis can serve as a shorthand descriptor—certain issues do need to be addressed for an athlete to perform optimally.

(8) If the focus is going to shift, do so with the client's knowledge and consent. Because of my clinical background, I may be more likely than those without such training to pay attention to or be attuned to serious issues reflecting past difficulties or present dysfunctions. If the client has not come to me expressing concerns in this area, I need to carefully negotiate with her or him whether and when we will address such problems.

(9) Maintain "boundary patrol," especially in situations that are different from "traditional" psychotherapeutic bounds and expectations. Because of my particular practice, I often function within some of the "traditional" boundaries of psychotherapy, such as the location of our meeting, the length of time that we meet, and how we interact. There are times, particularly with sport psychology consultation, when it makes sense to change one or

another element. A sporting event may be coming up this weekend and we agree that it will be useful to meet twice this week. A client comes to work with me from a distance, and so we meet less frequently, for longer periods of time. I go to a client's game and meet his parents for the first time—and am expected to sit with them and other family members and friends. A client is training elsewhere, and so we "meet" via Skype (an Internet video calling service). In each instance, I need to be clear about what my role is, discuss anything relevant with the client, and recognize and attempt to prevent potential pitfalls (McCann, 2000).

(10) I have an obligation—to my clients and myself—to make use of what I know and to continue learning. Over the years, I have worked with clients on a variety of issues and learned a number of techniques. In relation to clinical issues, for example, if an athlete has a history of trauma or troubled parenting, is dealing with disordered eating, is clinically depressed or manifests trait anxiety, I am familiar with these disorders and various treatment options. Depending on the client, I may suggest techniques more common in traditional psychotherapy or counseling, including a variety of methods for keeping personal journals or the use of Gestalt methods such as dialogues or "empty chair" techniques. Some of these methods can be augmented by encouraging specific relevant sport psychology readings. Timothy Gallwey's various "Inner Game" books, for instance, exemplify relevant elements of mindfulness.

I also feel a sense of obligation toward being open to my own learning, growth, and change. This may occur through learning from clients, whether it is about their specific lives, attitudes and beliefs, style of change, or sport. My own growth occurs by learning through reading, workshops, organizational involvement, and consultation with others. The following case study— masked to protect the client's identity—illustrates the features and principles I have described.

CASE STUDY

Crista was a self-referred, 24-year-old equestrian who—as happens with increasing frequency these days—found my name, practice description, and contact information on the Internet. As someone who has enjoyed riding for many years, and because of the complexity of consultation regarding a "team" sport in which one member is not only not present during consultation but also non-verbal in team interaction, I was intrigued with her request. Crista was seen for a total of 30 sessions over a one-year period. (This is a longer period of time and considerably more sessions than typically occurs in my brief intervention approach.) All sessions were held in my office.

Initially, Crista described panic and problems for the past three years, stemming from a minor accident while show jumping her horse. Tearfully, she explained: "I have a lot of fear and anxiety over not leading [to the jump] from the perfect spot and crashing my horse—I don't want to hurt my horse."

The youngest of three daughters in an intact family, Crista alternated between completing her undergraduate degree and competitive riding, assisting at a nearby stable and being instructed numerous times per week. She described herself as almost continuously anxious: her heart racing, her stomach feeling "nervous." She said that she could panic in a second: "My mind goes blank, I react without thinking." Typically, she would "pull up" (i.e., stop) her horse just before a jump, and then feel frustrated, embarrassed, and defeated.

I followed a general initial interview protocol (Taylor & Schneider, 1992) that included information about Crista's current situation, its antecedents, relevant history, and attempts at solution. Crista appeared bright, thoughtful, capable, and determined. She had had a few prior brief encounters with sport psychologists and counselors. As none had been especially helpful, she was dubious that this contact might be different. She felt, however, that she was currently making some gradual progress in overcoming her fears, while also feeling that she couldn't sustain this progress on her own.

During the session, in addition to obtaining information, I instructed Crista on the basic elements of diaphragmatic breathing. I suggested that she rate herself on a 10 point scale, where 1 would be totally relaxed, while 10 would describe her at her most anxious. Crista responded well, and noted that she was able to shift from an "8" to a "5" while supine. I wrote out a detailed training sequence such that ultimately she would be able to use diaphragmatic breathing while riding.

Eager to please, Crista was also heavily invested in change. She was conscious of the irrationality of her attempts to control and be perfect in a sport that involves two participants in non-verbal synchrony. She was intrigued by the idea of paying attention to those thoughts and developing more constructive attitudes, initially via a modified thought record, but mostly through observation and free journaling.

Over time, it became clear that her anxiety and perfectionism were considerably more widespread than just in relation to her riding. She acknowledged issues with "social anxiety," both self-described and diagnosed and treated with medication. Anxiety, it turned out, was really a life-long issue, affecting all aspects of her life. She was passionate about riding, but it wasn't until she was able to truly enjoy the experience that she could recognize the ways in which she had ridden for so many years *despite* the anxiety.

Crista felt intimidated by her coach. He urged her to just push through her fear, encouraging her to go at jumps over and over again. She would become more frightened and tearful, yet felt unable to let him know the methods that she found most helpful. Through role play, I assisted her in figuring out how to speak with her coach about what she would like. When she did, hesitantly, speak with him, she came to understand that what she had experienced as anger and demand was his ineffective attempt to find a method that would help her overcome her fear. She was able to explain to him her need for very gradual increases in jump difficulty and decrease in frequency of lessons, so that she could practice more on her own and learn to be gradual in her own expectations. He modified his behavior; Crista now found his instruction informative and helpful, rather than terrifying.

We developed a desensitization hierarchy and made use of it over a number of sessions. The hierarchy involved not only the type and height of jumps but, not surprisingly, the presence or absence of others. As Crista made use of these tools, she began to be able to "tune in" to her thought process. Recounting a recent experience, she could immediately recognize the ways she had set herself up for panic and failure. She was exhilarated when she began "catching" and then challenging her self-conscious, unrealistic, and perfectionist expectations. She became excited at the idea of beginning a cumulative list of "aha!" moments.

We had started our work in late spring and continued through summer. By the approach of fall, many of the techniques we had discussed had become incorporated into Crista's way of being. Progress in jumping was quite steady. The beginning of the school year, however, was daunting. When classes started again, she felt overwhelmed (as well as drowsy from medication). She was intrigued to think about ways in which she could apply what she had learned from riding to the experience of being in class.

With her appreciative agreement about a change in focus, much of the work that we did over the next few months involved cognitive and behavioral activities related to making some connections with other students, being able to speak with her professors, and preparing for and delivering class presentations. Although she did not develop a great deal of comfort with the presentations, she got through them adequately, decreased her reliance on medication, and all in all had a much better year at school than ever before.

Sessions had become less frequent both because of time constraints and decreased need. With the end of the school year and the beginning of showing season, Crista felt confident enough about her riding and jumping that our work together was terminated, with the understanding that she could return at any time. I assured her that clients return not infrequently, typically for a "booster shot": A few sessions helps remind them of what they know and what skills work well for them. I recognized that there were still some issues that, in a classic therapeutic relationship, I might have suggested working on further. Crista had, however, come away from this experience much more capable, in a much wider range of her life, than anticipated. I thought that she would be able to continue learning and growing on her own, perhaps with occasional support.

References

American Psychological Association (2006). Evidence-based practice in psychology: APA presidential task force on evidence-based practice. *American Psychologist, 61*, 271–285.

Andersen, M. B. (2000). Introduction. In M. B. Andersen (Ed.), *Doing sport psychology: Process and practice* (pp. xiii–xvii). Champaign, IL: Human Kinetics.

Aoyagi, M. W., & Portenga, S. T. (2010). The role of positive ethics and virtues in the context of sport and performance psychology service delivery. *Professional Psychology: Research and Practice, 41*, 253–259.

Berg, I. K., & deShazer, S. (1993). Making numbers talk: Language in therapy. In S. Friedman (Ed.), *The new language of change: Constructive collaboration in psychotherapy* (pp. 5–24). New York, NY: Guilford.

Borkovec, T. D., Robinson, E., Pruzinsky, T., & DePree, J. A. (1983). Preliminary exploration of worry: Some characteristics and processes. *Behaviour Research and Therapy, 21*, 9–16.

Côté, J. (1999). The influence of the family in the development of talent in sport. *The Sport Psychologist, 13*, 395–417.

Csikszentmihalyi, M. (1990). *Flow: The psychology of optimal experience*. New York, NY: Harper & Row.

Ericsson, K. A. (Ed.) (1996). *The road to excellence: The acquisition of expert performance in the arts and sciences, sports and games*. Mahwah, NJ: Lawrence Erlbaum.

Gardner, F., & Moore, Z. (2007). *The psychology of enhancing human performance*. New York, NY: Springer.

Gucciardi, D. F., & Mallett, C. J. (2010). Mental toughness. In S. J. Hanrahan & M. B. Andersen (Eds.), *Routledge handbook of applied sport psychology* (pp. 547–556). New York, NY: Routledge.

Hanin, Y. (1999). *Emotions in sport*. Champaign, IL: Human Kinetics.

Hardy, L (1996). Testing the predictions of the cusp catastrophe model of anxiety and performance. *The Sport Psychologist, 10*, 140–156.

Hays, K. F. (2006). Being fit: The ethics of practice diversification in performance psychology. *Professional Psychology: Research and Practice, 37*, 223–232.

Hays, K. F. (2009). *Breathing: Our first mental skill.* Association for Applied Sport Psychology, Salt Lake City, September 16, 2009.

Hays, K. F. (2009). Introduction. In K. F. Hays (Ed.) *Performance psychology in action.* Washington, DC: American Psychological Association.

Hays, K. F., & Brown, C. H. (2004). *You're on! Consulting for peak performance.* Washington, DC: American Psychological Association.

Hellstedt, J. C. (1995). Invisible players: A family systems model. In S. M. Murphy (Ed.), *Sport psychology interventions* (pp. 117–146). Champaign, IL: Human Kinetics.

Lyubomirsky, S. (2007). *The how of happiness.* New York, NY: Penguin.

Maher, B. A. (Ed.) (1969). *Clinical psychology and personality: The selected papers of George Kelly.* New York, NY: Wiley.

McCann, S. M. (2000). Doing sport psychology at the really big show. In M. B. Andersen (Ed.), *Doing sport psychology: Process and practice* (pp. 209–222). Champaign, IL: Human Kinetics.

McGrath, J. E. (1970). A conceptual formation for research on stress. In J. E. McGrath (Ed.), *Social and psychological factors in stress* (pp. 19–49). New York, NY: Holt, Rinehart and Winston.

Miller, G. A. (1969). Psychology as a means of promoting human welfare. *American Psychologist, 24,* 1063–1075.

Norcross, J. C. (2003). A primer on psychotherapy integration. In J. C. Norcross & M. R. Gottfried, *Handbook of psychotherapy integration* (2nd ed.) (pp. 3–23). New York, NY: Oxford University Press.

Pope, K. S., & Vasquez, M. J. T. (2011). *Ethics in psychotherapy and counseling: A practical guide* (4th ed.). Hoboken, NJ: Wiley.

Prochaska, J. O., Norcross, J., & DiClemente, C. (1995). *Changing for good.* New York, NY: Harper.

Sachs, M. L., & Buffone, G. W. (1984). *Running as therapy: An integrated approach.* Lincoln, NE: University of Nebraska.

Smith, R. L., & Smoll, F. L. (2001). *Way to go, coach!* Palo Alto, CA: Warde.

Taylor, J. J., & Schneider, B. A. (1992). The sport-clinical intake protocol: A comprehensive interviewing instrument for applied sport psychology. *Professional Psychology: Research & Practice, 23,* 318–325.

Whiston, S. C., & Sexton, T. L. (1993). An overview of psychotherapy outcome research: Implications for practice. *Professional Psychology: Research and Practice, 24,* 43–51.

Recommended Readings

Andersen, M. B. (2000). *Doing sport psychology: Process and practice.* Champaign, IL: Human Kinetics

Csikszentmihalyi, M. (1990). *Flow: The psychology of optimal experience.* New York, NY: Harper & Row.

Ericsson, K. A. (Ed.). (1996). *The road to excellence: The acquisition of expert performance in the arts and sciences, sports and games.* Mahwah, NJ: Lawrence Erlbaum.

Hanrahan, S. J., & Andersen, M. B. (2010). (Eds.). *Routledge handbook of applied sport psychology*. London: Routledge.

Hays, K. F., & Brown, C. H. (2004). *You're on! Consulting for peak performance*. Washington, DC: American Psychological Association.

Lesyk, J. L. (1998). *Developing sport psychology within your clinical practice*. San Francisco, CA: Jossey-Bass.

Lyubomirsky, S. (2007). *The how of happiness*. New York: Penguin.

Maher, B. A. (Ed.). (1969). *Clinical psychology and personality: The selected papers of George Kelly*. New York, NY: Wiley.

Murphy, S. M. (Ed.). (1995). *Sport psychology interventions*. Champaign, IL: Human Kinetics.

Pope, K. S., & Vasquez, M. J. T. (2011). *Ethics in psychotherapy and counseling: A practical guide* (4th ed.). Hoboken, NJ: Wiley.

Prochaska, J. O., Norcross, J., & DiClemente, C. (1995). *Changing for good*. New York, NY: Harper.

Sachs, M. L., & Buffone, G. W. (1984). *Running as therapy: An integrated approach*. Lincoln, NE: University of Nebraska.

Singer, R. N., Hausenblas, H. A., & Janelle, C. M. (Eds.) (2001). *Handbook of sport psychology* (2nd ed.) New York, NY: Wiley.

Van Raalte, J. L., & Brewer, B. W. (Eds.). (2002). *Exploring sport and exercise psychology* (2nd ed.). Washington, DC: American Psychological Association.

Williams, J. M. (Ed.). (2009). *Applied sport psychology: Personal growth to peak performance* (6th ed.). New York, NY: McGraw-Hill.

6

Dr. Keith Henschen

PROFESSOR EMERITUS, UNIVERSITY OF UTAH

Dr. Keith Henschen is a professor emeritus in the Department of Exercise and Sport Science at the University of Utah with an area of expertise in applied sport psychology. He has published over 200 articles, 35 book chapters, and five monographs; co-authored five books; and has made over 400 presentations. He has served as president (1997–98) of the American Alliance for Health, Physical Education, Recreation and Dance (AAHPERD) and was also president (2001–05) of the International Society of Sport Psychology (ISSP). He has consulted with numerous Olympic, professional, and world class performers, and has been the sport psychology consultant for the Utah Jazz NBA team for the past 26 years.

AUTOBIOGRAPHICAL SKETCH

I grew up in the northern portion of Indiana in a blue collar, industrial environment. My childhood was normal with my two brothers until, at the age of six, our mother suddenly passed away from cancer. The next few years were crucial to my development because, being motherless, I was allowed to "run the streets" and learned to be pretty independent and self-sufficient. Subsequently, much of my childhood was spent playing sports at the community center, at the YMCA, in church leagues, and in age group sport organizations. I loved sports (baseball, basketball, and football) and played year round. Being from a relatively poor family, at age 12, I started working a paper route in order to have some money. Actually, this also helped me be a little more responsible. Playing sports from an early age, I also learned to be highly competitive (probably too much so)!

I do not know much about my mother, but she and my father both graduated from high school. My father was valedictorian and a good tennis player. Neither parent attended college because it was the "Great Depression." They did instill in me the desire to do well in school. I rarely studied but had no trouble getting good grades. This was important because I had more time to play sports. After playing basketball and running track in high school, I received a number of scholarship offers in basketball and eventually decided to attend Ball State Teachers College. I studied physical education and psychology during my undergraduate years. I wanted to be a teacher and coach. The emphasis in psychology was because I had a sincere interest in human behavior. If I did not decide to pursue teaching and coaching, I also wanted to be prepared to possibly become a professional somewhere in the field of psychology. In essence, I wasn't sure of what I really wanted to do. Upon graduation, I took a teaching/coaching position in my home town at a junior high school and played semi-professional basketball. I was promised the next high school assistant coaching position that became available. After one year, a coaching position opened, but the administration decided to hire someone else with more experience. I felt betrayed and resigned a week later just as school was starting. Ball State had contacted me and asked if I would return and teach as an instructor. It is strange how some things work out. Because of this incident, I reexamined my life's objectives and came to the conclusion that coaching was not a very secure occupational choice, and I then proceeded to consider other career avenues. One fact was obvious though—if I was to actually attain something in life, I would need additional training. With the help of my wife, I decided to pursue a doctoral degree. I taught at Ball State for two years and finished my master's degree during this time. I then applied and was accepted to the doctoral program at Indiana University. Here again I studied physical education and minored in educational counseling. The field of educational counseling may appear somewhat confusing as a minor for my doctorate, but I was still intrigued with working with human behavior. It was also about this time that I became aware of a field called sport psychology. I felt that I had the sport experience and psychological training for this discipline; but needed to receive more counseling skills to become a professional in this new field.

In 1971, I received my doctorate from Indiana University and accepted a position at the University of Utah with the challenge to develop a graduate program in the psychosocial aspects of sports. This field (sport psychology) was relatively new and just emerging in higher education. During my doctoral studies, I attended a couple of national conventions in physical education and frequently listened to presentations on various aspects of sport psychology (i.e., motor learning, motor behavior, and applications of psychology to performance). I quickly decided that sport psychology would be a discipline of the future and I wanted to be part of that future. I realized that I had a lot to learn, and was excited about the challenge. After 39 years, I retired (Dec. 31, 2009) from the University of Utah. I must admit that through the years, I have been extremely fortunate to have excellent graduate students. They have been my inspiration and taught me more than I have taught them.

I believe my competitiveness, learned in sports from an early age, readily transferred to academics and was the motivation to attempt to excel. My sports background has allowed me insight into the nuances of the mental aspects of performance as well as to "talk the language" of performers. My training in psychology and counseling has taught me to listen adroitly and thus identify the real issues that frequently confront the struggling performer. In my case, the following old adage is very appropriate: "We are when we are old what we learn when we are young!"

I really don't know if my approach to the practice of sport psychology is unique because I have not had the opportunity to observe a great number of colleagues ply their trade. I will say that what I do is "whole person development." I am interested in the person, not just their athletic skills and abilities.

THEORY OF PERFORMANCE EXCELLENCE

Obviously, performance excellence is multidimensional and therefore evades the possibility of a single theory that adequately addresses the various components and also encompasses the uniqueness that each performer brings to the fore. Performance, I believe, is the "on demand demonstration of learned skills and abilities." It is a combination of psychological, emotional, behavioral, physical, and personal perceptions and experiences. Performance excellence only occurs when the mind is liberated from the analytical processing of information and free to enjoy the execution of automatic responses in an effortless and pleasurable fashion.

This type of performance (optimal) rarely happens, but when it does we normally label it with such terms as "flow," "being in the zone," or having a "peak performance." The characteristics of this phenomenon are readily recognized and eerily consistent across individuals and circumstances. So, most professionals in sport psychology are cognizant of what optimal performances look and feel like, but we are at a loss on how to replicate them—on demand—or even study them in a research setting. Thus, in order to attempt to understand this performance puzzle, a number of professionals (who have had a modicum of success in helping others attain this level of performance) have been asked to contribute to this book.

I wish the solution to achieving performance excellence were a cut and dried recipe that works for everyone, but of course that is not the case. It is unique to each performer and that is the reason it is so difficult to acquire. In order to shed some light on this subject, I will discuss my thoughts on the various components of "performance excellence" and how I deal with each area.

It is important to understand my philosophy on working with performers at this time: "Meet them where they are, take them where they need to be!" I know this sounds a little bold, but to help a performer reach performance excellence consistently, I need to know a great deal about how a performer thinks, reacts, and behaves.

PSYCHOLOGICAL. To optimally perform from a psychological perspective, I believe it is essential that individuals have high confidence, have a little fear of failure, be focused, and be able to become absorbed in their performance. Since confidence is a relatively abstract concept, I need to clarify what high confidence entails. This means a performer has no expectations about the eventual competitive outcome and strives to do one simple task—give maximum effort all the time. Actually, confidence is best enhanced two ways: (a) be in great physical condition, and (b) have previous experiences of feeling confident.

At first blush, having some fear of failure appears to be a negative, but I beg to differ. During my initial years in applied sport psychology, I believed that *good* performers had a greater motive to achieve success than to avoid failure. As my career continued and I started to consult with *great* performers, I found that they fear failure more than they have a will to win. This fear impels them to strive for excellence more than any other psychological characteristic. I think this is so because failure is an assault on their ego.

Being focused means that a performer has mastered all of the attentional styles and employs these appropriately (Nideffer, 1985). Concentration skills are rarely acquired because no one seems to teach them; yet, everyone is assumed to possess them. Many errors in performance are due to a lack of appropriate attentional style.

The final psychological characteristic essential for optimal performing is the ability to become absorbed in the moment. This definitely takes time and experience to develop. It is the skill "of losing yourself to find yourself." Children can reach this state more readily than adults. Children are attentive and enjoy what they are doing. Great performers have somehow attained this awesome ability. It is like the ego (or critic) has been temporarily banished and the performer is hedonistically doing it for themselves.

EMOTIONAL. From an emotional perspective, I think an athlete should be aroused, intense, and positive to the degrees that are unique to them. Most books dwell on the idea that athletes need to be relaxed to optimally perform. I slightly disagree with this viewpoint. The uniqueness of each athlete should be serviced here. Being relaxed and composed prior to performance conserves energy and is probably a wise skill to have, but the optimal level differs for each individual. Very important is the idea that the athlete be appropriately aroused, mentally and physically, throughout the entire performance. Many athletes use the actual competition to "work into" the proper arousal, but this can be a mistake. They should start at their effective level and adjust from there. Arousal does have a high correlation with the ability to concentrate: As arousal increases, the ability to concentrate narrows.

In terms of intensity, I want athletes intense but not tense. Many athletes confuse these two concepts. Tenseness limits the body to move with spontaneity and fluidity which is essential in performance excellence. Intensity equates to being highly aware and focused on the task at hand.

Being positive is not really an emotion but this frame of mind elicits a number of enhancing emotions (e.g., enjoyment, pleasure, confidence), while perceiving situations negatively is the gateway to sorrow, unhappiness, and depression. A positive attitude does not guarantee success, but it does influence how we react to whatever happens to us. Approaching performance from a positive perspective allows an athlete to approach competitions as challenges, while the negative approach generates more fears, which are very debilitating.

BEHAVIORAL. Performance excellence is more of a happening instead of a planned event. It happens to athletes more frequently when they are having and enjoying competition. Great athletes are not threatened by competing against the best; rather, they relish this opportunity. They also prepare themselves in such a way as to enhance their self-efficacy for whatever they are performing. They have learned that "trying harder" is not the way to become more proficient. The mentality that trying harder leads to better performance is a myth. In fact, I frequently tell those athletes I work with that "on the most important days of their competitive lives, they must learn to try less hard and just trust their training." Extra perceived stress (especially of importance of outcome) does not normally contribute to ideal performance.

Another behavioral characteristic that inhibits performance excellence is an athlete's lack of ability to avoid frustration (or at least handle it effectively). When athletes become frustrated, they now are faced with two problems: (1) getting rid of the frustration, and (2) refocusing on performance. Of course, the problem is that frustration is a powerful emotion that negatively affects behavior and takes time to overcome. Competition does not wait for a person to get it together again. Avoiding frustration is not possible in competition, but learning to handle it is essential to performance excellence.

The final aspect of behavior that affects performance excellence is the skill of "not thinking" and allowing oneself to respond automatically. An example would be a basketball player who tries to decide to shoot or not. It is already too late and he or she should pass the ball. A baseball player who tries to think at the plate will be a strike out victim. Performance is instantaneous and our minds get in our way in an effort to try to help us. Performance excellence only occurs when we cease the analytical thinking and trust our ability to just react.

PHYSICAL CONDITIONING. Very simply, an athlete who is in great physical shape has a better chance of experiencing peak performances. There is something about confidence and being in top physical condition that go hand in hand in attaining performance excellence. I have never worked with an out of shape athlete who has peak performances.

PERSONAL. There are three personal characteristics that seem to permit or encourage being in the zone more frequently. The major prerequisite is to be genuine and just be you. Too many athletes have a proclivity to watch and try to imitate what other performers do. Every athlete should study what works for them and then perfect the ability to execute these things. One size does *not* fit all and each athlete is special because they become a product of their personal experiences. When they are at peace with themselves and know what works for them, then they can perform optimally more frequently.

A second factor in the personal category is to have HEART. (Heart is not an easy phenomenon that most athletes have acquired.) Heart has two com-

Figure 6.1. HEART: Athlete motivation.

ponents—intrinsic motivation and an unquenchable work ethic (Figure 6.1).

Most athletes have one of these two attributes, but rarely do athletes have both. When a person has both of these, performance excellence becomes easier, more enjoyable and happens more often. I would venture to say that all the "great ones" have heart and the "good ones" are hopefully in the process of developing this characteristic.

A final thought in the personal area would be the concept of hating to lose. Most athletes have a will to win, but very few hate to lose. This may seem trite, but those who hate to lose give every ounce of energy to be successful and thus perform optimally on a regular basis. They refuse to not give maximum effort every competition.

EXPERIENCE. The great ones do one thing that other athletes do not do to ensure performance excellence. They "play forward." Through experience great performers learn to not dwell on mistakes or errors as they compete. The most important play in any performance is the next one. Mistakes will always happen, but to analyze them during the competition mitigates the possibility of performance excellence. Thinking is the death knell to the spontaneity of performance excellence. Performing defensively never allows performance excellence.

In summary, rather than provide a theory of performance excellence, which I do not believe is possible, I have presented a number of areas that need to be considered in order to reach this level of performance. Psychological, emotional, behavioral, physical, personal, and previous experiences all factor in or contribute to performance excellence.

THEORY OF PERFORMANCE BREAKDOWNS

Again, I am not bright enough to develop a theory on performance breakdowns; but I believe there are 10 primary problems which cause negative or less than performance excellences. These are, in no particular order: (a) over thinking, (b) fears, (c) trying too hard, (d) perfectionism, (e) comparisons,

(f) confidence issues, (g) anxiety, (h) goals/expectations, (i) fatigue, and (j) trying not to lose.

The above list reflects approximately 90% of the issues that I have encountered with athletes over my career. Of course, there are other issues such as relationships, coaching problems, eating disorders, dealing with injuries that occur, but not as frequently as the 10 listed, that can affect performance in a negative way.

OVER THINKING. It is almost a curse, in terms of performing, to be bright and have good analytical thinking skills. What makes a person successful in most of life's endeavors (e.g., academics, occupations) does not lead to success in performing. In order to perform well, the mind must "go on automatic" because thinking slows down the ability to react quickly. This concept is difficult to teach because most situations in life require analytical processing.

FEARS. Fear is such a powerful emotion that when it exists, it always takes center stage in the mind. Without counseling and education concerning the area of fear, it will continue to affect performance. All fear has an object and this needs to be identified in order to deal with its ramifications. Also, each athlete's method for dealing with fears is unique to that athlete. All injuries have fears associated with the actual incident as well as with the rehabilitation. Fear of success and fear of failure are types of fear that are also common with performers. Associated with injuries, the fears of success and failure are a little different than what was discussed previously. Fear of success in this context does not insinuate they are afraid of being successful; rather it means they fear that they will never be successful again. The fear of failure with injuries is actually in retrospect. The athletes are focused on beliefs that they have failed themselves and significant others because they have allowed themselves to be hurt.

TRYING TOO HARD. One of the great misconceptions of our society in general and sports in particular is the idea that working harder will always guarantee better performances. The problem becomes that trying harder frequently evokes tension, which negates the benefits of the extra effort. The so-called "football mentality" of "you can never work too hard" and "the more the better" has ruined many athletes. Obviously trying hard is important, but not too hard. Instead of trying harder, I advocate "trying smarter." Try hard, but do not over try.

PERFECTIONISM. Perfectionism is a double edged sword. It is good in that it forces an athlete to work hard and to rarely be satisfied. On the other hand, perfectionism also causes some athletes to work too hard, especially on what they are doing wrong. Thus, they practice errors instead of correct techniques. The laws of frequency in motor learning then kick in and the wrong technique becomes a part of their response. I believe, to be a really good performer, an athlete must have some perfectionism; but they must keep its effects in perspective. The bathtub test is ideal to illustrate perfectionism:

> Have the athlete place about two inches of water in the bathtub or shower, then take their shoes and socks off and step into the water. If they touch porcelain, they are not perfect; so they need not treat themselves like they need to be.

COMPARISONS. Many athletes, because they are so competitive, identify another athlete as a threatening rival. This other athlete becomes an enemy and someone they cannot get out of their head. Comparing yourself to someone else is a major threat to motivation. I emphasize to performers that they have control over only one performance—their own! They are wasting valuable energy on someone over whom control is not possible. I have a humorous little technique that helps an athlete cease the comparisons. I ask the athlete who is making the comparison "How much are you getting paid (by the other person) for renting a room in your head?" They find this humorous and answer nothing. I then tell them to evict the other person from their head. If they are not receiving any profit from the other person, then it is not a good idea to keep them around.

CONFIDENCE ISSUES. Most sport psychology consultants readily admit that confidence is a key ingredient in performance excellence. We all seem to know what this phenomena is, but we hardly ever agree on how to develop it. I think confidence is a state and not a trait. No one is confident in all areas, but most of us are confident in some situations. I also believe that learning the cardinal skills of performance (relaxation, concentration, imagery, self-talk, and a pre-competition mental routine) is a great way to help develop state confidence. Once an athlete has mastered these skills, confidence seems to grow.

There is one technique that seems to be effective for increasing confidence and that is self-rewards. I ask athletes what their favorite candy bar is and then have them purchase a bag of these "small" bars. Every day I ask them to take one bar with them. Each day they are to select something that they wish to accomplish that is difficult but realistic and achievable. If they succeed, they eat the candy bar. If not, they take the bar home and bring it back the next day.

The objective of this exercise is to make our successes as emotional as our failures. Athletes seem to spend more energy (emotional) on mistakes instead of successes. They need to at least make them emotionally even. Another example of counter balancing negative emotional energy with positive emotions would be, after each negative thought, have the performer focus on repeating a positive cue word at least 10 times.

ANXIETY. We exist in a very complex world. The stresses faced continually cause a great percentage of people (and athletes) to experience high anxiety. For athletes, managing anxiety is crucial because as anxiety increases, a person's concentration ability literally goes out the window. To complicate this issue, women generally manifest more anxiety than men. Suffice it to say that anxiety greatly affects performance excellence. I believe this is one emotion that should be treated first because it influences performance so drastically. Relaxation techniques are a good start.

GOALS/EXPECTATIONS. In all my consulting experience, I have never had an elite athlete tell me that they were thinking about their goals as they were optimally performing. Every sport psychology textbook lauds the practice of goal setting, but I believe this concept is greatly misunderstood and overstated. Goals/expectations are important in practice situations where there are opportunities for "do overs." But in actual competition, the type of thinking that facilitates goals/expectations is analytical, and this is not appropriate in competition. Plus, even in the heat of competition, as a goal is not attained, this frequently leads to immediate negative thinking which then mitigates confidence. As sport psychology consultants we need to be more precise in using this psychological intervention.

FATIGUE. It is my opinion that all excellent performances occur only when the performer is in great physical condition. A great football coach (Vince Lombardi) once stated "fatigue makes cowards of us all." This idea has high relevance to us in the field of sport psychology. Performance starts with the physical and the psychological is the frosting on the cake.

TRYING NOT TO LOSE. It is very important to understand if an athlete has high success orientation. When performing, are they consistently trying to win or do they try not to lose? Those who optimally perform always try to win. If the mindset reverts to trying not to lose, the athlete subconsciously enters a defensive position instead of an offensive mode. A defensive mindset allows the opposition to gain momentum and confidence. Performance excellence demands a success orientation throughout the entire competition.

CONSULTING PROCESS

The manner in which I consult is fairly straightforward, and I teach primarily the same psychological interventions as other applied sport psychology consultants, but with a few exceptions. As mentioned previously, my approach is whole person development and the skills I teach are life skills, and they are not presented to be used solely in the sport environment. I talk about these skills in a way that the performer understands how to use them in many aspects of his or her life. I believe there are five "cardinal skills" that should be mastered: relaxation, concentration, imagery, self-talk, and a pre-competition mental routine. I am also adamant that these interventions be taught in that specific order. They build on each other. You may notice that one of the popular interventions (goal setting) is absent from the list. I explained why in the previous section of this chapter. Each of the cardinal skills contributes greatly to increasing an athlete's overall abilities, confidence, and perceived control.

UNIQUE FEATURES

I am not sure if my consulting process is really unique because I have not had the opportunity to watch my colleagues in action. I have witnessed my doctoral students at work, but not my peers. Following is how I normally consult.

Allow me to state at the outset that I have never in my career advertised my services. All of my clients come to me by "word of mouth." My first meeting with a prospective client is always free and I explain to them what I do, how often we will meet, how long the process will normally take, and I answer any of their questions. If the client is under the age of 18, I require either one or both parents to be in attendance for the initial meeting. They are also free to attend any or all of the subsequent sessions if they so desire. At the end of the first meeting, I ask them to take a few days to determine if they feel comfortable working with me. If not, it is fine. If yes, then a subsequent meeting is arranged.

During the first meeting I explain that the consulting will only be productive if they make a commitment to perform all the exercises I give them. I explain that I will give them homework to do every time we meet. We will meet about every two weeks for the next four to six months.

Probably one unique feature of my applied work is that I have each client complete three psychometric assessments as we are getting started. These tests assess anxiety, concentration skills, and success or failure orientation.

Once I receive these tests, I share the results with the clients. These assessments serve two purposes: (a) provide crucial information and (b) build rapport with the client. The athletes many times ask "how do you know all that about me?" Of course, it is not difficult because they provide the information. The tests provide a basis for where I begin with the skills learning process with each person.

For each of the cardinal skills I have a number of exercises (the homework) that the clients need to work on to become better performers. For example, for relaxation we would practice a muscle to mind technique (progressive relaxation) for a couple of weeks and then work on a mind to muscle technique (autogenic training) for the next couple of weeks. I believe you need to expose your clients to a few different techniques for each intervention and allow them to select the one that best works for them.

Another unique feature of my style of consulting is that as we progress through the four to six months training period, they realize I am interested in them as a person. They are more than athletes, or musicians, or whatever roles they play. First of all, they are people. I am interested in them growing and developing and I do not just define them by their skills. At the end of the skills training, I want them to consider me as a friend. Also, once we finish initially, I encourage them to come back whenever they think I can be of help.

Probably the most unique aspect of my consulting is my intuitive ability to read the client (both from what they are saying and what they do not say) and identify the real issues that need to be addressed. My style can be realistically categorized as unorthodox, but it has been effective through the years. The approaches discussed in popular sport psychology textbooks are too simplistic, sterile, and superficial to be useful for my personality. Again, one size does not fit all. The art of consulting is as important as the science.

CASE STUDY

Bree (a pseudonym) was a 15-year-old gymnast when her father first contacted me. She was considered to be a sure thing to be on the next Olympic team the following year. She was ranked as one of the top five gymnasts in the world. From the outside, it looked like Bree's life was all roses. From her perspective, life was anything but rosy. Bree's parents were in the midst of an emotional divorce and Bree was experiencing the problems associated with puberty. Her disposition had changed from a happy, fun loving teenager to an unconfident and sometimes sullen young lady. During our initial meeting, the father did a lot of talking and Bree was silent until I asked her to tell me how she was feeling about gymnastics. She was pretty candid and said she, just recently, was feeling anxious and fearful. I then asked her to describe her life in general. She began to cry. Next, I asked the father if I could talk to Bree privately for a minute. He said yes and waited in another room. I told Bree that I had a very close friend (a lady) whose specialty was adolescent psychology that I felt could really help Bree understand the emotions she was experiencing. Without hesitation she agreed to see my friend. I also told Bree that the things that were happening in gymnastics were normal during puberty and that I would be happy to help her work through these emotions. She said that would be good. I then asked the father to return and Bree and I told him what we would like to do. He agreed and I contacted my friend (the adolescent psychologist) who was willing to see Bree. I asked her to call me when she felt Bree was ready to face her performance issues.

About a month later, my friend called me and said Bree was progressing nicely and was ready to see me. Her father called me the next day and I started meeting regularly with Bree every two weeks. The initial meeting this time was to discuss what happens during puberty, both psychologically and physically. I told Bree that every gymnast (Olympic and college) that I had ever worked with had experienced what she was going through. In other words, she was normal. She then took the psychometric tests; we discussed the results, and started a program of psychological skills training. Each session was about 45 minutes to an hour long. She was a very dedicated learner and quickly mastered some skills (relaxation) to decrease the anxiety. It took a little longer to mitigate the fears,[1] but that also eventually happened. She became more confident, less anxious and made the Olympic team. Her performances continued to improve and after high school she accepted a college scholarship in gymnastics. Bree graduated from college where she was a multi-All American, married, and is now leading a normal life. We have remained friends through a number of years and she has always been appreciative that I recognized her as a person that needed help and was not just concerned about her athletic talent. Working with fear is also a possible unique aspect of my consulting style. Bree, over the years, has called me periodically and asked a number of questions about how to handle her children, who are also excellent athletes.

EPILOGUE

Every contributor to this text will arrive at their expertise by a different route. All will have been successful because they were dedicated, inquisitive, persevering and brought their uniqueness to the forefront and then exploited it in a positive way. In my particular case, my experiences in sport, academia, and the powerful influences of some individuals molded my career to its ultimate destination. My interest in people and recognizing that athletes are not special people, but rather people with special physical talents have provided a foundation for my working relationships. Working with the whole person and not just the athlete has been beneficial. Understanding performance has been a lifelong journey. My thoughts and practices have changed over this journey. I have been blessed with wonderful colleagues, exceptional students, and a loving life partner. I believe I have been genuine, forthright, and willing to learn. As an applied sport psychology consultant, I have tried to stay in the background and rarely share the limelight with my clients. They do the performance, and I am just a resource. I have respected the thoughts of the performers themselves and those who coach them. Their successes are my reward.

It is important that all applied sport psychology professionals be influenced by theories and published books, articles, and research from many different areas—thus the included reference list. Equally important though, I believe my career has been immensely influenced by colleagues and students. One special mentor to me was Dr. Bruce Ogilvie. He was always willing to share his expertise and vast experiences with me even though I never really studied under him. In terms of applied sport psychology with elite performers he was unparalleled. A second great influence on my career was my association with a group of peers called the Utopians. We are a group of close friends who are always available to provide support and share perspectives on challenging issues. Every individual in sport psychology needs a trusted support group.

References and Recommended Readings

Adler, A. (1927). *Understanding human nature.* New York, NY: Garden City Publishing Company.

Bandura, A. (1969). *Principles of behavior modification.* New York, NY: Holt, Reinhart and Winston.

Gallway, T. (1974). *The inner game of tennis.* New York, NY: Random House.

Griffith, C. R. (1926). *Psychology and athletics.* New York, NY: Charles Scribner's Sons.

Heil, J. (1993). *Psychology of sport injury.* Champaign, IL: Human Kinetics Publishing.

Jacobsen, E. (1930). *Progressive relaxation*. Chicago, IL: University of Chicago Press.

McClelland, D. C. (1951). *Personality*. New York, NY: William Sloan Associates.

Nideffer, R. M. (1985). *Athlete's guide to mental training*. Champaign, IL: Human Kinetics Publishing.

Ogilvie, B. C. (1984). The sport psychologist and his professional credibility. In P. Klavora & J. V. Daniel (Eds.), *Coach, athlete and sport psychologist* (pp. 98–111). Toronto: Toronto University Press.

Ogilvie, B., & Tutko, T. (1966). *Problem athletes and how to handle them*. London: Pelham Books.

Orlick, T. (1990). *In pursuit of excellence* (2nd ed.). Champaign, IL: Leisure Press.

Rogers, C. R. (1961). *On becoming a person: A therapist's view of psychotherapy*. London: Constable and Company.

Unestahl, L. E. (Ed.). (1983). *The mental aspects of gymnastics*. Orebro: Veje.

Endnote

1. Fear is a very, very powerful emotion which seems to be ever present. As a performer progresses through puberty, experiences injury, or returns to competition/performance fears will naturally occur. I approach fear as a beneficial defense mechanism on one hand, but a debilitating factor on the other hand. My main technique for handling fear is to *educate*, and then to provide interventions for the specific type of fear on an individual basis.

7

Dr. Sean McCann

UNITED STATES OLYMPIC COMMITTEE

Sean McCann has worked for the US Olympic Committee as a sport psychologist for 20 years, including 12 years as the head of the department. He has traveled with the last nine US Olympic teams as a sport psychologist during the Games. In his work for the USOC, he works directly with teams and coaches, both at the Olympic Training Center, and on the road with teams at training camps and competitions. In addition to his work for the Olympic Committee, Sean works with professional athletes from a variety of sports, from ball sports to auto racing and with high performers in business settings. Sean is a past president and fellow of AASP, and has received the Distinguished Professional Practice Award from AASP for outstanding contributions in applied sport psychology.

AUTOBIOGRAPHICAL SKETCH

I majored in psychology as an undergraduate because I have always been fascinated by the motivations and interactions of people. However, the department at Brown University was stronger in the laboratory study of newborns and rodents than in other areas of psychology, and I did not see psychology as a career for me. After college, while bike racing and working in various teaching jobs, I met a clinical psychologist who focused in rehab psychology with head-injured patients, and I realized there was a career where my natural interest in people might be useful and helpful to others.

I left New England and headed west for the PhD program in clinical psychology at the University of Hawaii. UH was strongly cognitive-behavioral in orientation, and this has influenced my thinking about applied work to this day. There I learned the most important lesson any applied psychologist must learn: Behavior is the bottom line. Thoughts and feelings are important, but if behavior doesn't change, then you haven't had an impact. This has proven to be a useful orientation in sport.

Academically, I wrote a master's thesis in cross cultural psychopathology and I had a plan to focus on practice with children and families. This academic and career plan all changed while reading my US Cycling Federation newsletter and seeing a small notice about a new research assistantship in sport psychology at the Olympic Training Center. After barraging the newly hired sport psychologist at the USOC with letters of recommendation and declarations of my willingness to do whatever he needed, Shane Murphy relented and hired me as his first research assistant. I arranged in 1988 to take a leave from my PhD program to pursue this interest.

That experience changed everything. When I returned to Hawaii to complete my PhD, I shifted my research focus to sport and health psychology, and created a dissertation project which looked at the cognitive strategies used by endurance athletes (bike racers) to deal with pain. Although I had found my passion, I knew there were no jobs in sport psychology, so I continued to develop a practical career path with an emphasis on clinical child psychology. I went to the University of Washington for my clinical internship and followed that up with a post-doctoral year, still focused on kids and families. Fortuitously, the AAASP conference came to Seattle while I was there, and I was able to present research that Dr. Murphy and I had done on pre-event anxiety at that year's conference. It was the geographical accident of that AAASP conference that gave me the last push I needed to risk pursuit of sport psychology as a career even though there was no career path. When Shane created a two-year fellowship at a little under $13,000 a year in 1991, I convinced my fiancée to leave her job and her beloved Hawaii to move to Colorado for "just two years." That was nearly 20 years ago.

During my two decades at the USOC, the field has changed, and the role of sport psychology within the USOC has changed. In the 1980s, every sport psychologist began their presentation by trying to justify the role of sport psychology. In the 1980s and early 1990s, within the sport science division of the USOC, it was very important for us to emphasize our science, so that we were taken as seriously as the exercise physiologists and biomechanists. While many coaches and athletes saw the value of sport psychology from the beginning of my time at the USOC, it took longer to get my organization to see the role sport psychology could play. At my first Olympics, in Lillehammer, Norway, 1994, the USOC "justified" my travel to the Games by having me hand out Olympic clothing to the team in Oslo before the start. Through the Sydney Games in 2000, I had to battle for credentials for myself and other sport psychologists up to and even into the start of each Games. In those first 10 years at the USOC, being a good politician was as important as being a good professional. In my second decade here, it has been very gratifying to see the USOC sport psychology area grow in respect, impact, and number. We have moved from one full-time sport psychologist to six, and our clear focus now is helping the teams we work with achieve performance excellence at the Olympic Games.

THEORY OF PERFORMANCE EXCELLENCE

While the bulk of my time observing performance has been spent in the world of elite sports, my perspectives on performance have also been shaped by time working with rising leaders in the corporate and non-profit world. I believe there are commonalities across various domains of human performance, but the world of sport is unique in that performance is measured so publicly, so regularly, and so specifically. Despite the accessibility and frequency of measurement in sport, there are still so many individual variations in sport performance that the best coaches talk of their profession as a mixture of science and art. I believe honest applied sport psychologists must frame their work in a similar way.

Applied sport psychology should be based on the best science available, but an applied sport psychologist often faces unique performance challenges and settings where there is no clearly defined answer in the scientific literature. When specific data or science is not available, a personal theory of performance excellence provides a framework for data collection, and this ongoing data collection helps shape and change the theory. A personal theory of performance excellence provides a compass heading that can help keep a sport psychologist from wandering in circles.

My personal theory of performance excellence starts with a cognitive-behavioral (CB) frame. The emphasis on behaviors as the bottom line in high performance settings fits well with this framework. So my theories and interventions begin with the idea that behavior change or behavior maintenance is the focus, and that thoughts and emotions are the pathways to impact behavior. If consistent behavior is the goal, then an athlete must have consistent thinking. If changed behavior is the goal, then the athlete must change thoughts. Thus, my theory of performance excellence is shaped by the knowledge that as a sport psychologist, I must eventually end up at the business end of theory—behavior on the field of play.

MULTI-FACTOR INFLUENCES ON PERFORMANCE—MENTAL SKILLS, PERSONALITY, AND ENVIRONMENT. Over my professional career, I have developed three beliefs about performance excellence: (1) I believe that consistent performance excellence is only possible with a broad set of mental skills, (2) I believe that an athlete's personality makes certain of these skills virtually innate or easy to develop, and the same personality may make other skills much harder to develop, and (3) I believe that an athlete's environment, including coaching and sport psychology exposure, can facilitate or block the development of key mental skills.

OFFENSIVE AND DEFENSIVE MENTAL SKILLS. Mental skills for performance have been described and categorized in many ways. A typical approach in sport psychology books is to list skills in the order you might teach them to athletes. This approach is practical, but it treats each mental skill as discrete, independent, and relatively equal in importance. In 2002, while preparing a general sport psychology presentation for elite coaches, I read the familiar team sport philosophy—"offense wins games, defense wins championships"—and it struck me that mental skills might usefully be divided into offensive and defensive mental skills.

Over numerous Olympic Games, I had observed that there were two very broad categories of "sport types" among the elite athletes I worked with at the Games. One type was the athlete with tremendous drive, excellent practice habits, and a relentless pursuit of high standards. The second type was the athlete who seemed remarkably resilient and able to cope with the crazy pressure at the Games. This was the athlete who could execute well, even with crowds five times larger than she had ever seen, an army of media personnel, and appearances on morning television shows. What struck me is that only a small minority of Olympic athletes had the skills of both of these two types. When an athlete had the skills of both types, they were by far the most likely to do well at the Games.

The first sport type possesses what I call *offensive mental skills*, or those skills that help create and channel the drive that leads to outstanding athletic behavior. Offensive mental skills produce very high skill level, commitment to excellence, and a level of talent necessary to make it to the big stage. These skills can make an athlete exceptional and dominant. The *defensive mental skills* possessed by the second type of successful athletes helped them manage the intensity and chaos of high pressure, and large events such as the Olympics. These defensive mental skills help facilitate consistent performances under pressure and resilient athletes who can manage difficult circumstances.

Offensive Mental Skills

Offensive skills are the abilities that let an athlete dominate a competition. Offensive physical skills might include the terrific top-end speed of runner Usain Bolt, or the very high VO2 Max of Lance Armstrong that allows him to drop other cyclists in the Alps. Unusual strength and quickness are offensive physical skills in a majority of Olympic sports. When these offensive skills are well developed in an athlete, other athletes know this athlete must be contended with. Offensive skills are absolutely necessary to be a great, truly exceptional athlete.

Offensive mental skills (see Table 7.1) also allow an athlete to dominate an event. The ability to maintain tremendous *competitive desire* helps an athlete put in the time learning new skills to take their game, and sometimes their sport, to a higher level (think Tiger Woods). Competitive desire also helps an athlete rise to, match, and surpass great efforts by the competition. Consistent ability to *set and achieve goals* keeps athletes striving for improvement, identifying and eliminating weaknesses, and keeps their training intense and focused. The *ability to visualize success* lets athletes practice for excellence and perform more automatically. *Self-talk* skills help athletes talk themselves through challenges and think in a positive and useful way under pressure. The *ability to develop effective competition plans* is a critical mental skill for athletes who compete in complex, dynamic sports with frequent decision making. A willingness and *ability to commit* to a plan of training and competition is an offensive skill that allows athletes to go 100% in competition, and get the most out of new and innovative training methods. *Comfort with risk* is an essential offensive skill in competitive situations where too much caution and avoidance of risk is the difference between a medal and 10th place. The *ability to maintain a relaxed "athletic" approach* is a related skill that allows athletes to act without hesitation and avoid the danger of cautious over-thinking. Finally, *confidence* in skills and competition plan allows athletes to stay on the offensive in important competitions.

The word that may best describe an athlete with very strong offensive

Table 7.1. Offensive Mental Skills

OFFENSIVE MENTAL SKILLS	IMPACT ON PERFORMANCE
The ability to create competitive desire	Helps motivate athlete to improve skills. Helps athletes "battle" for the win in a tight contest or when competition improves.
Consistent ability to set and achieve goals	Helps the athlete achieve personal bests and constantly improve on the process of training and competing. Keeps intensity high.
Visualization skills	Allows athletes to see a path to success. Lets athletes keep their thoughts simple during competition.
Self-talk skills	An athlete skilled in self-talk is aware of the language in their head, and actively adjusts it to keep it positive and action oriented.
Competition planning	This skill helps athletes make decisions before competition, so that during the event they can simply execute rather than decide.
Ability to commit	This skill allows athletes to go 100% during competition. In addition, this skill lets athletes stay with new approaches long enough to see a benefit in training (such as changing technique).
Comfort with risk	An athlete with this skill understands that some events reward taking risks, and that a winning approach sometimes requires a willingness to lose (fear of losing may prevent risk taking).
Relaxed athletic approach	When athletes are "athletic," they are relaxed, mainly visual, looking for opportunities rather than danger, and don't hesitate. They do not over think their situation.
Confidence	Confidence is the overarching offensive skill that makes it easier to set high goals, see and believe success, and execute good competition plans.

mental skills is "PREDATOR." This athlete is focused, intense, athletic, looking to win, and ready to take advantage of the opportunity for success that competition provides. Without these offensive mental skills, an athlete may be good, but will never be great.

Defensive Mental Skills

Defensive skills are the abilities that help athletes succeed consistently and in all conditions. Defensive physical skills might include the ability to handle tremendous training loads, the ability to quickly recover from the effort

Table 7.2. Defensive Mental Skills

DEFENSIVE MENTAL SKILLS	IMPACT ON PERFORMANCE
Maintaining excellence in training	Train as they compete. Practice more useful, efficient. Helps athletes avoid the problems of overtraining and under-recovery.
Controlling competitive anxiety	Allows athletes to stay in control. Especially critical as the event gets "bigger" and competition becomes vulnerable to anxiety.
Controlling anger and frustration	Allows athletes to save energy for competition, control thoughts, and stay on task, even when real problems exist.
Energy management (raising intensity)	Allows an athlete to "ramp up" energy when the situation calls for it.
Energy management (recovery between efforts)	Allows an athlete to use whatever recovery time is available, so that athlete has energy at the finish when needed.
Energy management (Adjusting energy)	Allows an athlete to be very aware of correct energy level needed for the situation and make quick adjustments up or down to be physically and mentally ready.
Recovery from performance setbacks	Allows an athlete to quickly "bounce back" from mistakes, defeats, or bad luck and still have positive and useful thoughts.
Flexible when environment changes	Allows an athlete to quickly adapt to changes, tolerate disruptions to routine, and see all changes as opportunities.
Focused despite distractions	Allows an athlete to stay on task, keeping all five senses oriented only towards useful signals, even when all five senses could get pulled away from the task.
Mental maintenance skills	Allows an athlete to be very self-aware, noting changes and variations, and then make the adjustments needed to keep thoughts simple and effective.

of the last race, the capacity to adapt and respond to surges in a 10K race by other runners, and excellent technique that holds up under pressure. When defensive skills are strong in athletes they are consistent performers, winning big events as well as small. They adapt to changes in their environment and are very resilient.

Defensive mental skills (see Table 7.2) also help athletes be resilient and consistent in any conditions. If offensive mental skills are necessary to *be* excellent, defensive skills are necessary to *maintain* excellence, handle adversity, and be your best at the biggest events, like the Olympics. Maintaining *excellence in training* helps athletes practice the way they should compete, and results in organized, efficient, and useful training. *Controlling competitive anxiety* becomes more important as the significance of the competition increases. The *ability to control anger and frustration* before and during competitions allows athletes to quickly gain balance and recover from errors or problems in the environment. *Control of energy levels* falls into three different defensive mental skills: 1) Ability to raise intensity high enough; 2) Ability to recover emotional energy between efforts; 3) Ability to adjust energy up or down depending on the competitive situation. The skill of quickly *recovering from performance setbacks* is a defensive mental skill that pays dividends in longer competitions or competitions with repeated efforts. *Flexibility in response to changes in the environment* may be most important at the biggest events (Olympics, Worlds), where the environment changes the most. The *ability to focus despite distractions* is also critical in big events where distractions increase exponentially. Finally, *mental maintenance skills*, or the ability to maintain simple, effective thoughts under pressure, are often the difference between having a great plan and executing it.

The key words to describe defensive mental skills include: BALANCE, RESILIENCE, and INVULNERABILITY. Athletes with strong defensive mental skills are those athletes you count on for consistent performance, competition after competition.

The Role of Personality in Developing Skills

There is no room in this chapter to review personality theory, or to debate how many personality factors exist, or whether personality is a fixed trait or a malleable moving target. What is important, for the purposes of this chapter, is to recognize that "personality" (as a shorthand) has a shaping impact on the development of skills necessary for high performance. A certain personality makes some skills easy to acquire and that same personality may make other skills nearly impossible to acquire.

For example, a highly anxious young athlete may avoid certain sport situations, such as taking a penalty kick in soccer, or taking the last shot in a youth basketball game. Avoiding these situations makes it impossible to develop the defensive mental skills necessary to succeed in these situations. In addition, over time, the lack of exposure to these situations may create an untested self-perception of the athlete such as: "I guess I'm not the kind of athlete that can take the last shot." Over time that self-perception will become a reality as the skills needed to successfully take that last shot are never learned, trained, or perfected. Conversely, that same anxious athlete may naturally attend to details and re-check that all aspects of preparation are completed. This athlete will likely discover the utility of to-do lists, goal setting, and training logs, all of which might help the athlete develop solid consistency in their sport career.

The powerful shaping impact of personalities, especially strongly defined personalities, is why many people in sport tend to lump skills and personality into a single assessment of an athlete's mental side. They may say something like: "That kid just doesn't have the 'go for it' mentality to be a ski racer," or "I don't think she has the leadership skills to be captain. She is too quiet and introverted." This type of assessment makes the common mistake of equating personality with behavior or skills. While all of us in applied sport psychology have worked with athletes whose personality and mindset made teaching certain mental skills easy, we need to be careful to distinguish between the personality and the skills/behavior. Sport psychology hasn't always made that clear distinction. The field has gone down this road in the past, trying to find the Holy Grail—the personality test that will "predict" sport excellence. Sport researchers ultimately discovered what personality researchers everywhere have found: In a battle between strong personalities and strong environments, bet on environments if you want to predict behavior. Personality plays a very important role in performance excellence, but luckily for coaches and sport psychologists looking for work, so does the environment.

Role of the Athlete's Environment in Performance Excellence

In sports there are a host of environmental factors that interact with personality to determine who develops the key mental skills for performance excellence. Perhaps the biggest variable is the grab-bag of factors you could call "athlete career circumstances." Included in this general theme would be family, luck (injury or not, born in January rather than November, a scout shows up at a practice to see someone else and spots an unknown player, and so on), specific team environments, exposure to a developmental sport structure, and timing of key events and relationships. Re-read that long but incomplete list and ask yourself if personality (or even physical talent) is all you need for sport success. The critical role of environmental factors has been well documented in recent years by a number of popular books including Malcolm Gladwell's *Outliers* (2008), *The Talent Code* by Daniel Coyle (2009), and others building upon Anders Ericsson's provocative "10,000 hours of deliberate practice" work from 1993.

In the limited space of this chapter, it is important to briefly emphasize two key environmental variables in producing performance excellence: coaching and sport psychology. Coaching is key because a coach can impact so many of the other environmental factors. A great coach can compensate for a wide variety of environmental deficits and structure the type of deliberate practice needed to develop specific skills. Of course, a bad coach is capable of doing the opposite and sentencing an athlete to a career of sub-performance excellences. One of the questions I ask teams when introducing the topic of goal setting is "Can an athlete be a world champion without a coach?" Eventually, even the most independent and optimistic athletes grudgingly admit that coaches are necessary to succeed at the highest level. When I ask why, they come around to three keys: direction, feedback, and support. Performance excellence is impossible without these things.

Of course, these three key elements are also part of a good sport psychologist's relationship with their client. I need to emphasize that the best coaches are usually excellent sport psychologists, willing and able to work on the mental as well as the physical and technical. However, in my world at the Olympic Committee, I find that head coaches are exceptionally busy and rely on specialists, such as sport psychologists, to help their teams with specific issues. Besides the focus of this chapter, and my own self-interest, I highlight the role of sport psychology here because our Olympic coaches and athletes consistently remark that the key to performance excellence (and the source of sub-performance excellences) at the Olympics is the mental aspect. I believe this truth is emphasized at the highest levels of sport, since most of the other factors have been optimized. In any case, the role of a sport psychologist is to identify and build key offensive and defensive mental skills, even if the personality, environment, and the athlete's lack of prior knowledge of the skills challenge the process (see Figure 7.1).

Figure 7.1. **Performance excellence.**

THEORY OF PERFORMANCE BREAKDOWNS

Performance Breakdown = Mental Skills Overmatched by Challenge

If performance excellence is the product of sufficient mental skills in an athlete, it follows that mental performance breakdowns occur when there is a deficit in an athlete's offensive and defensive mental skills. Specifically, I am referring to the situation when the sport challenge is large enough to overwhelm the athlete's mental skills. To clarify, however, a performance breakdown is not the same as an athlete failing to win. Given the multiplicity of physical, environmental, and mental performance factors that are needed for success, a top 20 performance in the Olympics might be a nearly miraculous performance for one athlete, while another athlete in the same event might have a serious performance breakdown to "blame" for a third place result.

Sport Psychology and the Anna Karenina Principle

> "Happy families are all alike, every unhappy family is unhappy in its own way."
>
> —Leo Tolstoy, *Anna Karenina*

To my mind, Tolstoy's famous beginning of the novel *Anna Karenina* is an appropriate metaphor for the successful and unsuccessful athlete. Like all happy families, all successful athletes have made it through and over the various hurdles that all must face. Although achieving performance excellence demands a complex collection of mental skills, the successful finished product looks similar across a wide variety of sports. On the other hand, there are so many varied causes of performance breakdowns—a deficit in any skill area can do it—that every performance breakdown is a breakdown in its own way. Thus, athletes with performance breakdowns come in all shapes, sizes, and circumstances (as do unhappy families as Tolstoy declares). The Anna Karenina Principle has been popularized by Jared Diamond (1997), and others, as a way of explaining failures in a wide variety of domains. I believe that the great variety of sport psychology problems make a general theory of breakdowns less helpful than a series of specific theories about specific types of breakdowns based on a strong understanding of performance excellence. As an applied sport psychologist, I believe my clinical training has been a useful foundation for developing specific theories and solutions for specific performance "breakdowns."

As an aside, I have wondered if this fact of highly individualized problems versus the similarities of high performers may help explain the regular conflict between sport psychologists trained via clinical psychology versus those educated with a mental skills training model. I think that there is a divergence of viewpoints of mental skills specialists and clinicians arising from the difference between the tasks of building a broad set of mental skills versus the more clinical task of addressing specific mental skill deficits in athletes.

To use a mechanical metaphor, it is the difference between designing and building a car versus working to keep the car running well. I saw this in one of the sports car race teams I worked with. In this team, the auto manufacturer had a high performance division that came to help the race team get the most out of their car. The factory engineers had exceptional and unique knowledge of their car, which helped determine basic parameters for the car's race set-up. But whenever things weren't working right, or the car just couldn't keep up with competitors, all of the brilliant engineers from the factory deferred to the crew chief, an amazing mechanic who knew how to make the most out of bad tires, a driver's idiosyncrasies, and a set-up that created a disadvantage on certain turns on a specific course.

The crew chief had to understand the theory of how the car worked, and why it was designed the way it was, but he didn't have to know how to build the car from scratch himself. As a crew chief who had worked on dozens of race cars from different manufacturers, he understood that every car has design strengths and weaknesses that create competitive advantages and disadvantages. His job was to maximize the advantages inherent in a car's design, minimize the weaknesses, and constantly tweak it to keep it competitive. I believe the work of an applied sport psychologist with an athlete is much more that of the race car crew chief than the factory engineer.

Engineering the best mental skills program to build those skills necessary to succeed in sport is a critical task, but that's not my task when I am asked to work with an Olympic athlete two years before the next Games. At that point, I am a sport psychology crew chief trying to maximize mental advantages, minimize mental weaknesses, and develop specific skills to help the athlete stay competitive. If my specific theory about how a mental skill deficit develops is accurate, I am sometimes able to retrofit a solution for the specific situation. Sometimes, however, there are too many mental skill deficits, or one deficit is so pronounced that there is a performance breakdown. The challenge has overmatched the mental skills.

It is important to note that this mismatch between skills and the challenge can occur both in and out of competition. Too often in sport psychology, we focus on the athlete who "chokes" under pressure, and forget about all of the talented athletes who didn't have the mental skills to *ever get* in that pressure situation. In the sports I work with, perhaps 5% of an athlete's time is spent in competition, with 95% of the time spent in preparation. There are many more athletes who never get to the highest levels of sport due to an inability to effectively train for competitions than there are athletes who fail at big competitions.

Before moving to the topic of the consulting process, I have to make note of two things not frequently noted in the sport psychology literature: the opportunity presented by performance breakdowns, and the danger of avoiding breakdowns. Research at the Center for Creative Leadership and elsewhere has demonstrated that great leaders in business show the greatest growth as a leader when confronted with failure or personal deficits. Surviving a failure can create an understanding of how things can go wrong, develop empathy, appropriate caution and humility, and result in greater diligence on key behaviors. I believe the same opportunity for growth is present in every performance breakdown in sport. For a sport psychologist, it is critical to take advantage of these potential "teachable moments."

It has also been my anecdotal observation that avoiding performance breakdowns for long periods (especially at the beginning of a career) can be very dangerous for an athlete. Early in my career at the USOC, a great Olympian and coach I know was talking to me about a rising star in his sport. He said, "She isn't going to make it. She is so talented that everything has come too fast and too easy. She doesn't know how to work through struggles." I thought his statement was a little silly, since she was nationally dominant and internationally competitive as a junior, but his prediction was dead on. I saw her flame out at two Olympic trials, failing to make either Olympic team. She left the sport, never having developed the defensive mental skills she needed to work through struggles. So perhaps the addendum to *Anna Karenina*, is that "all happy families have successfully worked through their unhappy situations." A well-timed performance breakdown here and there may be necessary for growth and greatness.

CONSULTING PROCESS

It is very difficult for me to divorce my consulting process from the environment I work in. The great majority of my work experience in sport psychology has been in the world of the Olympics, and in particular the world of the US Olympic Committee. It is a strange mix of consulting situations, ranging from one-time and first-time meetings the night before an Olympic competition, to the opposite extreme of a 12-year relationship from the beginnings as a junior through the end of an athletic career. Some consultation is exclusively in my office, and I have worked with athletes for a decade who have never seen my office. Some consultation is team–based, with frequent group presentations and heavy coach involvement, while some consultation is with individual athletes whose coaches have no idea about our work. Identifying genuinely consistent processes in these wildly varied situations is a challenge, but there are some common themes in my approach.

Direction, Feedback, Support

As I mentioned earlier, effective coaches provide three things for athletes: direction, feedback, and, support. I believe the presence of these same three elements makes an effective sport psychology consultant. In the sports world, there is sometimes the impression that a stereotypical warm and fuzzy sport psychologist would emphasize support more than direction or feedback. In my experience, all three factors are critical, and all can be a challenge to provide.

In some ways, direction is the element most impacted and enhanced by the experience of the sport psychologist. I see this role similar to the role played by a veteran mountain guide, or even that of an old local by the side of the country road when asked for directions by a tourist. (Growing up in New England, the famous joke was the old codger saying "you can't get there from here." I am sometimes tempted to throw that line out to athletes.) Providing direction is not simply a matter of knowing how to get from point A to point B. Providing direction requires making a quick assessment of (a) where the athlete is, and (b) determining where it is possible to go in a certain time. Once A and B are determined, multiple options for the specific path from A to B of this specific athlete must be generated, sorted, and then chosen and presented by the sport psychologist. I will talk more about this later in the section of "unique elements."

Feedback is the element most shaped by my cognitive behavioral training. I am very comfortable giving "homework" to my athlete clients. I believe this helps the consulting in a number of ways, including ensuring that athletes will receive feedback on the psychological aspects of their sport. Sport is a feedback-rich environment, but much of the feedback comes in the form of outcome results, and frequently that feedback can actually interfere with the development of certain psychological skills. Enhancing feedback by providing homework can highlight certain thoughts and behaviors necessary for skill development.

For example, if I am working with an Olympic Rifle athlete, we may be working on a new shot process (a thinking and behavioral routine that makes the shot easier to take under pressure), but a bad score in a training match might distract the athlete from the process and cause them to prematurely quit developing the process. I might ask the athlete to keep track of how many shots they were able to use their process effectively, by using a counting tool, then writing down those numbers for four days and then bringing the results to our next session. The homework helps to create a consequence of doing or not doing the work, and it also provides a source of feedback in addition to (or even in conflict with) the score or outcome feedback. Of course, in this example and in most sport psychology interventions, the new process better eventually improve the score or any other result! Being fired as a sport psychology consultant is direct and powerful feedback as well.

I find that I talk much less about the support aspect of sport psychology to Olympic coaches, in part because I still worry about the stereotypical perception that a sport psychologist will "coddle" athletes who need to "toughen up." The reality is, however, that support *is* critical, in part because support is so rare in many elite sport cultures. An athlete who loses hope in his ability to rebound from a bad competition loses self-confidence for the next competition, and support can make a critical difference for that athlete wavering between self-doubt and self-confidence.

However providing support to athletes is not such an easy task for a sport psychologist. Saying "I feel your pain," or being too "warm and fuzzy" raises red flags for many athletes who may see their pain or vulnerability reflected back at them and worry that they are going soft. Because toughness is so prized in sport, support must be presented skillfully and sometimes even stealthily by a sport psychologist. Frequently, support takes the form of a more objective analysis of results, reminders of the progress made, reframing "failure" as "challenge," or as a story of similar struggles by other athletes who went on to success. But, if failure is challenge, sometimes the role of the sport psychologist in elite sport *is* to challenge and teach when things are going badly. In elite sport, it is often critical to say, "Yes, that was terrible. Let's figure out why." This statement acknowledges the performance reality, but quickly supports the athlete by joining together to find a solution.

In regard to solutions for performance problems, I suppose I need to re-emphasize a point I have made previously (McCann, 2008). Focusing on solutions to performance problems doesn't mean that serious clinical issues are off the table. In my world, everything is a performance issue, especially if that issue surfaces in the once every four years (or once in a lifetime) crucible of the Olympic Games. Therefore, clinical issues are regularly on the table with clients, but the nature of our world necessitates a solution-focused approach rather than a problem-focused orientation. A need for efficiency and rapid movement to solutions does not mean that serious issues get superficial treatment. Rather, the external context of the athlete's career situation can strongly influence the timeline and the nature of the work. At an Olympic Games the work might focus on rapidly stabilizing the situation, while at the Olympic Training Center, the emphasis may be more on a thorough understanding of how the issue has evolved over time and teaching new skills to change the future impact of the issue.

UNIQUE FEATURES

There are many practitioners who seem to believe science-based practice is an admission of limitations rather than a foundation for excellence. When sport psychology becomes a profession, uniqueness will be valued less than competence. Still, even in the most developed professions, individual practitioners will always be unique. Exploring the unique factors in sport psychology practice may be particularly useful at this stage in our development as a field and as a profession. In my case, my unique factors are a product of my personality and my environment. The environment at the USOC has shaped me uniquely by regular exposure to a wide variety of athletes in a wide variety of sports. In part because I have worked with so many athletes, I have seen a variety of ways to get from here to there. I believe that at this point in time, the strongest element of my own consulting is providing direction.

My personality also draws me to a focus on direction. I'm an extrovert, drawing energy from people, and I'm a conceptual thinker, drawn to challenges of context and perception. I love the first few meetings with athletes, figuring out who they are, how they got to be in this situation, and what the future might hold. As someone who has always loved maps, exploring, and finding shortcuts, I see my role in those first meetings as providing a "lay of the land." I believe I have become skilled at providing perspective and drawing a clear map of the road ahead. The job of quickly making an assessment of an athlete's personality, background, present capabilities, and future hurdles is an intellectual challenge and something I love.

Operationally, I work much better with clients as active partners. I don't work well with passive clients, in part because I am less structured and more distractible than many sport psychologists. With passive clients, my lack of structure can lead to sessions that drift away from the central challenges. With active clients, and more of a partnership, I am more certain to provide what the athlete really needs, because the active client lets me know when I drift away from their needs. In addition to partnering with athletes, I have come to see coaches as natural partners in performance enhancement.

In my initial meetings with athletes, we talk about confidentiality and the potential benefits of active involvement of coaches in the work we do. Not every athlete is comfortable or interested in working with a sport psychologist and coach simultaneously, but there can be significant advantages in working as a performance team, together. I find it a challenge to get the perfect balance of private work (only the athlete and I), and public work (the athlete, coach, and I all with the same data), but I believe the extra work and vigilance to get the balance right has paid off in Olympic medals. With a psychologically sophisticated coach, a little more information at the right time can head off potential disasters. This balance comes easiest with teams that I spend a great deal of time with, but even when I am pulled deeply into the coaching team, I always stand a bit apart, due to my unique role as a psychologist.

Stylistically, I try to ask as many questions as possible, both to get information and to prevent me from speaking too much. I like to talk, as it helps me think, but it can also push the relationship from partnership to teacher and student. I frequently catch myself having gone on for a few minutes and will call myself out for being in "lecture mode" and ask for input or reactions. Although I love telling stories, drawing analogies, and using metaphors, I also know that the correct question can be worth a thousand of my words. If I know where we are and where I think we need to go, I can lead the way by telling a story or by asking questions that help the athlete to tell their story. When I do draw from experience to tell a story, I need to make sure that my storytelling is meeting the athlete's needs rather than mine.

CASE STUDY

Olympic Trials Meltdown: Coach Brian, Athlete Lauren.

It has come down to one spot available for the women's Olympic Rifle team. The favorite for the Olympic team spot is Lauren, who has been the best American in this event over the last six years. She has won silver at the World Championships, and numerous international World Cup medals over the last three years. Unfortunately, at the last Olympic Trials, Lauren had a terrible performance on the last day and fell one place out of making the Olympic team. Lauren, her coach Brian, and I had many conversations in order to get past the trauma of failing on such a big and public stage, and how best to prepare for this Olympic Trials, four years later.

I am staying at the same hotel as the team, and I drive the 30 minutes to the range every morning with Brian. Brian had been a shooter himself, and he had been on the national team, although he had never made the Olympic team. He has had a long career as a very successful college coach, and this is his first exposure to Olympic Trials as a coach. During a conversation, Brian tells me how stressed he is, and I am able to normalize this by sharing with him the results of a poll of our Olympic coaches, which indicated that they were most stressed at trials. Brian also mentions noticing some differences in Lauren seemingly related to stress/anxiety, and wonders if he should approach her about this.

At this critical point in the session, I, like Brian, have a choice to make. It's the last day of a three day trial, and the athlete has a lead. It's an almost identical situation to four years earlier at the last Olympic Trials when the athlete failed. It's the 500 pound gorilla. Will she choke again? Should anybody say, "Hey there is a big gorilla right here!"? Is it better for Brian to keep quiet and hope that it won't come up, or is it better to talk about this with Lauren in the limited time he has to talk to her this morning before her competition?

When I first began in sport psychology at the Olympic level, I would have likely answered Brian's question with a question and pushed the decision about whether Brian should say something to Lauren right back to Brian. This was partly due to my training, and partly because I assumed the coaches probably knew what they were doing, otherwise, why would they be the Olympic coach? At this point in my career, however, the reality is that I have been to 10 times more Olympic Trials than Brian has. I may not be able to answer the question, but I can provide a map of the options and the possibilities of success and failure for each potential route. Ultimately, it is Brian's choice, but the guidance I provide is a sum of my knowledge of Brian, of Lauren, and of the situation about to unfold. I am wary of Brian's tendency to over-coach under pressure, and I know that we have developed a very good and very limited script for moments such as this, and I remind Brian that this has worked successfully in the past. Brian agrees that this simple approach should help shape Lauren's thinking and addresses her natural anxiety without an explicit mention of "what if?"

So, when Lauren approaches me this morning, about 90 minutes before the start of the match, I am expecting a brief check in. Instead, Lauren tells me she is "freaking out" and her eyes well up with emotion as she talks. Lauren can be very intense, and I have seen her get emotional in a number of other competition situations. Nonetheless, I am alert and aware that this is not going to be a quick check-in.

L: I didn't sleep well. I have been warding off thoughts of disaster this entire trip, and last night I was convinced I would sleep through my alarm and miss the Trials. So I woke up at 3:45 a.m. instead of 6:30 a.m., and I lay there worried that not sleeping well might screw me up. Then I started thinking about four years ago. (Lauren starts crying, and I start walking and moving our conversation around the corner, out of sight of other competitors).

S: Well, we knew this was a real possibility, so this is no big surprise, right?

L: Yeah, but things were going so well so far, and mentally, I was just focused on performing and I've been thinking the right things the last two days, and now, when it really matters, I feel like I'm going off the cliff!

S: Woah there. Are you off the cliff?

L: No, I guess not, but I feel like I could melt down like last time.

S: All right. Big difference there. Feeling like you could versus actually doing it. You have known about that cliff, we have known about that cliff for four years, and we talked about it. We have a plan for it. You have the skills to manage this situation. Right?

L: Yeah, I guess so.

S: You guess so? OK. Let's prove that you have the skills. Tell me what your plan has been for the last four days.

L: Focus on international standards, don't worry about my domestic competitors; use the Trials as preparation for the Games.

S: So, how's that been going?

L: Good, obviously. But I feel different today, and I'm worried I might slip back into doubt.

S: OK, the doubt is the cliff. The doubt is the thought. And we talked about the feelings and behaviors that thought can produce unless you have a plan. That's why you made your plan.

L: Right.

S: So, what's the plan for the doubt?

L: Okay. Expect the doubt. Don't fear it, but understand why I need to respect it. Then I go back to basics. Who am I at my best? What do I think about at my best? How do I feel when I am at my best? What do I do when I am at my best?

S: Can you answer those? (She nods, beginning to smile) Humor me; can you say them out loud?

L: Okay, Sean! At my best, I am the world's best. And that's not bragging. It's true, based on what I have achieved. When I'm at my best, I think about excellence. When I'm at my best, I feel relaxed, aggressive, and confident. When I'm at my best, I trust my hold, my technique, and I execute my shot plan without hesitation.

S: Okay! Listen Lauren. We knew this would happen. We talked about this for a reason. It's not just you. This is true for all champions. It's part of the path, being challenged like this. I can tell you, if you weren't challenged like this here at the Trials, it wouldn't be such good preparation for the future. You need this to be hard. Just like Worlds and the Pan Am Games. Remember how you felt at those?

L: Yeah. Nervous. A little crazy.

S: And what happened? You followed your plan, used your skills and succeeded. You know what they say; courage isn't the absence of fear. It's when you feel it, but still do what you need to do.

L: Yeah. Yeah.

S: You have shown me time and again you have courage and do what you need to do no matter how you feel.

L: F-in-A right! (said with a laugh)

S: Yeah, what you said! Okay. Specifics: What are you up to until the match?

L: Well, I've got about 75 minutes, so I need to do my normal warm-up, then . . .

Lauren breaks into a detailed pre-match and match plan. We spend another two minutes as she runs through a number of details of her pre-match routine.

One of the things I have found in situations such as this one, there is a great temptation to give a speech. Through trial and error, I have found that asking questions, rather than giving a speech, is a better way to go for me. In a way, by asking the questions, you preview the self-talk the athletes will need to use in the competition. Of course, the self-talk comes easier when, as in this case with Lauren, the talk has been developed through many discussions about the ideal mental state for performance.

As Lauren heads back into the range to prepare for her match, I am feeling confident that she has avoided turning a crisis of confidence into a disabling major meltdown. I have seen too many sports events to feel confident that she will perform well enough to win and earn her Olympic Team slot, but I know that she has made it through the mini crisis of doubt.

References and Recommended Readings

Albee, G. W. (1986). Toward a just society: Lessons from observations on the primary prevention of psychopathology. *The American Psychologist*, *41*(8), 891–897.

Hanin, Y. (2000). *Emotions in sport*. Champaign, IL: Human Kinetics.

Kellman, M. (2002). Enhancing recovery: Preventing underperformance in athletes. Champaign, IL: Human Kinetics.

Martens, R. (1979). About smocks and jocks. *Journal of Sport and Exercise Psychology*, *1–2*, 94–99.

McCann, S. (2008). At the Olympics, everything is a performance issue. *International Journal of Sport and Exercise Psychology*, *6*(3), 267–276.

Meehl, P. E. (1954). *Clinical versus statistical prediction: A theoretical analysis and a review of the evidence*. Minneapolis, MN: University of Minnesota Press.

Meichenbaum, D. (1985). *Stress inoculation training*. New York, NY: Pergamon Press.

Meichenbaum, D. (1977). Cognitive behavioral modification: An integrative approach. New York, NY: Plenum Press.

Nideffer, R. M. (1976). *The inner athlete: Mind plus muscle for winning*. Thomas Crowell.

Orlick, T. (1986). *Psyching for sport mental training for athletes*. Champaign, IL: Leisure Press.

Staats, A. (1975). *Social behaviorism*. Dorsey Press.

8

Dr. Richard T. McGuire

UNIVERSITY OF MISSOURI

Rick McGuire is the director of sport psychology for Intercollegiate Athletics at the University of Missouri, and graduate professor of sport psychology in the Department of Educational, School and Counseling Psychology. For 27 years he was Missouri's Head Track and Field Coach. Under McGuire's tutelage, Missouri athletes earned 143 All American recognitions, 110 conference champions, 27 USA National Team members, seven NCAA Champions, three collegiate records, and five Olympians, with two winning Olympic silver medals. He was the founder and chairman for 27 years of the USA Track and Field Sport Psychology Program, and served on the staff for 11 USATF National Teams, including the 1992 and 1996 Olympic Games in Barcelona and Atlanta. Rick has been a significant contributor to the cause of coaches education, has written extensively, and is a prominent speaker, having delivered over 200 professional presentations. Rick was a founding member of the Association for Applied Sport Psychology, in the initial class of AASP Certified Consultants, and has been honored with the recognition of AASP Fellow.

AUTOBIOGRAPHICAL SKETCH

I am a coach! And I am proud to be a coach! To be a coach is the most special, most important, most impacting, most contributing and most honorable thing that I can do with my life. I am a coach. And here is how it all happened. I grew up on our family's dairy farm, five miles outside the picturesque upstate New York village of Salem. My dad was a dairy farmer and national agricultural leader; and my mom was a music and kindergarten teacher. Together they taught and modeled for my sister, brother and me that our most important role in life was to love, to share and to serve others.

Coach Kana was the coach for everything in Salem, and he introduced me to the dream world of sport and to the magic of being the coach. But Coach Kana left after my 7th grade year. The new basketball coach had enormous energy and passion for the game, and he was a brilliant teacher. But he also had a violent temper and a penchant for using intimidation, humiliation and fear as his means of motivation. As players, we feared his wrath and were motivated to do whatever it took to avoid his verbal and physical abuse. Rarely did we succeed, but we did succeed at winning basketball games! In fact, we won nearly all of them.

As I continued playing basketball at the collegiate level, I realized avoiding punishment, public humiliation and shame had become the defining characteristics of my sport experience. I felt like I was living in a different world. How could this be? How could we have an experience as potentially wonderful and uplifting as sport, and at the same time, have the mechanisms to get good at it and achieve success driven by intimidation and shame? I had realized that my personal experience was not very unusual. That, in fact, my coach's techniques were pretty normal, and if they led to winning championships, they were also generally accepted by the athletes.

I was incensed! There had to be a better way to teach and coach in sport, and I was going to find it. Right out of college I became a junior high school math teacher and basketball coach. And when it was time for my first practice, I had not yet found the best coaching method. As I prepared for my first official practice, I really had no idea how I should coach, or what I should do. But I absolutely did know what NOT to do! And so, I understood that if I was going to be loud, I should be cheering and encouraging. If I was going to be physical, I should hug them and not hit them. And that words like "awesome, fantastic, super, great, way to go, you can do it, nice job, and I'm really proud of you" should be utilized liberally, consistently, persistently and relentlessly.

Along the way, I had my first great epiphany regarding being a coach. When I first held our newborn daughter, Wendy (and repeated and reaffirmed two years later when her brother, Mick, arrived), I realized an entirely new and overwhelming understanding of LOVE. I knew that I would never allow anyone to do to this special child what had been done to me. It was then that I first realized that every student in my classes, and every athlete on my teams, was some other mom's and dad's most special love!

At that moment, I realized that I did not coach basketball, but rather I coached basketball players. I didn't coach the high jump, but rather I coached the high jumper. I didn't coach sport, but rather I coached kids. And I loved my kids, and I could share that love for everyone else's kids. And I could make the magic of sport happen in their lives, just like Coach Kana!

I was now free to study what I really wanted: coaching. I enrolled in a master's program in physical education with an emphasis in athletic coaching at Alfred University. It was here that I met Dr. Warren Bouck, and he taught me the critical nature of the relationships amongst philosophy, truth, values, thought and behavior. He also convinced me to take a course in personality theory, and I realized that this was the piece of coaching that I really loved. I loved coaching the kids! I cared about the kids! They trusted me. They shared their lives. I helped them try to figure out their puzzles. I was fascinated by psychology, and I wanted more. Two years later, seeking to learn more about that better way of coaching, I enrolled in the sport psychology program at the University of Virginia to study with Bob Rotella, later becoming his first doctoral graduate. He not only introduced me to the field of sport psychology, but even more importantly, he encouraged me to find my own answers to the questions that were most important to me.

Certainly my time at the University of Missouri has provided both the platform and the opportunity for my career in sport psychology to unfold. In 1983 I was hired to be the head track and field coach at Missouri, first with the women's team, and then in 1988 for the combined men's and women's team. In 1984 I was invited to teach an undergraduate course in sport psychology, followed in 1986 with our first graduate courses and master's degree opportunity. By 1988 we had admitted our first doctoral students. In 1991 Richard Cox joined our faculty as department chair, and we formed a collaboration that lasted 17 years until his retirement. With the foundation of a prominent counseling psychology program, our sport psychology program flourished and brought to us many outstanding students.

Through all of these years, I remained both head track and field coach and graduate professor of sport psychology. This allowed me a totally unique experience unheard of anywhere else in our field. To have the daily accountability of being responsible for the preparation and training of a team of 100 highly competitive NCAA Division I athletes kept me current and informed about the challenges of the real world. This was the test for taking theory to practice! It challenged me to be constantly engaged in developing and refining credible, valid theory and application. This made me a better teacher. This interaction with the academic world and the search for new knowledge challenged and equipped me to be a better coach.

In 2010, I retired from the track coach role and became the director of sport psychology for Missouri's Department of Intercollegiate Athletics, and continued as graduate professor for our master's and doctoral programs, as well as developing the Missouri Institute for Positive Coaching. But possibly the most significant and defining experience in my career in sport psychology began in 1983 when Dr. Harmon Brown asked me to become the first chairman of the USA Track and Field Sport Psychology Program. The charge was to develop and deliver a comprehensive set of sport psychology services for the coaches and athletes of the US Olympic and World Championship Track and Field teams. Over the next few years I shared my vision with colleagues and recruited several of the finest sport psychology professionals in the world to join me in this volunteer service program. Ralph Vernacchia, Gloria Balague, Keith Henschen, Rich Gordin and Jim Reardon became the executive committee and central core of the program. Together we built one of the finest models for sport psychology service delivery ever seen.

From the Family Farm to the Olympic Games: What Did I Learn?

SPORT PSYCHOLOGY IS "THINKING RIGHT IN SPORT!" It's really pretty simple. Wrong thoughts hurt sport performance. Right thoughts help sport performance. Recognize the difference. Learn to *Think Right!*

KIDS MEET SPORT AT THE COACH. The coach can MAKE or BREAK each kid's experience in sport. We need to get all of those great understandings that we have in sport psychology to all of the coaches, so that they can make the experience of every athlete positive, successful and fulfilling.

MY PURPOSE AND ATTENTION. To place my life in an intersection where I would predictably meet and have opportunities to share my life with others, so that when they moved on, they would move on with their lives being better because we met. That is my life's work—to serve others so that their life experience is better.

THEORY OF PERFORMANCE EXCELLENCE

Building from two of the points that I made in concluding the autobiographical sketch, I will attempt here to share the key theories or concepts that help me to understand the process of helping others achieve performance excellence. I begin from the understandings that through sport psychology I am trying to help athletes "Think Right in Sport," and an enormously high percentage of these athletes, these "Kids Meet Sport at the Coach." For any of my theory to help athletes prepare better, achieve more and have more fun doing it, I must first teach these theories to their coaches in ways they can be easily utilized. Thus, a central part of my "theory" is the critical nature of coach education.

Winning Kids with Sport, Not *Winning Sport with Kids!*

I am a coach. And I'm proud to be a coach. I know that right after being a husband and a father, to be a coach is the most important and most special thing that I can do with my life. I am so proud to be a coach because it allows me to share my life with kids through sport, and to potentially *win kids with sport.* For many, there is nothing in our lives more important than our children. And so, it really matters that we win in the lives of all of our children. Thus, I am a coach. I'm proud to be a coach not because sport is important, but because kids are important!

At its absolute most basic and fundamental level, sport psychology is all about "Thinking Right in Sport." If wrong thoughts can hinder sport performance, then logically, right thoughts can facilitate and enhance athletes' abilities to perform. Thus, in a nutshell, the focus of sport psychology is to assist others in "Thinking Right in Sport." Wrong thoughts hurt. Right thoughts help. Learn to Think Right.

From a "Fix It" Model to a "Build It" Model

Unfortunately, however, sport psychology is all too often viewed in the context of a "Fix It" model. Sport psychologists are frequently approached by coaches and parents with the question, "I have a kid with this problem, can you fix it?" Or an athlete will ask, "I have this problem, can you help me?" When something is broken sport psychology is seen as having the answers for how to fix it. Yet, many, if not most, of these problems could have been avoided; this is where sport psychology can make its greatest contribution and have its most profound impact. Let's first provide understandings and answers from sport psychology in the building of the sport experiences, in both preparations and in performances! Let's change the sport psychology paradigm from a "Fix It" model to a "Build It" model.

Construction Model vs. Destruction Model

Construction: to build something up. With our athletes, it is about having an understanding and making a plan for teaching, modeling, developing, nurturing and building the athlete's psychological capabilities. It is about building them up into bigger, stronger, happier, more confident and trusting people. Destruction: to tear something down. There are many settings where we observe coaches who employ a "destruction model" of coaching, and engage in tearing down their athletes, with the rationalization that they will then build them back up better than they were before. What possible logic could conclude that you can build people to be bigger if you first cut and tear them down, rather than if you just started building them up from where they were when you first met them? There is no logic to support this. This is about building a construction model, where our intention and purpose is to build our athletes up, without needlessly tearing them down.

Positive Coaching vs. Negative Coaching

Communication is the key to coaches being able to provide a great sport experience for their athletes. Communication is the conduit through which the coach translates all of these important understandings and values into instructions and experiences and then delivers them to the athletes. Communication is the bond that connects coaches to athletes, builds relationships, and establishes the basis for trust and belief. At the heart of all great sport experiences is great communication.

Great coaches are also great communicators. All great coaches do not necessarily communicate in the same way or with the same style. Most have had to work hard at learning more about themselves and their athletes and developing a wide repertoire of ways to best deliver their message. Regardless of the coach's method or style, we can all be well served by the simple reminder to remember the "Golden Rule" (Do unto others as you would have them do unto you). This is to say, communicate with those you lead, as you wish to be communicated with by those who lead you. If coaches use this principle, they almost can't go wrong.

There is No "I" in TEAM . . . But . . . There is an "I" in WIN!

Nearly anyone who has ever participated in sport has been challenged by the iconic sport cliché "There is No 'I' in TEAM!" This directive of course is meant to exemplify the importance of playing together as a team, and that for the team to win everyone must cooperate and collaborate by carrying out their own role and doing their very best for the good of the team. Unfortunately, this simple phrase has been morphed into the message and mandate that "Only the TEAM matters. The individual does not matter."

The individual absolutely does matter, and it is critical that each individual knows and understands that they do matter. Each individual has the opportunity to then develop into the biggest, best, proudest athlete that they can become, and is then motivated to deliver their very best performance for their team with each and every opportunity that they are given. Kids play sport. Sport is not sacred. Winning is not sacred. Kids are sacred. Let's "win" every kid, first!

SuCCCCCCCess vs. Winning

Nearly every coach and athlete would prefer to win in their athletic contests. I am a fan of winning. In fact, if I could, I would pick getting the "win" every time, for my team or for me personally. But you don't get the win by just focusing on winning. You must perform. And in every athletic contest, performance comes before the outcome. Performance comes before winning.

The key is to perform one's best, every time on demand. More potential victories have been lost because the team or individual did not deliver their best performance than for any other reason. Performance comes before winning; so the challenge is to deliver one's best performance first. The focus must be on preparing to perform and then delivering our best performance. Being suCCCCCCCessful in delivering your best performance gives you the best chance to get the outcome that you desire, to get the win that you want.

SuCCCCCCCess = Ability × Preparation × Effort × Will

This formula reminds us that we all are challenged to take whatever abilities (i.e., natural genetic talents) that we have, and to work diligently every day to develop those abilities into greater capabilities (i.e., practice). We then take those developed capabilities into the competitive arena and give the greatest effort that we possibly can to deliver all of that capability, to play the very best that we can. And, sometimes, maybe regularly, we may find that even though we have delivered great performance, to the point that we may feel nearly or completely exhausted, that we are still behind in the scoring or in the race, and time is running out. At this time, no matter how hard the challenge, we must exercise and engage our will power to choose to go again, and again and again, to find that little extra energy and effort hidden in our reserves, to find that little bit more that is necessary to get the score in our favor. This is the challenge for the athlete in every contest.

Motivation Matters!

From Maslow (1943) we learned that for individuals to be motivated to strive to become the very best they can be (self actualization), they must first have their subsistence needs, their safety needs and their self worth needs met.

For athletes, this would mean good basic nutrition and an ample home in which to live and sleep. It would mean a safe life away from sport, and a safe environment in which to experience sport. Safety in life and sport would include both physical safety and psycho-emotional safety. Self worth needs are primarily met by fulfilling one or more of our needs to feel competence, achievement or acceptance. In sport, our society and coaches deliver this message to athletes very clearly. Practice a lot. Get good (competent). Then go win (achievement). And, then we will love you, because we love winners (acceptance).

And yet, as a coach I know that I can't always guarantee that athletes will feel competent. Competence is generally judged relative to others, and depending on the level or the setting, an athlete may not experience the sense of competence to support feeling good about where they stand in the group. Similarly, I cannot always guarantee achievement. Our opponents play a major role in our winning opportunities. Gaining self worth through achievement and winning simply may not be guaranteed or even predictable. Still, our athletes' need to feel worthy must be met from one of these three sources: competence, achievement or acceptance.

Acceptance is the key. Although I cannot guarantee every athlete that they will feel competent or achieving, I can absolutely guarantee every athlete that they will be and are accepted; that they belong; that they are loved. Because, as the coach, I can provide that acceptance, belonging and love for each and every athlete. The key is that my love for them must be unconditional. That I love them regardless of how good an athlete they are. They cannot gain any more of my love by how well they perform, nor can they lose any of my love by how poorly they perform! All the athlete has to do is to accept that love, and to recognize the freedom that it provides them to now dare to strive to become the very best athlete that they can be.

From this foundation, athletes can and should be instructed and encouraged to experience an intrinsic, internal, approach, and positive orientation to their motivation, as opposed to the more common extrinsic, external, avoidance, and negative orientation seen so predominantly in sport experiences at nearly all levels.

The Foundations of Positive Coaching

Building a personal "Construction Model for Positive Coaching" involves a person's values, philosophical perspective, personal mission and passionate intention. To this end, all coaches would be well served to consider the questions, "What do you value most? What is really important to you? What gives meaning to life? What is defining about your life? What are your most real and most basic priorities? What guides you in making key decisions, or every day decisions?"

Here are my statements of my *Foundational Beliefs* as they apply to my role as a coach. They lead me in the development of my own personal "Construction Model for Positive Coaching." To be an effective and successful coach of young athletes, a person must: (a) have a genuine love for young people, (b) have a sensitivity to the priority and special nature of the lives of young people, (c) have a passionate commitment to contribute to the joy and happiness of young people through sport, and (d) find personal enjoyment and fulfillment in seeing excitement in young people's eyes and smiles on their faces. (McGuire & Schloder, 1998). It is the intention of Positive Coaching: (a) to develop the desire to strive wholeheartedly toward excellence, (b) to develop the realization that nothing of any real value is ever achieved without hard work and dedication, (c) to develop a healthy attitude toward competition, (d) to develop a spirit of cooperation, (e) to develop self confidence through one's ability to make decisions for oneself, about oneself and by oneself, and (f) to develop the desire to have fun (Vernacchia, McGuire, & Cook, 1996).

Principles of Positive Coaching

Principle #1: *Build a Foundation for Future Success*—physically, psychologically, socially and morally—both in sport and in life. Principle #2: Create, nurture and protect each individual's *feelings of self worth*. Principle #3: *Allow athletes to have fun*—to experience the sheer joy and excitement of playing sport. Principle #4: *Communicate with those you lead as you would wish to be communicated with by those who lead you.* Positive Coaching! It's about mission, intention, designing, building, developing, teaching, encouraging, and coaching.

THEORY OF PERFORMANCE BREAKDOWNS

First, let me make an important comment and observation on performance generally. There are many factors that affect performance, and the mental game is only one of them. At the time of performance, the whole athlete performs, and all of the athlete's capabilities are homogenized into one unified whole that is then delivered. It is very difficult, and usually unfair, to attempt after the fact to identify one aspect of the athlete's total capability to either credit for great performance or blame for poor performance. It is a task somewhat similar to taking the chocolate out of the chocolate milk. You can't do it.

With that said, I believe that the two greatest factors that negatively influence athletes' performances are the influence of our society/culture (including family) and the influence of the coach. Sport has become so valued, such a high priority, that it has distorted and undermined many other critically important values in our lives (e.g., family, health, education, respect). Our kids hear the message loud and clear. If you want to be someone, be an athlete on a team. If you really want to be someone special, be an athlete on a team that wins a lot and becomes the champion. Kids meet sport at the coach. The coach has the power to make or to break the sport experience for every kid. Coaches get the message from society, too. Great coaches win the big games, while bad coaches lose the big games. Really bad coaches lose lots of games. Bad coaches are "losers." Losers get fired and shamed. Coach, you had better win!

This leads all too many coaches into their own version of the "Disabling Focus on Winning." Motivational techniques become driven by extreme versions of extrinsic, external, avoidance, and negative motivation. As already stated previously, this is especially true when considering the issue of negative coaching. Tragically, sport at every level is filled with many coaches who use negative coaching.

CONSULTING PROCESS

My most prominent consulting role has been as the leader of the USA Track & Field Sport Psychology program, and in this capacity I have served in a variety of roles, including being the primary service provider, recruiting, training and assigning the primary service providers, developing training programs for service delivery, developing training programs for coaches and athletes, and educating the administrative and organizational leaders of US-ATF regarding both the scope and limitations of services provided by a Comprehensive Sport Psychology Service Delivery Program. But, by far, my greatest work both in volume and impact has been in the area of coach education. The absolute primary focus of my consulting efforts has been to deliver sport psychology to the people of sport. Whether it is through formal educational course curriculums, speaking at coaching seminars and clinics, or working directly with coaching staffs with universities, colleges, high schools, or community recreation programs, my consulting focuses on providing applications of sport psychology that coaches can implement immediately to make both their coaching more effective and their athletes' experiences in sport more suCCCCCCCessful and fulfilling!

In all of these approaches to consulting, I am focused on teaching others that it is all about two simple principles—*Thinking Right* and *Building*. No matter what the question is, eventually the answers are found in *Thinking Right* and *Building*. I first attempt to orient the coaches' (or athletes' and parents') understandings regarding *Thinking Right*, particularly what it means to be a SuCCCCCCCess!

What are the "Cs" of SuCCCCCCCess?

We start with SuCCCCCCCess = Ability × Preparation × Effort × Will, as discussed previously. Several times now, I have referred to the concept of being a SuCCCCCCCess! A person cannot experience great SuCCCCCCCess without having some very important "Cs" right in the middle of that SuCCCCCCCess. Our athletes need to have:

Confidence: trust that they will deliver their best.
Concentration: control of the focus of their attention.
Composure: control of their physiological and emotional arousal.
Courage: their desire and confidence is greater than their fear.
Commitment: final decisions are made before meeting the challenge.
Control: take the reigns of their own thoughts.
Choice: choose to control their thoughts.

Each of these "Cs" is critical to being a SuCCCCCCCess, and each of these is a thought. Yes, they are all thoughts. They are not things. They are thoughts. And because they are just thoughts, we can all have them in our experience, and in our athletes' experience. Because they are each just a thought, we can take **Control** of them and have them be our thoughts. How do we take control of them? It is really quite simple. We make the **Choice** to have them be our thoughts. We choose what we think. We can choose to think in ways that help us to become and to deliver our very best. We, and only we, can **Control** our **Confidence, Concentration, Composure, Courage and Commitment**. And, the ONLY way that we can take **Control** of each of them is to first make the **Choice** to develop and to engage our **Confidence, Concentration, Composure, Courage and Commitment**! Control—YOU take it. Choice— YOU make it. This is *"Thinking Right in Sport!"*

Coaches understand this. They get it. And, they want it. In a word, this is FOCUS. What all coaches want is for their athletes to show up on competition day totally focused and intending to deliver their greatest performance ever. Maybe even more than that, coaches want their athletes to show up in practice every day totally focused. If they are focused every day in practice then they will develop greater skills and capabilities, and they will have a better game. They will have practiced being focused every day, so they'll be really good at being focused. Now when they show up on game day totally focused to deliver their best, their best will be an even better game. And when they deliver that best ever game, they have the best chance of being SuCCCCCCCessful. Coaches want to know how to teach their athletes to focus. With this as the cornerstone to *Thinking Right*, I next move to helping the coaches build the foundation for their own "Construction Model for Positive Coaching."

What are the Goals and Purposes of Sport?

As I stated earlier, building a personal "Construction Model for Positive Coaching" involves a person's values, philosophical perspective, personal mission and passionate intention. To this end, I engage all coaches in considering the questions, "What do you value most? What gives meaning to life? What is defining about your life? What are your priorities? What guides you in making decisions?"

Typically, when groups of coaches share in generating such a list of what they value, it would include, but not be limited to, such things as: faith, health, family, acceptance, friends, trust, kids, teaching/career, love, learning, life, and challenge. Next, I ask them to consider, "What are the Goals and Purposes of Sport? What will my children gain from having you as their coach? What are your goals and purposes, your intentions for all the kids on your team?" Again, when groups of coaches are asked to identify the goals and purposes of sport, their composite list typically includes: confidence, respect, patience, pride, fun, and many more.

Whether these would be on your list of important goals and purposes of sport is not critical. Certainly many of them would be. And, just as certainly, it is obvious that most of these represent those attributes, skills, strategies, values, understandings, and knowledge that define "Coaching the Person" and developing that all-important "Core Confidence" that is critical in "Coaching Mental Excellence." Nearly every coach understands that these are the key elements that we are responsible for teaching and coaching with our athletes. Unfortunately, the passionate need and motivation to get the win, often overrides the motivation to teach and develop these values. Winning distracts us from SuCCCCCCCeeding first.

For sure, all of these can be learned through sport. However, they are not automatically learned in sport. Many people, even many coaches, are under the assumption that sport teaches confidence, pride, courage, respect, etc. But the truth is that sport doesn't teach anything. For every athlete who ever learned **confidence** in sport, many learned to **doubt**. For every athlete who ever learned **pride**, others learned **shame**. For every athlete who ever learned courage, others learned **fear**. For every athlete who ever learned to **respect others**, many learned to **hate**. This may be discouraging, but it is the truth. No, sport doesn't teach anything. Only the teachers of sport, the coaches, do the teaching. Whatever the coaches choose to teach usually gets learned.

Another unfortunate reality is that while nearly all coaches develop great training and practice plans for developing physical capabilities and skills, very few coaches actually have similarly intricate detailed plans for developing their athletes' psycho-emotional-mental skills, attributes and capabilities. But that's about to change right now. This is the focus of my consultation work with coaches.

Building a Construction Model for Positive Coaching

First, the construction model concept is built upon the presence of valued intentions, purposeful planning, skilled instruction coupled with active learning experiences, and positive modeling, all provided in a safe, supportive nurturing environment. Next, the coach must identify specific activities and experiences that will support and allow for the learning and development of the desired psycho-emotional attribute or skill. For example, coaches have many things for athletes to do to develop their physical capabilities and attributes. Coaches employ appropriate combinations of these activities to develop seasonal, weekly and daily training plans intended to help the athletes become more capable physically and technically.

So, now we simply apply the same planning principles to helping athletes become stronger and more capable psycho-emotionally and mentally. The following outline of questions will provide appropriate guidelines for creating this plan. For each of the attributes, skills, strategies, values and understandings that the coach has identified, these four questions should be asked and answered in sequence: (1) What will I *never do* in practice or anywhere else with my athletes, because it will destroy or undermine the nurturing and development of X?, (2) What will I do *generally* in practice to develop and nurture X?, (3) What will I do *weekly* in practice to develop and nurture X?, and (4) What will I do *daily* in practice to develop and nurture X? (See the Appendix for example construction models).

This is exactly how I approach the vast majority of my consultation work. I understand that *Kids Meet Sport at the Coach*, not at the sport psychologist. I understand that the kids and the coach are to be center stage in sport, not the sport psychologist. As a sport psychologist, I should never be a threat to the coach. And I am never trying to get between them and their athletes. When I am really good at leading coaches to understand how to build and deliver their construction models, they become amazed at how utterly simple it is. They then insist that I work with their team. So then we work together, me occasionally, the coach every day with the athletes, and we're all needed, wanted and happy.

UNIQUE FEATURES

This is undoubtedly my unique feature—that I am a coach! For 41 years my primary professional role was that of being the coach. In sport psychology I found that knowledge, understanding, answers, and truth can help athletes, parents, and coaches have a better experience in their sport activities. I have found and developed understandings, applications and approaches that will allow athletes to become more effective in their practices and preparations. This increases the probability of delivering outstanding performances more consistently, and with that gain more fun and greater achievements and successes, leading to the athlete experiencing personal pride, satisfaction, fulfillment and ultimately more motivation to dream and work and strive for even more.

I intend to get all of this information to coaches and to athletes and parents through their coaches. The coaches are our most efficient and effective distribution network for sport psychology. Coaches are the teachers of sport. Kids meet sport at the coach. I am the teacher of the coaches, and I am encouraging and enlisting my colleagues to do the same. If I have anything unique, this would be it. I am a coach! And I am proud to be a coach!

CASE STUDY

The case study that I am providing illustrates two significant aspects of sport psychology consultation. The first is the meeting with the prospective client, in this case the university football coach. The second is the identification of needs and the subsequent development of the service program to meet those needs.

The Collegiate Football Coach

In early February, our senior associate director of athletics for student services, a former doctoral student of mine and my soon-to-be new boss, came to me with the alarming news that the football staff had become interested in gaining the services of a sport psychologist, and they had the name of a person that they were exploring. He felt that it would be wise for me to schedule a meeting with the head coach and share with him my plans for the coming year and the services that I would be offering. The senior associate athletic director and the assistant director of athletics for performance accompanied me to the meeting. As we entered the football office suite, the coach's first words were "Welcome" and then, "Coach, I'm eager to hear more about what you are going to be doing with sport psychology for the rest of the department next year. I think that is such an important area, and I am interested in hearing all about it. But, I want you to know that we have another guy who we really like and think that he can help us. So we are going to go in a different direction and we aren't going to be using you in this role. But I am interested to hear your ideas. We have a few minutes. I just want to be up front and be sure you understand that we are going in this different direction."

As far as the beginning of an important potential job interview goes, that's about as bad as it can get. Basically, we're NOT HIRING YOU, but we can talk if you want. I thought that the other two guys' jaws were going to hit the floor. Now in total truth, I did not have my job riding on this meeting. I was being hired to develop a model program to provide a comprehensive array of sport psychology services, and to integrate them throughout the department's sport teams and support services. I didn't need to have football to keep my job. At the same time, it would be a devastating setback to have the very first thing known about my new program be that it wasn't good enough for the football team, so they were going with some other guy's services. This was not an encouraging start to the meeting.

But, the "game was on," and the conversation had just begun. After a very few minutes of cordial small talk, I said to the coach that I wanted to share a few things with him about sport psychology and about me, personally and professionally. I then elaborated briefly, but directly, about these key points: (a) I am a sport psychologist and a coach, and thus I understand that coaches never want anyone between them and their team, so I always work with and through the head coach and the coaching staff, and not independently; (b) sport psychology is not counseling athletes with mental/emotional problems, fixing them in confidential meetings, and then sending them back ready to play. Certainly there would be a few athletes on any team that had counseling needs, and that when and where those needs existed, I would refer them to the appropriate counseling professionals; (c) the primary focus of sport psychology is "Thinking Right in Sport!"; (d) sport is not 90% mental as the trite cliché suggests. In fact, if anything, it is 90% physical, but, at the moment of delivery, the mental piece has an enormous impact; (e) with all that said, my years as a coach, and my years as a sport psychology consultant, I believe what all coaches want is for their athletes to show up on game day, totally focused and intending to deliver their greatest performance ever, right now, today. Maybe even more than that, coaches want their athletes to show up in practice every day totally focused, so that now practice will work. If they are focused every day in practice then they will develop greater skills and capabilities, and they will have a better game. And they will have practiced being focused every day, so they'll be great at being focused. Now, when they show up on game day totally focused to deliver their best, their best will be an even better game.

At this point, the coach broke into the conversation and said, "I can't believe it! I just got done talking with our coaches about how our team needs to learn how to focus. I keep yelling focus and, they still can't do it! We're a young team, but if we could learn to focus, and to re-focus before the wheels come off, we could be a very good team. Are you saying that you can teach our football players how to focus?"

Coach told me that football was a six-second game. Players had to go hard from the snap of the ball to the referee's whistle, and that averaged about six seconds. I asked what they did from the whistle to the snap. He said make substitutions, get the next play, and get ready for the snap. I suggested that we needed to look at this time frame, that it was during this 20–45 second window that the players needed to do the focus and re-focus skills. We needed to teach them how to use this time to make them better players and a better team. We would teach them the skills of focusing so that we could win games "from the whistle to the snap."

"From the Whistle to the Snap"

We put together a task specific mental skills training program for the football team to equip them with the skills of being able to focus and re-focus for every play throughout the entire game. We titled this program "From the Whistle to the Snap," and created six lessons to teach the skills of *focus* (i.e., thinking right, being in the present, positive self-talk, composure, concentration, confidence). Each lesson was 30 minutes in length, with 10–15 additional minutes for questions/discussion. Then, each skill was integrated into the activities of their workouts. The mental skills were not being learned and reinforced separately, but integrated right into the activities of regular practice. I met with the coaching staff to review the lessons exactly as the players had been presented them, and identified appropriate coaching behaviors necessary to complement and further support integrating these new skills into daily practice. I brought Dr. Jim Reardon (Columbus, OH) into the program as a consulting counseling psychologist for the football team. Jim and I had worked together for over 20 years, including the 1995 World T&F Championships and the 1996 Olympic Games. We did some specific testing and assessment and held individual meetings to follow up and review the results and to make plans for developing approaches to establish greater effectiveness and consistently proficient play. We provided regular follow up with players throughout the season, and maintained regular communication with the coaching staff on a weekly basis, more frequently if needed.

This proved to be a very positive experience for the players, the coaches, the support staff, and for the sport psychology professionals. The team had a very successful season, and the team and staff spoke openly to the public through the media regarding the difference that their new sport psychology program was making.

Recommended Readings

I have been influenced by many individuals from across several fields. Here are several who have intrigued and encouraged my thinking. Psychology: Abraham Maslow (motivation), Albert Bandura (Social Learning Theory), Martin Seligman (Learned Helplessness, Learned Effectiveness, Positive Psychology), Carol Dweck (Mindset), Mihaly Csikszentmihalyi (Flow). Applied Sport Psychology: Ralph Vernacchia, Bob Rotella, Gloria Balague, David Cook, Keith Henschen, Ken Ravizza, Susan Jackson, Dick Coop, Terry Orlick. Popular Life Application: Stephen Covey, John Maxwell, Ken Blanchard, James Dobson, Tony Robbins, John Eldridge. Sport: Clair Bee (Chip Hilton series), Tony Dungy, John Wooden, George W. Kennedy (Sport and Sportsmanship, 1931).

References

Maslow, A. (1943). A theory of human motivation. *Psychological Review*, *504*(4), 370–396.

McGuire, R. T., & Schloeder, M. E. (1998). *Coaching athletes: A foundation for success*. Marina del Rey, CA: Health for Life.

Vernacchia, R. A. (2003). *Inner strength: The mental dynamics of athletic performance*. Palo Alto, CA: Warde Publishers, Inc.

Vernacchia, R. A., McGuire, R. T., & Cook, D. L. (1996). *Coaching mental excellence. It does matter whether you win or lose*. Portola Valley, CA: Warde Publishers, Inc.

Appendix

EXAMPLE CONSTRUCTION MODELS

1. I Intend to Build PRIDE with my athlete(s)/team.

a. What will I NEVER DO because it will undermine or destroy the building of PRIDE?
- I will never humiliate an athlete by yelling or screaming.
- I will never demean my athletes.
- I will never belittle or degrade my athletes.
- I will never purposely ignore progression, breakthroughs, milestones, or brilliance.
- I will never take credit and shuffle blame.
- I will never provide negative feedback.
- I will never show favoritism.
- I will never criticize an athlete or staff member to another athlete.
- I will never lose control of my emotions or behaviors.

b. What will I do GENERALLY to build PRIDE with my athletes?
- Involve athletes in individual and team goal setting.
- Use language that builds and encourages the athlete.
- Give positive feedback for accomplishments.
- Take pride in what I do. Be knowledgeable and prepared.
- Show class! Lead by example.

c. What will I do WEEKLY to build PRIDE with my athletes?
- Allow ownership. Give athletes choices.
- Praise hard smart work.
- Give credit where credit is due.
- Acknowledge great efforts, school records, PR's in front of the whole team.
- Create successes. Create meaningful drills and activities that are challenging yet able to be accomplished.
- Create a healthy learning environment for athletes to feel the positive aspects of sport.
- Allow for mistakes to be learning tools for development.

d. What will I do DAILY to build PRIDE with my athletes?
- Provide positive and constructive feedback.
- Create activities that promote skill development.
- Offer support through active listening.
- Encourage risk taking, responsibility and openness.
- Keep our area clean. A clean area is a beautiful area. Beauty = Pride
- Arrive on time and be prepared. This shows respect. Respect = Pride
- Develop a warm up that can be done well. Competency = Pride
- Be as positive as I possibly can be.

2. I Intend to Build CONFIDENCE with my athlete(s)/team.

a. What will I NEVER DO because it would undermine or destroy the building of CONFIDENCE with my athletes?
- Point out mistakes without offering suggestions for improvement.
- Question my athletes' abilities.
- Make rewards contingent only on winning.
- Display extreme negative emotion in response to mistakes.
- Focus only on weaknesses.
- Call athletes out if front of everyone, make a negative example of.
- Show favoritism.
- Use negative communication with the athletes.
- Accept a low standard for excellence.
- Limit the opportunity for success.
- I will never belittle or demean any of my athletes.
- I will never go to practice without a plan.
- I will never make the outcome of a performance a personal issue.
- I will not teach my athletes that their confidence should be predicated on their last practice or last competition.
- I will never allow my athletes be overly negative about themselves, especially out loud.
- I will not use sarcasm or put downs to motivate my athletes.
- I will not allow athletes to belittle another team member.
- Give them unrealistic, unattainable challenges during training.

b. What will I do GENERALLY to build CONFIDENCE with my athletes?
- Provide unconditional belief and confidence in my athletes
- I will be confident in myself.
- I will be calm in difficult situations.
- Develop realistic goals.
- I will treat the opinions and ideas of my athletes with respect and open-mindedness.

- I will focus on the process of performance, not on the outcome.
- I will teach that confidence is the belief that you can deliver your personal best.
- I will proactively teach my athletes positive responses they can call upon when needed during competition.
- Develop training sessions that allow opportunities for athletes to succeed.
- Teach my athletes that confidence is a choice. And it is their choice!

c. What will I do WEEKLY to build CONFIDENCE with my athletes?

- Spend time developing relationships with each athlete.
- Model confidence and positive self talk
- I will provide a situation where there will be a little pressure, with a reasonably attainable challenge at least once a week.
- I will reflect on and praise great efforts.
- Allow athletes to provide instruction and/or feedback for teammates

d. What will I do DAILY to build CONFIDENCE with my athletes?

- Treat athletes with respect and value their ideas and opinions.
- Encourage athletes to take risks, and not be afraid of the occasional poor performance.
- Give positive feedback and communication.
- Not allow use of the words "I Can't."
- Use the "sandwich" approach for providing feedback (one positive, one constructive instruction, one positive).
- Show belief and confidence in the program, the athletes and in myself.
- Commit daily to high work ethic in practice.
- Provide training that will build their competence.
- I will teach them how to be independent, not dependent on the coach.

9

Dr. Bruce Ogilvie

PROFESSOR EMERITUS, SAN JOSE STATE UNIVERSITY

Left to right: Diane Ogilvie, Patrick Baillie, and Bruce Ogilvie

Bruce Ogilvie, PhD, enjoyed a professional life with many facets. After completing his doctoral degree in 1954, he soon began work at San Jose State University, dividing his time between an academic appointment and responsibilities as the director of the new student counseling center. As a researcher, he began to accumulate a massive database of information from testing completed with thousands of elite and professional athletes—as well as with other high-level performers. In 1966, he and Tom Tutko authored the seminal "Problem athletes and how to handle them." Bruce retired from San Jose State in 1979, but he continued to write prodigiously, to work with countless athletes, and to consult with various police departments in the south Bay Area who sought to hire and train the best possible police officers. With Dr. Don Greene, Bruce developed the *Learning Styles Profile* and the *Competitive Styles Profile*, building on his years of experience in measurement of key performance attributes. Bruce died in 2003.

Dr. Ogilvie's chapter was written by Patrick Baillie, PhD, LLB, a psychologist and lawyer based in Calgary, Alberta, Canada. Through his doctoral dissertation research with retired elite and professional athletes, Patrick came to know and work with Bruce. Patrick provided assistance with statistical analyses required for the development of the *Learning Styles Profile* and the *Competitive Styles Profile*. He was able to use these measures in his work with some of Canada's best athletes, at Olympic and professional levels. Patrick continues his involvement in sport psychology, in part, through risk management services provided to the Canadian Sport Centre Calgary. His full-time role is as a senior psychologist with Alberta Health Services.

Bruce C. Ogilvie (1920–2003)
AUTOBIOGRAPHICAL SKETCH

I am a Canadian by birth and an American by history. My childhood and early adolescence were risky, with my father absent from the home and my mother, well, more attentive to herself than to me. I had no rules, so my behavior was often lacking in any controls. I spent much of my childhood at the beach or at the park, only occasionally dropping by school. At the age of 12, I found out I couldn't even read.

But one teacher at Mission High made me his project and I started to add some academic intelligence to my obvious skills in sports. Sport was the stabilizing influence in my life—not just in my adolescence. I was the quarterback of the high school football team and several colleges recruited me. When World War II started, though, I signed up for the Army and soon found myself in Texas.

One day, I was in the gym at the base, working out, when a Staff Sergeant suggested I could make some cash as a professional wrestler. As a result of the wrestling—and an arrest by the military police—I met a Major, who told me of the big plans he had for me. The Major and I worked to set up a rehab clinic at the base. There, I learned that recovery is as much about the soldier's head as it is about his body. The Major wanted me to pursue medicine and was deeply disappointed when I opted for psychology.

After the war, I completed my bachelor's degree in psychology at the University of San Francisco, and then attended Portland State for my master's degree. With my beautiful wife, Diane, and two children, Terrie and Doug, we moved to London, England, where, in 1954, I completed my doctorate. Hans Eysenck was my supervisor and, as the years passed, a great friend.

Following the completion of my degree—financed in part by Diane singing in cabarets throughout Europe and by my wrestling—we moved back to the United States. I joined the faculty at San Jose State University (SJSU), with a half-time teaching load and the rest of my time spent setting up the student counseling center. On campus, I worked out regularly and came to know many of the student athletes. Coaches began to contact me, raising concerns about a particular athlete, and asking me if I could work with their "star." Bud Winter—who was a USA Track and Field Hall of Fame coach—was one of the first people to ask me to work with an athlete with a performance issue. As I look back, I find that many of the coaches who came to me in those early days would later enter the Hall of Fame, having always been willing to try new approaches. Applying the principles learned in my doctoral studies, about personality and psychopathology, the field of applied sport psychology might have found its roots. Still, though, my credibility came far less from having a doctorate in psychology than it did from being a person who was athletic, who knew and had experienced their world of sport.

Over the years, I was invited to work with dozens of professional and Olympic teams, and I accumulated test data on over 12,000 elite athletes. For me, though, the focus was always on the individual athlete. My goal was to ensure that no emotional, psychological, or personality factor would stand in the way of the athlete's ability to achieve their peak performance. The elite athletes with whom I worked all had unique motor skills; they sought my services in order to uncover the blocks that interfered with those skills being allowed to flow naturally. I should emphasize, though, that many, many of the athletes I worked with had amazing physical talents and were nationally ranked, record holders, or professionals *long before I ever met them*. They were referred to me not for what is now called "performance enhancement," but to overcome some block that was getting in the way of each athlete achieving their full potential. They could do it in practice or they'd done it before; why couldn't they do it now?

I retired from SJSU in 1979 and was fortunate to have another 24 years of practice ahead of me. Every morning began with reading a scientific journal (or one of my favorite alternatives, the *Skeptical Inquirer*) and I would be at my Mac computer by 8:00 a.m., working on a paper. I wrote hundreds—once recording over 20 publications in a single year—but there are so many that I never finished.

Sport is where I came from and family is what sustained me. No day was ever complete until I had done my workout and then headed off to dinner with Diane. In 2003, we celebrated our 60th anniversary, even if we never found the marriage certificate.

THEORY OF PERFORMANCE EXCELLENCE

Over the last half century, the field of applied sport psychology has grown from its somewhat-misinformed infancy[1] into an area of legitimate training and practice. Starting as a clinical psychologist on the San Jose State University counseling center staff, my sessions with athletes often referred to performance crises and became the impetus for seeking knowledge about the difficulties faced by athletes. The problems presented in these early years were beyond what I had experienced or observed as a young therapist. During counseling sessions, I was watching or hearing about symptoms that ranged the pathological scale, inhibiting effective behavior in general. So often the performance issue or conflict took the form of phobias, denial and irrational beliefs, obsessive or compulsive behaviors and thoughts, and symptoms of depression. The challenge for me was to determine how I could become more effective in applying my prior clinical training as an eclectic therapist to the role of consultant for individual athletes, coaches and teams.

My tendency, at that time, was to see myself as taking a "humanistic" approach to problem solving with clients, showing active concern with the "whole person." My experiences with conflicts and issues of high performance men and women in such occupations as law enforcement did provide a limited background for treating sport-related conflicts. It appeared, though, that the stresses of competing at the elite level were introducing negative human reactions that were unique to sport participation. The presenting problems were often related to a failure to perform up to potential. Coaches saw the athlete as capable, as having the motor potential, but somehow experiencing some type of psychological block. The talent was obvious but their performances were unreliable. For me, there were few things more painful than seeing an athlete who had great physical abilities, but, when it mattered, simply could not perform. Whether the problem was a function of a disconnection in coaching or of something mental, I wanted to help.

No one should be surprised that, as a student of Eysenck, I was a strong believer in the notion of science as the key method of discovery. Collecting psychometric data upon samples of intercollegiate athletes was also motivated by my first, naïve impression that competition at elite levels appeared to have a deleterious effect upon many young athletes. In a 1971 article in *Sports Illustrated*, I was quoted as having originally been "ready to conclude that all jocks were 'overcompensating, psychoneurotic kooks,'"[2] but I thought that a more rigorous analysis of personality variables in athletics might give me a different perspective. I sought, then, to answer the question posed by my generalization: What are the negative effects that accrue from seeking to excel as an athlete?

Occasionally the performance crises appeared to be manifestations of deep-seated emotional problems, expressed behaviorally in the sport setting. These experiences, then, gave birth to the studies of exceptional athletes that I completed since 1958. These studies provided data that became the source for the approaches, methods and strategies that underlie the consultation style that has evolved over these many years. The findings contributed most to our learning how best to serve our athlete clients, recognizing the inimitable nature and character of men and women who were elite performers.

Certainly, there are demands that are unique to this service population. I found the most difficult demands to be the treatment expectations of administrators, athletes and coaches. The most stress I experienced over the years flowed from an expectation that the source of the problem would be identified quickly and effective treatment programs designed immediately. There was a widely held belief that the individual would be back on the field, court, ice or other venue performing at his or her previous levels within days. These were often athletes who were critical to team success such as contributing points to a tournament victory. These unrealistic expectations were to reinforce my concern about the health and welfare of elite young men and women. Was this another example of general stress of competition producing symptoms observed in the clinic? Unrealistic expectations were to cause me to alter both the form and style of my clinical approach to problem solving.

As reflected by my training, every elite athlete with whom I have worked has been subjected to extensive psychometric study. In the early days, in this select sample, modest trends were to appear when compared to the university norms for the instruments employed. The variables measured by these instruments were not assumed to measure sport-specific attributes. Such assessment instruments were yet to be developed and standardized.

Initially, we[3] used the following battery: Minnesota Multiphasic Personality Inventory; Cattell's 16PF (Sixteen Personality Factor Questionnaire); Edwards Personal Preference Inventory; Jackson Personality Inventory; and Nideffer's Test of Attentional and Interpersonal Style. Each instrument was considered by us to be the best standardized measure for the attributes we were investigating. Our expectation was that these instruments would generate significant insight for those athletes seeking to overcome the psychological issues or blocks that were negatively affecting performance.

Beginning in 1960 we were able to extend the elite population samples by including Olympic, National Team and professional athletes with the growing population of intercollegiate athletes.[4] In experiences as consultants with these elite athletes, the dramatic need for valid assessment and acceptable crisis intervention strategies became even more apparent. Time pressure to produce measurable positive effects was an ever-present reality. These consulting experiences continually reinforced an awareness that graduate and post-doctoral clinical training had not provided a sufficient background for working with this client population.

What did become obvious during feedback sessions with each of these elite athletes was a need to develop and standardize assessment instruments that measured sport-specific behaviors. The phenomenon of individual differences prevails wherever we seek to understand behavior, emotions and cognitions of individuals who seek our counsel. In working with athletes, there existed a need to determine those questions that will enhance self-reflection and self-evaluation of the most significant performance factors. For the 50 years of my career, my quest was to find the most important, the most effective, the most probing, and the most relevant questions to ask to an athlete in crisis, with a goal of providing insight in order to alleviate the crisis.

In my early research, significant differences between high level athletes and recreational athletes were found. Only 4–5 % of male high school athletes were able to continue their competitive involvement in college athletics. (In the early years after the institution of Title IX, the figures for females ranged between 1.5 to 2 %.) We assumed these collegiate athletes represented a more select sample with regard to performance skills.

As mentioned, through the 1960s, I was fortunate to work with various Olympic teams, professional sports teams, and elite individual athletes. Only with these populations included did we begin to see significant differences in trait discriminations, with the national team and professional athletes showing higher scores on measures of need for achievement, emotional integration, and self-assertion. We also found that traits such as autonomy and independence were high for those athletes participating in individual sports, but remained within normal limits for those athletes engaged primarily in team sports.

I mention these elite sport experiences because I decided that I had learned enough to now begin to write about the diagnostic implications of assessment findings. I felt it more important to communicate with those in the coaching professions, so published modest articles in journals that would appeal to such an audience. These early attempts—to define specific performance problems and to provide insights into both the meaning of symptoms while guiding these professionals in approaches to problem remediation—proved most fortunate. These papers attempted to document how individual differences played such a significant part in how athletes responded to the stresses and demands associated with the perfection of their performance skills. With my colleagues, I wrote articles with titles such as "Unconscious Fear of Success," "Is Competition for Women Unfeminine?",

"Unable to be First," "Potential Realizer—Potential Failure," "Unconscious Fear of Failure," "Importance of Trust," and "Uncoachable Athlete."

What followed from these modest publications was that, between 1962 and 1969, I would make an average of 16 presentations per year to professional groups or audiences. I found that there were small pockets of researchers and consultants in the sport area in every developed country. There was an explosion of literature in social, psychological and physical factors based upon samples of elite athletes.

Once psychometric instruments had been specifically designed, we were able to begin to measure what appeared to be the most critical performance attributes. After gathering data on literally thousands of young men and women—all of them elite athletes—the most critical variables associated with high performance excellence were identified and various myths and possible misconceptions based on race, gender, and age finally could be addressed.

In 1966, Tom Tutko and I co-authored *Problem Athletes and How to Handle Them.*[5] Over the years, I came to loathe the book's title, given that it reflects only the negative side of athletic performance and that it reneges on my long and firmly held belief that we *work with* our athlete clients, never *handle* them. The book drew on our early research and used personality dynamics as a way of explaining impaired performance. Our intended audience for the book was the coaching community, many of whom are good applied psychologists. Our basic philosophy was that psychological investigations would provide important information about the athlete that could then be used to enhance and complement coaching skills. We believed that when coaches developed better insight into their athletes, the relationship between coach and athlete would be strengthened, sport performance would be enhanced, and, frankly, the athlete would be given an opportunity for personal growth.

I emphasize that *Problem Athletes* was written for coaches—or, I guess, for up-and-coming sport psychologists who wanted to take over the coaches' jobs. We wanted to explain certain psychological concepts to coaches and offer them advice on how to strengthen their relationships with athletes. Without a doubt, we were asking coaches to consider changing their behaviors, rather than always assuming that it was the athlete who needed to make the changes.

For example, when discussing anxiety, we wrote:

The two most general human responses to any cue are characteristically either to fight or to escape. Certainly, there are gradations between these two extremes, but in the concluding analysis of any behavioural segment we will ultimately have to conclude that, to a degree, one or the other is in evidence. The words, fight or escape, may be too emotionally loaded to represent what the individual actually feels. Subjectively, when we are placed in a stress situation, we say to ourselves that we are tense, uneasy, or ill at ease; we don't often admit that actually we feel dread or fear. In our culture we so often fail to stress the psychological values with the honest, subjective admission, 'Boy, am I scared.' Too often a useless value has been expressed by an attempt to teach youngsters that it is unmasculine to admit fear. It doesn't follow that such an admission of fright leads to a deterioration of behaviour or athletic performance. We have observed, when it is treated intelligently by the coach, that it can be a valuable insight and lead to a lessening of unreasonable fear and anxiety.

We would make the following unequivocal generalization: the coach who, because of his own personal needs, refuses to allow fear to become a conscious experience or expression will create by this refusal an atmosphere that will condition feelings of guilt within his anxious team members. He will achieve a compounding effect which causes the fear feelings to be repressed from conscious experience; and, as a result, the fear effects will become more manifest in the athlete's behavior. His subconscious need to hide his fear creates a barrier that in time becomes increasingly difficult to break down. The longer this barrier has functioned in order to hide the real feelings, the greater the time necessary to reduce or alter its effects.[6]

As another example, we also wrote about the impact of success, stating:

Becoming a champion can be terrifying to the dependent, overprotective athlete, because he can no longer look to others; they look to him. His dependency needs are ignored; as a curious reversal, he must begin to take care of others.

For the athlete who is sensitive about being liked and accepted by others, whose primary needs are to 'belong,' this can be equally dramatic; for now he becomes a target, and he can no longer be seen as 'one of the boys.' In practice he must compete among his team mates; while in track meets, the other athletes seek to unseat his position. His need for being liked is threatened; to continue to produce will only alienate more people; yet to lose means that he's less loved by those who supported him. The dilemma is inescapable.

Becoming a champion also presents a curious role reversal conflict for the hostile, aggressive athlete. He suddenly finds the tables reversed; for, rather than aiming at a target to vent his frustration, he is the target. He can no longer look up to the 'big challenge,' but must defend himself. He finds that he loses his justification for being hostile and aggressive. He has reached his peak.[7]

As these excerpts may suggest, and as I have hinted earlier in this chapter, my fundamental belief is that when elite athletes are suddenly unable to continue performing at their previous level of excellence, there is usually some trauma, some event, or some new belief that has rapidly come into play that has bumped the athletes out of their usual mental game. Often this trauma causes a distraction; more commonly it causes a disruption. From a treatment point of view, I begin with a thorough assessment and then seek to uncover the intervening factor that has caused the performance decline. From our decades of research, we know what makes an athlete mentally successful. We also know that helping an athlete in crisis is a far more individualized process and usually involves working with a client who is particularly vulnerable and wounded.

Perhaps predictably, over the years I was criticized for having, in *Problem Athletes*, glossed over the issue of race. For me, given that I work with individuals who are unique and need to be understood in terms of that uniqueness, race is not a singular concept, but is certainly another factor that may influence the internal dialogue of an athlete. To be clear, race is always a factor, though I still have to work with the athlete to understand how that factor affects them. In short, I listen to the athlete, rather than subscribing to stereotypic notions of how different racial groups act. When someone suggests, however, that *leaving out* race somehow makes me racist, of course, I bristle at the superficial analysis.

Here is what Tommie Smith had to say in his 2007 autobiography, about the reception he received back in the United States after his famous podium act at the 1968 Olympic Games in Mexico City:

Now, it was not as if no one with a title or prefix on his name at San Jose State stood with us in 1968. Dr. Clark, for one, spoke up for us after Mexico City at great cost to his standing on campus and with his peers in other parts of the country. Also, at least two professors at San Jose State will always stand out in my mind as men who helped shape me when I needed shaping the most: Dr. Bruce Ogilvie and Dr. Thomas Tutko. Their names ought to be recognizable as, respectively, the foremost sports psychologist and sociologist of all time, men who pioneered in their fields. When either of them spoke in the years after I graduated, I made a point to go see them if I could, no matter how long the drive was. Dr. Ogilvie in particular was special. I took his class as a junior, and in that class and in personal conversations with me, he truly made me understand that I was not dumb. At that time, convincing me of this took some doing, because of my own background and the campus culture. He was amazing.[8]

Again, for me, that kind feedback reflects my core approach to intervention: You can do nothing that is effective until you know all about the athlete *with* whom you are working. There are no canned strategies, no easy solutions, and certainly no standard assumptions. Everything is about respecting the individual as unique. The athlete has to know that you care, and that message is conveyed by being authentic, compassionate, engaged, and attentive.

With the Athletic Motivation Inventory (AMI) (Tutko, Lyon, & Ogilvie, 1969), we focused on traits likely to have relevance to performance success and likely to lend themselves to counseling interventions. After a number of iterations—evolving on the basis of data—the 11 traits that came to comprise the AMI were these: Drive; Aggression; Determination; Guilt Proneness; Leadership; Self Confidence; Emotional Control; Mental Toughness; Coachabililty; Conscientiousness; and Trust.

In validating the AMI, we asked coaches to rank their athletes on each of the 11 traits, and some consistent findings began to emerge. Most notably, while coaches could reliably rank their players on the more overt dimensions (e.g., Drive, Aggression; Leadership; and Coachability), coaches were unreliable when attempting to assess the more covert dimensions (e.g., Mental Toughness, Emotional Control; and Conscientiousness). Whether with the AMI or with another instrument, given their inherent, concealed nature, these dimensions needed to be assessed in a reliable and valid manner. I would spend the next 30 years looking for another measure (and another colleague with whom to work) until Don Greene and I developed the Competitive Styles Profile (CSP) and the Learning Styles Profile (LSP).[9] My dear friend, Rich Gordin, has very kindly stated that he thinks the CSP and LSP "are by far the best instruments ever used in our field"—and he has used them hundreds of times.

In the CSP, Don and I put together a measure that was both quick to administer and easy to interpret. Bar graphs showed how each athlete scored on the five core dimensions (i.e., Determination, Concentration, Orientation, Poise, and Mental Toughness) and on the 24 categories that contributed to these dimensions. The categories measured such constructs as Will to Win, External Distractability, Extrinsic Motivation, Fear of Failure, and Self-Confidence. In the LSP, the four core dimensions were TriModal Learning, Learning Preferences, Teachability, and Optimal Learning, with underlying categories that included Kinesthetic Learning, Caution/Risking, Willingness to Change, and Frustration Tolerance. While the potential existed for athletes to answer as they thought we wanted them to, when answered honestly the CSP and LSP gave us great insights into an athlete's style and suggested possible directions for interventions. I never used testing to assist teams in making draft picks, only to inform teams about what strategies in coaching and other leadership would likely help to get the most out of their star players. An aspiring rookie may want to present an unrealistically positive version of himself or herself, but such useless information, in the end, only limits the coach's ability to get the best out of that athlete.

CONSULTING PROCESS

Of course, there is no such thing as a standard session, since every case and the circumstances surrounding it vary. Sometimes, the coach has made the referral and the athlete has arrived at my office rather sheepishly; sometimes, the athlete calls me. Sometimes, the consultation happens during the off-season and we have time to work together in smaller pieces; sometimes the intervention occurs just before the playoffs and results are needed right now. What is typical for me, though, is that close to every intervention will include formal psychological testing.

Early on in my career, I used hypnosis to help me get into an athlete's inner thoughts, but there were limitations with this. I became more comfortable—and so did the athletes—when using the less maligned tense-and-relax approach. Having athletes engage in extreme tension of various muscle groups, followed by complete relaxation, assisted the athletes in doing what I call "clearing the field," which was also accomplished by the use of imagery.

Once the athlete was relaxed, I would ask him or her to visually replay a performance that had gone wrong. This guided imagery was used to work with the athlete to understand his or her internal dialogue—what was the script playing inside their head? Self-punishment, doubt, and other negative factors in self-talk interfere with positive mental processes. We have to create the right mental attitude and that means writing a script that silences criticism while emphasizing excellence.

More often than not, the voice of criticism has a particular origin in some person (e.g., a parent, a coach, a girlfriend or boyfriend) or some trauma (e.g., an injury, a loss, a tragedy). When we find that, we work through it, clinically, using everything from systematic desensitization to rational emotive therapy to psychodynamic approaches. I cannot tell you the countless numbers of athletic careers I've seen cut short by the over-involved parent who foolishly believes that anything less than perfection must be met with profound (and usually loud) criticism of their athlete-child. These instances are often replayed, for years, and can seriously hinder the athlete's ability to let his or her natural skills simply flow.

After working through the trauma, the next step is to have the athlete tell me about their best day: The day when everything went right, when the hoop was huge and every shot went in, when the defense couldn't stop you, when the competition couldn't keep up. The script has just one message: "I can do this." I call it "wholesome arrogance," the firmly held belief—the emotional commitment—that "I will own you!" We rehearse the new script until it becomes firmly planted in the athlete's conscious (and, I believe, unconscious) mind, being the new dialogue that will allow the athlete to perform to his or her potential.

Over the years, there have been some athletes who have become regular visitors to my home office. I welcome their continued trust in me. For many, though, the interventions have occurred over only a brief-but-intense period of time. We have worked together and, for the athlete, excellence has become a reliable partner.

CASE STUDY[10]

This case study establishes rather clearly the difficulty we have in terms of labeling behavior patterns of athletes in a direct cause-and-effect form. This is the case history of an athlete who failed to live up to the general consensus of coaches that he would be the best on the Pacific Coast in his particular event. This young athlete differed in a number of respects from the typical athlete who we have been studying in that he sought out one of the authors because he was becoming extremely distressed by his failure to live up to the standards he had set for himself as a performer.

Here are a few of his statements during his first interview at the Counseling Center. "I don't know what's bothering me, Doc, but I haven't felt like myself all season." When asked what he most remembered about his change of feeling and when he became most aware that he was not functioning as he felt he should, he referred this change to his sophomore year of competition. At 19 he was aware that the press, his family, and former coaches had constantly reminded him that he was destined for stardom and that it was simply a matter of time before he would achieve this greatness. He stated, "Now I seem to be all tied up in knots; much of the time I feel sorry for myself. If I didn't have my girlfriend to talk to, I am sure that I would quit school, athletics, and just get the hell out of here." He was asked if there were other things unrelated to sports that might be bothering him. He stated that he was not able to sleep well and hadn't [had] a complete night's sleep for about five weeks. He was unable to concentrate on his studies and had been finding excuses for not keeping up with his class work. He stated, "If only my girlfriend could come up from Southern California and spend more time with me, I am sure she could help me overcome this mood."

During the first interview he was approached with the inquiry as to his interest in taking the psychological tests included in our studies of athletes. It was explained to him that we would be able to gain insight into many aspects of his personality in the shortest amount of time possible. Also, as he was now in the last half of his season, time would be important if we would help him to be a more effective person. When it was explained to him that, should he be willing to take five different tests we use to study athletes, we would have them scored and meet with him. Within the next three days he expressed an immediate interest. He was given the test material and left the room, only to return about four hours later with all tests completed.

His test profiles were compared with the norms we have established and presented to him both visually and verbally. He was informed that these were the things he had said about himself and that he was free to make any corrections should there be inconsistencies with the way he felt about himself. (Author's note: We have had individual interviews with approximately 500 athletes, using the same method of allowing the individual to respond to the actual data we have collected from our tests as an attempt to increase the validity of our findings.) Each point on his test profiles was compared with the standards we have gathered over the last four years. The following is a selected number of the important differences between this young athlete and samples of outstanding athletes. (It is at this point that we would like to make reference to our opening remarks with regard to labeling behavior and arbitrarily assigning significance to particular symptoms or cause of symptoms with extensive data about any individual performer.) This is of considerable importance when time is of such vital concern to both the coach and the athlete. Gaining clinical insight into the most important emotional factor that was having such a crippling effect upon this athlete made time our particular enemy. We had six weeks in this case to help provide this athlete with psychological insight that would begin to free him from the emotional bondage he found himself in at this time of his life. The clinician's concern in this case of such a young man as this would be focused more on his basic depressive mood; possibly this would have been our focus too without the extensive psychological information he was able to give us from his tests. Yes, he was depressed; but, as we have tried to explain, the hyper-anxious athlete has been engaged in a long-term fight not to be overcome by his anxiety and only succumbs at the point of emotional exhaustion.

These are the important psychological clues that he provided on his tests that can be used as a reference for more effective handling and coaching of this athlete.

1. He was a warm-hearted, basically shy individual with high-average college-level intelligence. He had the capacity to be flexible in the use of his above-average mental ability.
2. He differed from successful athletes in that he tended to be disorganized and careless about details. He tended to bypass rules and regulations and would have preferred to make up most of his rules as he went along.
3. He was very resistant to setting high goals for himself at this time of his life and was reluctant to express any desire to be a front-runner or be on top. His psychological endurance was quite low, and his ability to apply himself over the long haul was greatly reduced.
4. He was very unstable emotionally and was prone to feel and act child-like when under particular stress. He felt over dependent upon others: his mother and girlfriend seemed to become unduly important to him as supporting figures. There was a general retreat to child-like forms of dependency. He expressed an exaggerated need to receive special attention and concern from his coach.
5. Team acceptance and public acceptance had become excessive concerns much of the time; he was physically bound because he could not afford to do anything athletically that might cause others to reject him.
6. At the time of testing, he was extremely guilt-prone and much inclined to blame himself when he did not live up to other's expectations. His test scores for tension, overwrought, drive and anxious were consistent with his behavioral descriptions of himself as totally without self-discipline or control. He was showing an increased concern with possible physical dangers in the world around him.

We asked his permission to share some of our insights with his head coach in order that we could provide a plan for psychological handling that could aid in limiting the influence of the negative features that were so pronounced in his personality at this time. We reassured him that we could reveal much information without violating our obligation to keep the information we had gained as private data.

Although we had never communicated with his particular coach nor worked with any of his athletes, we found him to be more receptive to our limited suggestion as to how he might more effectively handle this particular athlete. The coach was made aware that this giant of an athlete was not sleeping well, nor had he been for the entire season; that he was feeling rather profound guilt for not living up to his great potential, feeling that he had let down the team and his coach. This was such a startling statement that the coach became very silent and then remarked that he was very disappointed about this young man's performance but had not singled him out for special criticism. We asked him if he had taken the opportunity to give him recognition when there was an act on the athlete's part that could be rewarded. The coach seemed to exhibit much surprise that this young man would ever respond to such treatment on his part because he always seemed to be so reserved and self-sufficient. The thing that concerned him most was the frequency of mistakes and blunders on the part of this athlete to the point that he, as coach, was beginning to feel that the failures were a reflection of his coaching ability. The coach stated that this athlete had made unbelievable mistakes that had contributed significantly to the team's failure over a period of five weeks. Neuromuscular co-ordination had been obviously a special problem as the increased stress of personal failure had continued.

The coach was asked to determine first how much sleep this athlete was getting each night and to have the team physician provide some form of medication that would assure him a full night's sleep. This was arranged so that he would get a full night's sleep on Thursdays to be sure that prior to Saturday's event he had at least one night of complete rest. The coach was asked to find some honest way to show his basic approval of this young man. We did not make any recommendations as to how to express this positive attitude toward him but to let it be an honest reflection of the coach's approval. What happened and how he showed his true feeling proved to us again that we must always limit our contribution to outlining the problem areas and leave the coach free to use the information in terms of his coaching intuitions and skills. This coach appointed this athlete team captain for the remainder of the season. Our fear would have been that this would have proven to be an overload of emotional responsibility for this young man, who was already burdened by guilt about his performance. What the coach could determine was the probability of success for the future events, and, on this basis, he risked the chance of making him captain of a winning team.

In the time allowed, the two most basic needs of this athlete were met:

one, to arrest this loss of sleep and the consequent physical effects which would continue the cycle of depression; the second need to have his sense of personal worth reinforced was accompanied by his being made the most responsible member of the team.

The three hours that he spent at the clinic were used mainly to inform him as to his test scores and to interpret the psychological meanings into behavioral terms as to how the negative traits might be expressed in his athletic performances. There was no attempt to be a psychotherapist to this athlete but simply to describe our psychological finding in an open and useful form that might allow him to determine for himself those which he could effectively change by remaining conscious of their influence in his life. Now we shall describe the immediate changes that occurred.

Whatever the combination of factors that led to a rather dramatic change in performance, the end effect was so remarkable that this case will read like a movie script. Two weeks later this young man was chosen athlete of the week by the sports writer of the area in which he competed. He was chosen by his own teammates as the most inspirational player. During the next four weeks he was to set a new record for his institution, breaking a record that had been standing for 18 years.

Once again we have an example of a young athlete that causes us to wonder about the potential value of early investigation simply as a precautionary measure, using the data in some preventative manner early in the career.

In that every case is truly unique, we can always learn to ask ourselves critical questions about his response to the responsible role of team captain. Our first speculation is that he saw this as a measure of new faith and respect in him and renewed his motivation to put his ability to the real test once more. It is possible that the gesture on the coach's part was interpreted as 'He values me as much or more than anyone else.' What we will never know is what would have been the effect of initial team failure under his captaincy. Would he have had sufficient emotional strength to continue to produce? As we are continually reminded by coaches in every sport, when you are winning, most problems take care of themselves.

FINAL THOUGHTS

After close to 50 years of trying to identify those elements of personality, learning and motivation that contribute most to success in athletics and other high-performance endeavors, I think that we now have a better understanding of what factors make a difference. Put simply, there are no substitutes for mental toughness and concentration; and, conversely, when these facets are impaired, performance almost invariably suffers. When an elite athlete suddenly is no longer able to excel, I believe our role becomes one of figuring what's gone wrong and then coming up, in collaboration with the athlete, with ideas on how to fix that.

I hope that some young star in our field will choose to pursue this line of inquiry. I used to hand score the tests and manually compute correlations and even alpha coefficients. Today, such analyses, of course, take seconds on a computer. The research can be carried on, with less difficulty and with the great promise of new discoveries. Perhaps that might be my legacy.

References and Recommended Readings

Ogilvie, B. C., & Tutko, T. A. (1966). *Problem athletes and how to handle them.* London: Pelham Books.

Ogilvie, B. C. (1974). Personality traits of competitors and coaches. In G. H. McGlyn (Ed.), *Issues in physical education and sport.* San Francisco, CA: National Press Books.

Ogilvie, B. C., & Greene, D. (1994). *Athletes in crisis: Histories of performance issues in sports.* Los Gatos, CA: ProMind Institute.

Ogilvie, B. C., Greene, D., & Baillie, P. (1997). *The interpretive and statistical manual for the competitive styles profile and learning styles profile.* Los Gatos, CA: ProMind Institute.

Endnotes

1. For those who call me "the father of applied sport psychology," responsibility for its childhood tantrums must also be mine.

2. Jares, J. (1971, January 18). "We have a neurotic in the backfield, doctor." *Sports Illustrated*, pp. 30–33.

3. Whenever I refer to "we," I wish to acknowledge the long list of esteemed colleagues with whom I had the pleasure of collaborating. People like Bob Nideffer and Tom Tutko, or, more recently, Jim Taylor, Glenn Brassington, and Don Greene, each challenged me in my thinking, kept me digging in the literature, and joined me in more than few laughs of celebration. Not all friendships endured as well as others, but each was important at whatever stage of my lifelong development I was working on.

4. Bud Winter was an assistant coach on the 1960 Olympic Track and Field team. With Louis Spadia as general manager and, later, president of the National Football League's San Francisco 49ers, I was invited to test and work with all of the players from the 49ers, Los Angeles Rams, and Dallas Cowboys. I also started what would be a long and immensely enjoyable association with Stu Inman (from SJSU) and the Portland Trail Blazers of the National Basketball Association.

5. Ogilvie, B. C., & Tutko, T. A. (1966). *Problem athletes and how to handle them.* London: Pelham Books.

6. *Problem athletes*, pp. 66–67.

7. *Problem athletes*, pp. 90–91.

8. Smith, T., & Steele, D. (2007). Silent gesture: The autobiography of Tommie Smith. Philadelphia, PA: Temple University Press.

9. Ogivlie, B. C., Greene, D., & Baillie, P. (1997). *The interpretive and statistical manual for the competitive styles profile and learning styles profile.* Los Gatos, CA: ProMind Institute.

10. This case example was originally presented in *Problem athletes* on pp. 81–85 and is reproduced here without modification.

10

Dr. Terry Orlick

UNIVERSITY OF OTTAWA

Terry Orlick has committed his life to fulfilling a dream of enhancing personal and performance excellence. He has helped people of all ages to learn essential focusing skills and perspectives that free them to become better people, better performers and contributors to a better world. He has charted new paths to performance excellence and quality living through his extensive ongoing consulting work with elite athletes and high level performers in many different domains. He has also created Positive Living Skills programs that empower children, youth and adults to lift the quality and joyfulness of their own lives and enhance the lives of others. Through his books and workshops, Orlick provides detailed guidelines on how to pursue and sustain excellence in positive ways and how to teach Positive Living Skills to enhance the lives of children, youth and adults throughout the world.

Orlick is a professor in the Faculty of Health Sciences, School of Human Kinetics at the University of Ottawa, Canada where he teaches and conducts applied research on performance excellence and quality living. He is a graduate of Syracuse University, The College of William and Mary and the University of Alberta and founder and editor of the

innovative free online *Journal of Excellence* (www.zoneofexcel
lence.ca). Terry continues to consult with athletes, share his ideas
through his writing, presentations and applied workshops on quality
living, performance excellence, and Positive Living, throughout the
world. He remains physically active on a daily basis and loves to run
on trails and wide open beaches, cross country ski, skate on lakes and
kayak in beautiful nature settings.

AUTOBIOGRAPHICAL SKETCH

My early sport and life experiences influenced my passion for helping others to enhance their sport and life experiences. I was fortunate to grow up in
a very positive, supportive and active family environment. My father, who
had been a circus performer, introduced my whole family to gymnastics and
acrobatics at an early age. Our family performed a number of different acro-
batic acts, which gave me many experiences performing in front of live audiences. I was also actively involved in many different sports as a child and
spent a great deal of time actively engaged in outdoor activities.

I had two internship experiences during my master's studies—one as a
guidance counselor in a local high school and the other with youth in a psychiatric hospital. Both were meaningful learning experiences that helped me
clarify what I wanted to do with my life. I wanted to work with highly functioning people who were passionate about their pursuits, and I wanted to
help young people learn the psychological skills or focusing skills that would
free them to live their dreams.

For the next two years, I was an assistant professor in the Department of
Physical Education at Montclair State University in New Jersey where I also
coached the varsity gymnastics team. I really enjoyed working with the athletes on that team, and they taught me many important lessons about how I
could help them live to their potential and keep the joy in their pursuits.

As an athlete and coach I was intrigued by the power of focus on learning and performance. I wanted to learn more about how we could challenge
ourselves and others to focus in positive ways to perform closer to our potential, consistently. I wanted to learn more about how we could become
more effective in focusing for personal excellence. While I was searching for
ways to expand my knowledge in hopes of learning and contributing, I stum-
bled across a poster advertisement from the University of Alberta stating
that they were looking for interested students who wanted to pursue a PhD
with specialization in sport psychology through their Faculty of Physical
Education.

I applied to this new program and was accepted. I wanted to learn as much as possible about the mental links to excellence and how to keep the joy in the pursuit for children, youth and seasoned athletes. I wanted to help people to live their dreams—regardless of what they were pursuing.

My personal performance experiences, coaching experiences, teaching experiences and life experiences taught me that certain skills were critical for consistent high level performance and for living life with a sense of joy and passion. I took a huge step forward in my understanding of the real applied performance enhancement field through my extensive consulting experiences—first with developing athletes and later with high level performers in sport and many other high performance disciplines. I took another huge step forward in my career and life through my extensive applied work with children and youth, which was aimed at enhancing the overall quality of their lives. My ongoing work, teaching, researching and nurturing of positive living skills began first with children, then youth, then adults. I was, and continue to be, open to exploring many different unique opportunities that present themselves that are related to quality learning, quality performance and quality living.

THEORY OF PERFORMANCE EXCELLENCE

The following models of performance excellence, optimal living, and personal excellence have grown out of real people's experiences with excellence in sport, other high performance domains, and life. These are the internal models that I have drawn upon and continue to use to help people and performers pursue their dreams in sport, work and life. For more detailed information on each of these models and how to use them to enhance performance—see *In Pursuit of Excellence* (2008) and *Positive Living Skills* (2011).

Wheel of Excellence

The Wheel of Excellence is based on 35 years of applied research and extensive one-on-one consulting work with high level performers in sport and leading performers in many other high performance disciplines. Extensive interviews, questionnaires and long-term consulting experiences with some of the world's best performers resulted in a clear understanding of essential mental skills or perspectives that empowered best performances for high level performers in sport and many other high performance disciplines. The most essential mental skills or focusing skills are presented on the Wheel of Excellence (Figure 10.1).

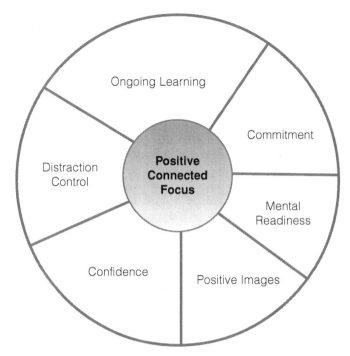

Figure 10.1. **Wheel of Excellence.**

The Wheel of Excellence was created to simplify the presentation and understanding of essential mental skills that are required to reach performance excellence in any challenging pursuit or to guide one's pursuit of the highest levels of personal excellence. The seven basic elements of excellence contained in the original Wheel of Excellence (commitment, confidence/belief, focus/focused connection, positive images, mental readiness, distraction control and ongoing learning) have not changed over the years. However, the center of the Wheel has been revised and updated based on more in-depth knowledge and experience that reflects a clearer understanding of how Focus (more specifically, how we direct and connect our focus) impacts on all other elements on the Wheel of Excellence. In the 2008 edition of *In Pursuit of Excellence*, **Focus** is clearly placed at the center of the Wheel of Excellence. This is because focus leads, directs, connects or affects all other components on the Wheel of Excellence—**Commitment, Mental Readiness, Positive Images, Confidence, Distraction Control** and **Ongoing Learning.** Your focus (and your client's focus) leads or directly affects your commitment, the extent to which you feel mentally ready, your confidence or lack of confidence, your ability to control distractions, and the extent to which you learn from each of your experiences and act or fail to act on the lessons learned.

The most accomplished performers I have interviewed or worked with over many years have reached that special place where they have all elements of the Wheel of Excellence working for them and certainly not against them—almost all the time. This is why they perform at or close to their potential almost all of the time. Performers who are less accomplished, more inconsistent (up and down) and do not perform close to their current potential typically do not have all elements on the Wheel of Excellence working for them. If you hand out the Wheel of Excellence to an athlete or group of athletes (or other performers) and ask them where they are strong and where they need work, they can usually instantly tell you—this is where I am strong and this is where I need work. Often all that athletes/performers need to do to improve the quality or consistency of their performances is to become more accomplished or consistent at focusing, distraction control and acting on lessons learned.

Bottom Line: The perspectives, mental skills and focusing skills presented on the Wheel of Excellence are required to perform at an optimal level. If athletes, students or performers in any other field really want to reach their potential and perform to their potential (or at their optimal level) on a consistent basis, they will need to develop and refine the essential performance enhancement skills outlined on the Wheel of Excellence.

Wheel of Highlights

The Wheel of Highlights is based on a lifetime of applied research, teaching, consulting and reflection on positive living and what contributes to and distracts from joyful living. Part of this discovery process included creating positive living skills programs and activities for children, youth and adults and having them record and identify the major sources of joy in their lives. The most essential sources of Highlights identified by these varied groups of people are presented on the Wheel of Highlights (Figure 10.2).

One thing that became clear to me in my work with high performance athletes and other high level performers is the imbalance that is a part of this journey for many people. The stress is high, the expectations are sometimes daunting (both internal and external), the demands are ongoing, there is very little time for rest and relaxation, and sometimes life on the road (away from family and loved ones) or in the fast lane is not that joyful. For these reasons I feel it is very important to help athletes and other high level performers to schedule time for relaxation/recovery and keep some sem-

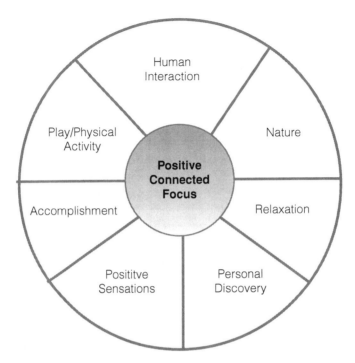

Figure 10.2. **Wheel of Highlights.**

blance of joyfulness in their lives. When athletes and other performers don't take care of their needs for rest, recovery, relaxation, positive human contact and simple joys away from the performance area, eventually it will bring them down in the performance arena.

One way of presenting the concept of balance to high level performers in any performance domain (sport, school, work, music, dance) is to introduce the Wheel of Highlights and challenge them to find some simple joys within and away from their performance arena. This will be of great potential value for their long-term pursuit of personal and professional excellence. This text you are reading is centered on different approaches to performance excellence and models of performance excellence. From my perspective, long term, ongoing performance excellence does not come only from preparing to perform and focusing on performing. It also comes from what you do and embrace within and outside your performance domain.

The Wheel of Highlights simplifies the presentation and understanding of essential *sources of highlights* that are available for adding joy, meaning and balance to everyday living and performing. The Wheel of Highlights can serve as a personal guide in one's pursuit of higher quality living. The seven essential *sources of highlights* contained in the Wheel of Highlights include: Positive Human Interaction; Positive Connection through Play, Games, Sport or Physical Activity; Positive Personal Accomplishments; Positive Personal Discovery; Positive Physical Sensations; Pure Relaxation; and Positive Interaction with Nature.

The center of the Wheel of Highlights is driven by the same core value as the center of the Wheel of Excellence—Positive Connected Focus. If you want to embrace highlights in any highlight domain, first you have to acknowledge and recognize potential highlights in your life and then connect with those potential highlights in a positive and fully focused way. If you are not open to noticing, recognizing and embracing highlights, then you will not experience them. One of the greatest values of embracing any positive experience, action, interaction or highlight (no matter how small it may be) is the positive energy it can give you and others.

If you direct and connect your focus in positive ways, there will be a direct positive impact on the extent to which you experience highlights (or positive energy gains) in your daily life. Your focus leads, connects and directly affects the extent to which you experience, or do not experience highlights or energy gains in every domain—every day of your life.

I believe we are doing a disservice to athletes and other performers if we do not teach them to embrace the simple joys of the journey—on and off the playing field. My ultimate goal is to help performers reach their personal performance goals and live a higher quality of life. We can do this by helping them develop positive focusing skills for enhanced performance and skills for positive living. If we help performers or students achieve performance goals and there is no positive benefit to their health or happiness, are we really contributing what we are capable of contributing?

A positive perspective and fully connected focus is required to continue to pursue positive dreams with passion and embrace life with an ongoing sense of joy. Embracing highlights in different parts of one's life will energize and sustain performers through the ups and downs of the journey. Finding simple joys inside and outside of the performance context or arena is essential for long-term ongoing performance excellence and joyful living.

Most performers who focus only on their performance pursuits at the expense of everything else in their lives ultimately lose the spirit and positive energy to continue to live and perform at an optimal level. To help people continue to perform at or close to their optimal level, over an extended period of time, we need to remind them of the importance of recovery time, moments of pure relaxation and embracing uplifting simple joys.

Performance excellence is not only about training, striving, working and performing. It is also about how you live your life optimally and what you do with your time and focus away from your performance site. This is why the Wheel of Highlights is essential for long term performance excellence. Some diversity in highlights is also extremely important for making positive transitions out of high performance pursuits to other meaningful endeavors. Performance excellence over time is not only about preparing, practicing and performing in the arena. It is also about living in ways that give you positive energy and keep you in a positive frame of mind. Embracing the Wheel of Highlights is important for sustainable performance excellence and optimal living, which for me is the ultimate goal. It keeps you and those with whom you work or consult centered on seeing and appreciating the positives in life.

Closely linked to the Wheel of Highlights is the Wheel of Appreciation. Nurturing a sense of appreciation for what you have, who you are, where you are, what you are doing, what you can do or become, the special people who are supporting you and the opportunities you continue to have in your life! This is extremely important for sustained performance excellence and quality living. Create your own Wheel of Appreciation by identifying all of the things, people, activities, contexts and opportunities that have added and continue to add joy, meaning and quality to your life. Share your appreciation with others who have helped you and continue to help you on your journey. Appreciation for everything that is positive and potentially available to you in your life gives you (and others) positive energy and makes your goals more attainable and your life more joyful.

Pillars of Focus

Those of you who know my work, have read my books, listened to me speak or done one-on-one consulting with me, know that *focus* is the center of almost everything I do. In my most recent book, *Positive Living Skills* (2011), I discuss eight Pillars of Focus that I believe are essential assets for high quality performance and high quality living. My experiences over the course of my life have taught me that positive and fully connected focusing is essential for optimal learning, performance excellence and optimal living. I also know that in many contexts (including school, sport, work, personal interactions, performing arts, etc.) people of all ages are expected to know how to focus effectively without anyone ever teaching them how to focus in more positive and fully connected ways.

Identifying eight essential Pillars of Focus (Figure 10.3) was an attempt on my part to begin the process of teaching children, teens and adults how to focus in more effective ways. The ultimate goal is to give all children, teens

Figure 10.3. Eight Pillars of Focus.

and adults the focusing tools that are required to learn what they have the potential to learn, perform closer to their optimal level in everything they do, live with more joy and compassion, and become what they have the potential to become as worthy, contributing human beings. The stronger one's Pillars of Focus, the more solid that person's foundation becomes for optimal learning, performing and living.

These eight Pillars of Focus include: Focused Listening, Focused Seeing, Focused Learning, Focused Playing and Performing, Focused Reading, Focused Feeling, Focused Love and Joy and Focused Reflection. Nurturing a more fully connected focus in any one of these areas has the potential to enhance the quality of that person's learning, performance or living.

Developing positive and connected focusing skills in all eight Pillars of Focus creates a very strong foundation for helping people to pursue and attain optimal levels of performance in multiple disciplines and also opens the door to more optimal living.

The Wheel of Excellence, the Wheel of Highlights and the Pillars of Focus are all aimed at helping people become what they have the potential to become—as people, learners, performers and contributors to a better world. The theory of Performance Excellence is the stated emphasis of this book. However, performance excellence is not always attained by focusing directly on performance excellence. There are many different pieces that need to be connected in positive and meaningful ways to attain and sustain performance excellence. I believe that the Wheel of Excellence, the Wheel of Highlights and the Pillars of Focus contain the most essential pieces required to live and perform at an optimal level over the course of your life. Each student/ athlete/performer begins at a different departure point and can choose the most relevant piece or pieces to work on at this juncture in their life. Performance excellence moves forward in a positive direction one little focused step at a time. A positive and fully connected focus in the preparation phase, performance phase and post performance phase (and continuing to respect the focus that works best for you) leads to performance excellence and optimal living.

THEORY OF PERFORMANCE BREAKDOWNS

Assuming that athletes/performers are physically healthy and rested, errors or performance breakdowns normally result from not respecting key elements of excellence outlined on the Wheel of Excellence. Distractions (internal or external) that lead to a disconnected or negative focus (or to not respecting the connected focus that works best for you) prevent most people from attaining or sustaining optimal levels of performance.

Performance blocks normally surface when athletes/performers do not respect the focus that works best for them. In some cases they have a weak link on the Wheel of Excellence or the Wheel of Highlights (usually distraction control or refocusing). In other cases they either do not have or have lost their passion for the pursuit.

CONSULTING PROCESS

For me the client is the person, athlete or performer with whom I am interacting or trying to help at that moment. I am simply trying to help this person do the good things that he or she wants to do with his or her focus, training, preparation, performance or life. Ultimately my goal is to empower people to believe in themselves and their goals or dreams, and help them to perfect or refine the focusing skills they need to get to where they want to go in the best way possible.

"Who," "When," "Why," and "How"

Who. I have worked with and learned from a wide range of people—from very young children to some of the most accomplished performers in the world. Every person, in every culture, at any age can gain something of real value from learning and living the skills we have to offer—because these skills can be directly applied to enhanced learning, improved performance and more positive living for everyone.

When. For most of my life, even as a child, I have drawn upon focusing skills to improve my learning, my performance and add joy to my life. I have continued to gain a clearer understanding of the value of connected focus and positive focus through my consulting experiences with others. As a young professional in this field, I began to coach and guide others on how they could continue to improve and perfect their focusing and refocusing skills. As a more seasoned professional in this field, I began to see and feel the huge potential for teaching these same skills to all people to enhance the overall quality of their lives and the lives of others.

Why. Why do I do what I do? I do it because I know from personal experience in many different contexts, that what I am doing and what I have learned from doing it can make a positive difference in people's lives. I do it because I love doing it. I love the connected feeling with others. I love the collaborative and creative process of helping people to pursue their dreams and make meaningful changes in their lives. I love the feeling of contributing to making a meaningful contribution in someone's life. I love the process of meaningful ongoing learning. I feel good about doing something that actually contributes to the quality of other people's lives—whether they are children, teens, young adults, seasoned adults, parents, performers or everyday people.

How. How do I do what I do? This is the big question that developing consultants often want answered. My simple answer is—I just do what works for me and for the person with whom I am interacting. I continue to learn from what works best and what doesn't work for me and the people with whom I am consulting. Parts of the process that I follow in my consulting and focus coaching are the same for every person or client. I do it with respect, with a connected focus, with belief, with attentive listening, with reflective thinking, and by suggesting to athletes or performers that they respect the focus that already works best for them (even if it only works for them in some performances or some parts of performances). Parts of what I do in every consulting interaction are different for each individual—because everyone is different and at a different phase of their journey. Everything I do in this context revolves around where that person is right now and what they feel is most important to them at this moment.

My overall goal is always the same—to help each person enhance their quality of learning, quality and consistency of best performances, and quality of living.

I respect the people with whom I am interacting, consulting or teaching. I respect their positive visions and goals. I respect the challenges they are facing. I listen to them closely to find out what they have already tried to move along the noble path they have chosen. I try to find out what has already worked for them—especially in terms of their focus when things have gone well. I believe in them and their mission. I challenge them to continue to do the good things they want to do. I encourage them to take concrete Positive Actions to free themselves to become the person and performer they really want to become. I encourage them to read some real-world stories from other athletes or performers that will lead them to reflect on "ways" to get to where they want to go. Some of those stories are written within *In Pursuit of Excellence* (2008), *Embracing Your Potential* (1998) and *Positive Living Skills* (2011) and some are available from other sources.

UNIQUE FEATURES

It is difficult to say how I might do things differently or the same as other consultants because I do not see their consulting practices when they are alone with athletes or performers. However, here are some ways I think I have probably followed a different path. First, I have worked with children my whole life and continue to do work and develop hands-on applied programs for children to enhance the quality of their lives, learning and performance. Second, I have done thousands of interviews, presentations and workshops with performers in many different high performance domains outside of sport. Third, I have probably written more (at least more books) than other consultants in our field.

With respect to the consulting process itself, I think I probably listen longer with full focus or more intently to athletes/performers than some other consultants. I remember being asked to do a one-on-one consulting session with a world champion athlete who was one of the world's best competitive shooters—and to do it in front of a group of other consultants, educators and coaches at a conference in Sweden. In private, I asked this athlete if she wanted to do this or if she would prefer to not do it. She was a very confident and grounded person and said she would be happy to do it.

So we sat down in two chairs facing each other (in front of this group). This athlete, as great as she was, had been struggling with focus in some major competitions that year. I began by asking her to tell me about what was going on in different events this year (good ones and then not-so-good ones). I wanted to know all the details about what was going on when things were going well and why she felt it was going well. Then I asked her to share what she felt was going on when it was not going well and why she thought it was not going well—again I was looking for details. Finally I asked her what she had already tried to fix it or make it better. I wanted to really understand what this great athlete had attempted that worked or didn't work and what she had attempted to do to try to solve or remedy the situation. This took about 20 to 25 minutes.

Up until this point, I never made a suggestion of any kind. I was just listening and asking more questions to learn from her wisdom and clarify the challenge she was facing and exploring possible solutions that lived within her. Only after gaining all that important information did I make any suggestions, because I know that most athletes and performers especially at this level have tried something to fix whatever it is they are dealing with and that whatever this athlete had tried had not worked to their satisfaction.

There were two consultants who wrote chapters in this book in the audience observing my interaction with this athlete. Right after that session one of them came right up to me and said, "Terry, I can't believe you waited that long to provide some advice. I would have jumped in right away in the first minute or two to give her some advice." What he realized sitting there in the audience and listening was that every suggestion he would have made two minutes in was something that she had already tried and it didn't work. The other consultant in the audience who is in this book also told me that he too was surprised by how long I just listened and asked questions.

I just asked questions and listened because I wanted to find out where her focus was in her best performances, where her focus was when she was struggling and what she had tried to do to resolve or improve her performance. When I make a suggestion to an athlete or performer I want to make sure that it is not something that they already tried that did not work. And I want to know the details of where their focus was connected when they tried to improve or resolve the situation.

For me, consulting is a very collaborative venture. The athlete or performer and I are working together and combining our wisdom and experience to come up with possible solutions or action steps that will get them back on track or take them to where they want to be. I have great respect for what they do, what they have tried, what they are trying to do, what worked and didn't work, and what we can do together to move forward in a positive direction.

CASE STUDY

Beckie Scott's Journey to Excellence

Beckie Scott, a member of the Canadian Cross Country Ski Team, placed 45th in her first Olympics in Nagano in 1998. I first began working with Beckie when she contacted me and asked me if I would help her in preparation for the 2002 Salt Lake City Olympics. I happily agreed to work with her and in Salt Lake City she won an Olympic gold medal. We continued to work together through the 2006 Torino Olympics where she won a silver medal. Beckie is now retired from racing, has two lovely children who keep her very busy, and lives near the mountains in Alberta with her husband Justin Wadsworth (a former cross country skier with US men's team and currently a national team cross country skiing coach).

My journey with Beckie was honest and open and collaborative in every way, and one from which we have both grown. Shortly after Beckie retired from competitive cross country skiing, I asked her if I could interview her about her journey to the top of the world in the very demanding sport of cross country skiing. Parts of this interview are presented below to give you an idea of one athlete's collaborative journey with me as a performance enhancement consultant.

Terry: What did we do together that helped you most in terms of pursuing and achieving your goals?

Beckie: I think initially, it was the very thorough and detailed process of planning, executing and evaluating that laid the groundwork for me and became the base for getting the best out of myself mentally in training, racing, and ultimately, life. It was a step-by-step, day-by-day process that was in motion year-round. The process was always dedicated to improvement, the highest quality, and getting to where I wanted to go. It began with really detailed work-sheets and a lot of careful thought, and later evolved to a process that would become second nature.

I asked myself almost every day, what am I going to do today to get closer to my goals? How am I going to do it? And at the end of the day I asked myself, what went well and what could have been done better? In the final year of my career, which I consider my most successful, I almost didn't have to ask the questions anymore. I knew exactly what I needed to do to reach my goals, how I was going to do it and where to turn for a little help and support when it was needed. I was confident that when it was all over I could look back and say, I did everything I possibly could to get the best out of myself.

Developing and implementing a detailed race plan was another one of the most crucial elements of my success. In the year before the Salt Lake City 2002 Olympics, we had the opportunity to race world cup races on the same courses that we would be racing at the Olympics. I learned a tremendous amount during those World Cups about how the courses "raced," and felt very confident that given the opportunity, I could capitalize on this education.

During the year leading up to the 2002 Olympic Games, I also spent a great deal of time at the venue either by myself, or with the team. I had decided to make a special effort to train on those courses as much as I could. When the Olympics rolled around, I had not only developed a tremendous level of comfort and familiarity with the environment and surroundings, I had also developed a very specific race plan for the pursuit race and felt confident that if I could handle the physical aspect of the race, I had the best strategy going.

On race day, the pursuit race was two 5k races separated by about an hour and a half. I had followed my first 5k classic race plan to the letter and was sitting in a perfect position for the second 5k, a few seconds separating a group of about six women. I knew every uphill, corner, downhill and flat on that course and when the time came to make a move, I did. I didn't know how the others racers would react of course, but I was even prepared for a sprint to the finish if it should happen—knowing I would swing wide out of the final corner and take the outermost lane if it came down to it. At the end of the day, that 10k Olympic race (two separate 5k races combined) was won by 1/10th of a second. I am confident in knowing that all the homework I did beforehand and executing my race plan and strategy with full focus and precision had everything to do with it.

Terry: Part of our plan for ongoing learning was ongoing evaluation and acting on the lessons learned—to pull out positive things from every performance, to assess your focus, and to learn from every experience. Can you comment on how you did that during the years we worked together?

Beckie: For five years (the entire time since we began working together), I sat down after nearly every single race, even time trials, and wrote out an evaluation that basically asked "what went well, what didn't go well, and what do I need to do in order to be better next time?" This was an absolutely critical process for me in ensuring that no experience, good or bad, was ever wasted and that I continued to grow both as an athlete and as a person from each time I stepped to the starting line—whether it was a roller ski time trial by myself with only my husband timing, or an Olympic medal winning race. On many occasions, through taking the time to go back and sift through what had happened, I picked up things that hadn't been obvious before. Every race was a learning opportunity.

Terry: What do you think was the most important lesson that you learned from me?

Beckie: If I work backwards from the present, more specifically this past season, I think the most important lesson I learned was the very powerful nature of the deciding process, and how things can be changed or affected by taking it upon yourself to just decide to do something. Even though that seemed to be one of the final chapters we worked on, I realize now it was present from the very beginning. Whether that was deciding to make every single day of training the highest quality possible with careful planning and evaluating, or deciding that adrenaline and nervous energy were a good thing and would help me ski faster instead of impeding me, or deciding that I was confident and fully prepared (even if preparations hadn't necessarily been ideal), or deciding to turn negative and potentially adverse situations into positive ones that could be beneficial or learned from. I think that virtually everything I was able to accomplish can be traced back to just beholding the responsibility of decision making and the power you have in just deciding something for yourself.

References and Recommended Readings

Amirault, K., & Orlick, T. (1999). Finding balance within excellence. *Journal of Excellence, 2*, 37–52.

Barbour, S., & Orlick, T. (1999). Mental skills of National Hockey League players. *Journal of Excellence, 2*, 16–36.

Bianco, T., & Orlick, T. (1999). Sport injury and illness: Elite skiers describe their experiences. *Research Quarterly for Exercise and Sport, 70*(2), 157–169.

Burke, S., & Orlick, T. (2003). Mental strategies of elite Mount Everest climbers. *Journal of Excellence, 8*, 42–58.

Coleman, J., & Orlick, T. (2006). Success elements of elite performers in high risk sport: Big mountain free skiers. *Journal of Excellence, 11*, 34–56.

Cox, J., & Orlick, T. (1996). Feeling great: Teaching life skills to children. *Journal of Performance Education, 1*, 115–130.

Gilbert, J., & Orlick, T. (2002).Teaching skills for stress control and positive thinking to elementary school children. *Journal of Excellence, 7*, 54–66.

Grand-Maison, K., & Orlick, T. (2006). Focusing lessons from an elite Ironman triathlete: Chris McCormack. *Journal of Excellence, 11*, 107–118.

Halliwell, W., Orlick, T., Ravizza, K., & Rotella, B. (2003). *Consultant's guide to excellence.* Chelsea, Quebec: Zone of Excellence.

Hester, K., & Orlick, T. (2006). The impact of a positive living skills training program on children with Attention-Deficit Hyperactivity Disorder. *Journal of Excellence, 11,* 1–33.

Kabush, D., & Orlick, T. (2001). Focusing for excellence in a high risk endurance sport. *Journal of Excellence, 5,* 38–62.

Kendrick, J., & Orlick, T. (2003). Introduction to executive coaching : An overview of the path ahead. *Journal of Excellence, 8,* 4–7.

Klingenberg, M., & Orlick, T. (2002). Teaching positive living skills to a family with special needs. *Journal of Excellence, 7,* 5–35.

Koudys, J., & Orlick, T. (2002). Coping with cancer: Lessons from a pediatric cancer patient and his family. *Journal of Excellence, 7,* 36–53.

MacDonald, M., & Orlick, T. (2004). Perspectives of exceptional adolescent athletes and musicians: Exploring the meaning and value attached to the performance. *Journal of Excellence, 9,* 45–66.

McMahon, S., Partridge, T., & Orlick, T. (2008). Positive living skills: Skating through adversity. *Journal of Excellence, 12,* 26–34.

Murphy, T., & Orlick, T. (2006). Mental Strategies to enhance quality performance of professional actors. *Journal of Excellence, 11,* 80–96.

Orlick, T. (1972). *A psycho social analysis of early sports participation* (Doctoral dissertation, University of Alberta).

Orlick, T. (1976). *Cooperative games and sports.* New York, NY: Pantheon Publishers.

Orlick, T. (1978). *Winning through cooperation.* Washington, DC: Hawkins and Associates.

Orlick, T. (1979). Children's games: Following a path that has heart. *Elementary School: Guidance and Counseling Journal. 14*(2), 156–161.

Orlick, T. (1981) Cooperative play socialization among preschool children. *Journal of Individual Psychology, 2*(1), 54–64.

Orlick, T. (1981). Positive socialization via cooperative games. *Developmental Psychology, 17*(4), 426–429.

Orlick, T. (1983). Enhancing love and life mostly through play and games. *Journal of Humanistic Education and Development, 21*(4), 153–164.

Orlick, T. (1986). *Coaches training manual for psyching for sport.* Champaign, IL: Human Kinetics Publishers.

Orlick, T. (1986). *Psyching for sport: Mental training for athletes.* Champaign, IL: Human Kinetics Publishers.

Orlick, T. (1996). *Nice on my feelings: Nurturing the best in children and parents.* Carp, ON: Creative Bound.

Orlick, T. (1998). *Embracing your potential: Steps to self-discovery, balance and success in sports, work & life.* Champaign, IL: Human Kinetics Publishers.

Orlick, T. (1998). *Feeling great: Teaching children to excel at living.* Carp, ON: Creative Bound.

Orlick, T. (1999). Profiles of excellence: Interview with Chris Hadfield—Astronaut. *Journal of Excellence, 2,* 84–91.

Orlick, T. (2001). Insights on excellence from an elite cardio-thoracic surgeon. *Journal of Excellence*, 5, 117–125.

Orlick, T. (2002). Excelling in the Olympic context. *Journal of Excellence*, 6, 5–14.

Orlick, T. (2002). Nurturing positive living skills for children: Feeding the heart and soul of humanity. *Journal of Excellence*, 7, 86–98.

Orlick, T. (2006). *Cooperative games and sports*. Champaign, IL: Human Kinetics Publishers.

Orlick, T. (2008). *In pursuit of excellence: How to win in sport and life through mental training* (4th ed.). Champaign, IL: Human Kinetics Publishers.

Orlick, T. (2011). *Positive living skills: Joy and focus for everyone*. Renfrew, ON: General Store Publishing House.

Orlick, T., & Botterill, C. (1975). *Every kid can win*. Chicago, IL: Nelson Hall Publishers.

Orlick, T., & Partington, J. (1986). *Psyched: Inner views of winning*. Ottawa, ON: Coaching Association of Canada. Available free on www.zoneofexcellence.ca

Orlick, T., & Partington, J. (1988). Mental links to excellence. *The Sport Psychologist*, 2, 105–130.

Orlick, T., & Partington, J. (1999). Modelling mental links to excellence: MTE-2 for quality performance. *Journal of Excellence*, 2, 65–83.

Orlick,T., Zhou, Q.Y., & Partington, J. (1990). Cooperation and conflict among Chinese and Canadian kindergarten children. *Canadian Journal of Behavioural Science*, 22(1), 20–25.

Partington, J., & Orlick, T. (1998). Modelling mental links to excellence: MTE-1 for quality practice. *Journal of Excellence*, 1, 76–94.

Partridge, T., & Orlick, T. (2008). Positive living skills for teenagers: A youth intervention. *Journal of Excellence*, 12, 1–29.

St-Denis, M., & Orlick, T. (1996). Positive perspectives intervention with fourth grade children. *Elementary School Guidance and Counseling Journal*, 31, 52–63.

Talbot-Honeck, C., & Orlick, T. (1998). The essence of excellence: Mental skills of top classical musicians. *Journal of Excellence*, 1, 61–75.

Taylor, S., & Orlick, T. (2004). An analysis of a children's relaxation/stress control skill program in an alternative elementary school. *Journal of Excellence*, 9, 89–109.

Towaij, N., & Orlick, T. (2000). Quality of life in the high tech sector: Excellence in work and non-work. *Journal of Excellence*, 3, 67–89.

Zitzelsberger, L., & Orlick, T. (1998). Balanced excellence: Juggling relationships and demanding careers. *Journal of Excellence*, 1, 33–49.

11

Dr. Anne Marte Pensgaard

**NORWEGIAN SCHOOL OF SPORT SCIENCES
& NORWEGIAN OLYMPIC TRAINING CENTER**

Anne Marte Pensgaard, PhD, has a joint position at the Norwegian School of Sport Sciences and as head of the Sport Psychology Department at the Norwegian Olympic Training Center. She has published extensively within the field of elite sport, motivation and coping with stress and also written several books and produced DVDs and CDs on mental training. She has been a credentialed sport psychologist at five Olympic Games and has worked with several Olympic gold medalists in soccer, handball and skiing. Currently, she is involved with preparing athletes for the Olympic Games in London 2012 and in Sochi 2014. She is also engaged by the University of Tromsø to contribute to build a center for excellence in sport where mindfulness is one major philosophy. In Spring 2011 she launched a CD on mental training and awareness together with the world-renowned jazz pianist Bugge Wesseltoft. In her leisure time, Professor Pensgaard enjoys extreme outdoor life and crossed Greenland in 1990 as part of the first all-female expedition. In 2000 she and Marit Holm used one month to ski Svalbard from north to south, again, as the first all-female expedition.

AUTOBIOGRAPHICAL SKETCH

It was an extraordinary day, late August in 1990. The sun was warm and made a startling contrast to the ice landscape that surrounded us and to the hilly mountains in the west. The journey had reached its conclusion. The first all-female crossing of the Greenland Icecap was a success, and together with Marit Sørensen and Katinka Mossin I took a last long look at the white horizon behind us and felt 100% present, content and alive! I felt completely present in that very moment and nothing more.

The Greenland crossing stands out as one of two key experiences that made me embark on the voyage of sport psychology. Marit Sørensen was my advisor for my master's degree in sport psychology and I also worked for her as a research assistant. When she asked whether I would be interested in being part of an expedition to cross the Greenland Icecap, I was thrilled with joy and could not believe what I heard and said "YES" before she had finished her words. As long as I can remember, I have had one aspiration in life and that is to live my life slightly differently from other people. My friends attended high school in my hometown, while I went to a skiing college on the other side of the country. Later, as an exchange student in high school, I went to Africa while most students chose the United States. I find it fascinating and inspiring to make slightly odd choices in life and take a different path. A strong feeling of belongingness to nature and a great passion for skiing also made it easy, of course, to seize this unique opportunity in Greenland.

Almost at the same time, a very different influence came through my part time job as a personal trainer for a young man called Eric. He was diagnosed with moderate to heavy depression combined with general anxiety and lived with his mother despite being in his thirties. For a long time Eric had had a strong desire to learn how to swim. This became my task as a trainer for Eric. We practiced every week. Watching how a gradual mastery of water affected this man, at first very shy and an introvert and later becoming more outwardly content and friendly, amazed me in a deep way. I will never forget his astonishment and then his ever so happy face when he had managed to swim across the small swimming pool. From that moment I knew what I wanted to do with my life. I wanted to assist people to achieve their goals; and that is still my aspiration today!

Early in my development as a PhD student in sport psychology, I had the great fortune to be introduced to people of high recognition in the field. I have gained insights and tremendous inspiration from Glyn Roberts, Terry Orlick, Daniel Gould, and Rich Gordin, and later, from Gloria Balague. It was, in fact, Terry who urged me to hold on to my unique background from expedition life when I at that time was taking on my applied career. Only today can I fully appreciate and be grateful for their contributions in my career.

After doing my PhD under the supervision of Glyn Roberts and Holger Ursin, I worked as a research fellow at the University of Birmingham with Professor Joan Duda, among others. I later on specialized in cognitive therapy and also became an instructor in mindfulness.

Since 2002, I have held a joint position at the Norwegian Olympic Training Center and at the Norwegian School of Sport Sciences. This possibility to combine research and applied work has been an important factor to me, and I have deliberately pursued both academic and applied work because I believe it provides me with a rather exceptional platform. Working with eager and curious students who constantly ask challenging questions keeps me on my toes. Additional frequent theoretical discussions with colleagues, who are not necessarily interested in performance but rather in well-being or outdoor life, are refreshing and motivating. This comfort of intellectual stimulation makes for a contrast when I meet up with athletes and coaches who are impatient, and who expect that you have the answers and are available and ready to act. Based on these two rather different worlds, I have developed an insight that I believe speaks well to the essence of performance excellence.

THEORY OF PERFORMANCE EXCELLENCE

The theory of performance excellence that I have developed during my career builds on the following concepts: faith, authentic identity, task orientation, positive response outcome expectancy and awareness.

Faith

A type of unwavering faith or strong belief, I believe, is key for any successful performance: a strong faith in your own and your team's abilities. If one of the two is faltering, the performance will never reach its true potential. Having worked with several teams over the years, I am more convinced than ever that this is the main reason why some teams succeed while others do not.

One particularly fascinating aspect working with a team is that while the team may perform well, some players will be dissatisfied and frustrated with the situation; some players will also experience contradictory emotions such as blaming themselves for not being as happy for the team as they think they should be when they find themselves underperforming. The ability or inability of a team to cope with these issues is an indicator of the strength of the belief. Will the faith in oneself and the team weather out the internal turmoil or will it erode? In these processes the work of a sport psychologist can be very valuable for a performing team. I find Albert Bandura's (1977) way of defining self-efficacy beliefs and also the role of collective efficacy very useful. I believe the guidelines he has outlined in order to enhance self-efficacy and collective efficacy work as important foundations for mental training.

Further, I am convinced that unless you are in tune with yourself, you will find it hard to reach your full athletic potential. By "being in tune with yourself" I mean being true to your values and personal convictions and not trying to measure up to a standard that one is not comfortable with. Being in tune with yourself might precede development of strong beliefs, but the opposite might be also true, that strong beliefs allow a person to be more in tune with himself or herself. Nevertheless, my experience is that they often co-exist and have a reciprocal effect on each other. Through performance accomplishments, athletes will enhance their beliefs and will also be more prone to trust their own judgments and convictions, which in turn will facilitate living life more consistently with their beliefs and values. Conversely, acting more in line with their own beliefs may lead to higher self-efficacy regarding various abilities, which may lead to a better performance.

Authentic Identity

Above all we have to nourish athletes' development of their own strong identities. In fact, we should assist them in trusting that they need to be in charge of their own development and, in a sense, be their own coach. Often athletes depend too much on advice and direction from their coach. Their ability to self-regulate is almost non-existent. This may function well for a while, but in the long run athletes have to be able to make decisions concerning their own life both when it comes to athletic development but also when dealing with more existential dilemmas. They must be authentic as performers. For a sport psychologist this authenticity piece can be a significant challenge when working with talented, young athletes at the center of the media's attention, typically attracting advice and guidance from everybody feeling they have something to contribute. Being able to assist the athlete in this process of self-development may be one of the most important tasks sport psychologists can perform. Balanced, mature and secure individuals who trust themselves are well equipped to meet the demands of top-level sports.

Task Orientation

A third cornerstone of the ability to perform optimally is a high degree of task orientation. My own conviction of how important this component is has grown stronger with each athlete and team I have had the pleasure to work with. An inherent drive for continuous development toward ever improving performance is one of the most noticeable characteristics of well performing athletes—especially those athletes who maintain a high level of performance relative to their direct rivals over longer periods of time display this disposition. Curiosity and the ability to critically evaluate suggestions and new ideas are typical expressions of the drive to improve. These athletes strive to learn and push their limits not only when competing but every day. They find their sport immensely fulfilling and show total commitment and involvement.

A high task involvement ensures that challenges and setbacks are met with a healthy approach where they are seen as opportunities to grow and develop rather than disasters. I always try to establish an athlete's or a team's level of task orientation. On the other hand, I never try to downplay the role of ego orientation (or comparing with others), but I spend as much time as needed in order for the athlete to understand the importance of high task orientation as well. As long as the athlete perceives a high level of relative competence (compared with other athletes she is competing against), a high level of ego orientation is not problematic. Indeed it can produce even more effort in such circumstances. However, a high ego orientation makes an athlete more vulnerable when the expectations are no longer met, thus a high task orientation is far more important to establish than maintaining a high ego orientation. I believe in educating athletes and coaches so that they comprehend why it pays off to develop a high task orientation due to being more self-referenced and more in control of one's own behavior. I am convinced that when the athlete sees the logic of this orientation, he or she is better motivated to do the necessary work. How much time we have to work on these dynamics and the shifts of motivational orientations also plays a role here, naturally.

John Nicholls, in his extraordinary 1989 book, provided me with the most vivid example that is always catching the imagination of Norwegian athletes, when he used the historical 1911 quest for the South Pole to illustrate the role of task and ego orientation. The two explorers, Roald Amundsen and Robert F. Scott, were the two contenders in this epic race. Amundsen is portrayed as a typical task oriented achiever while Scott is the classic ego oriented striver. Both individuals were equally eager to win. As we know,

Amundsen came out on top, becoming the first man on the South Pole while Scott met his ultimate destiny and died while trying to return to base camp after realizing he had become the second man on the Pole. With this example at hand it is a grateful task to convince Norwegian athletes of the importance of high task orientation and also "provide evidence" that high task orientation will not weaken their determination to win.

Positive Response Outcome Expectancy

Positive response outcome expectancy (PROE) is a concept that originates from Ursin and Eriksen's (2004) Cognitive Activation Theory of Stress (CATS). They argued that having a Positive Response Outcome Expectancy when faced with challenges in life was a predictor of how a person would endure those challenges and also the extent to which an individual would thrive in stressful situations. This is, in fact, Eriksen and Ursin's definition of coping. This concept was first examined while studying military personnel and later developed further through studies of extreme expeditions as well as astronauts on space missions. The results were convincing; individuals who had high positive outcome expectancy generally handled stressful situations better. When tested among athletes who attended the Olympic Games (often considered the most stressful competition any athlete can experience) these results were confirmed: Having a high PROE predicted better athletic outcomes.

I find this concept of being overall positive and having a strong belief both interesting and intriguing. Firstly, the fact that the way we, as sport psychology consultants, choose to view new challenges seems to be of critical importance. When working with athletes, coaches, and other support personnel, we need to be aware of how we ourselves meet new challenges on a daily basis. We tend to focus on how the athletes act, but we rarely focus on ourselves. Are we appropriate models in this respect? Secondly, I am curious about the extent to which this perception can be influenced by training. An intervention study where this is tested has yet to be conducted.[1] My belief, however, is that one's inclination to respond to challenges with PROE is indeed something one can influence through training and I encourage all athletes and coaches to work with their perceptions of challenges and stressful situations with this in mind. It will not suffice, though, that only the athletes make this cognitive shift; it is equally important that the coaches, the medical doctor, the physiotherapist, the massage therapist and the sport psychologist also have a high PROE so that the environment surrounding the athlete is permeated by this ambiance. High PROE becomes reflected in the way you talk, your body language, and your mood of which all can be contagious for better or worse.

Awareness

The final aspect of my theory of performance excellence involves awareness. Awareness and mindfulness have seen remarkable revitalization the last few years both in general psychology and in sport psychology. Peter Haberl from the United States Olympic Committee first introduced me to mindfulness and to Kabat-Zinn's writing. The systematic model of mindfulness training developed by Kabat-Zinn (1990) in his famous book *Full Catastrophe Living* was for me akin to coming home. He put into words how Norwegians for generations have used nature and outdoor life as both a place to meditate[2] and to simply feel at peace and alive. To be present where you are is in many ways the essence of life. If an athlete can let herself be absorbed in the task in front of her and fully trust her training and experience, then the possibility to achieve performance excellence increases.

I see a synergistic interdependence linking these building blocks of my theory. If you are able to improve on one component, you will also experience progress in the others. For example, athletes who develop strong positive outcome expectancy will increase belief in their own abilities and will also focus more on their own development rather than comparing themselves with others. Further, an increased awareness will also help with coming to terms with what is important for them and, thus, will facilitate developing a strong identity and being authentic both as an athlete and as a person. Having worked with Olympic gold medalists and world champions in both individual and team sports, I found that there are several similarities among athletes who succeed (which I have described in this section), and yet, they all follow their own distinct and unique path to success. Champions can be introverted, extroverted, hardy or neurotic, but all of them are highly committed to follow their dream to excel in their sport.

THEORY OF PERFORMANCE BREAKDOWNS

It is devastating to watch talented athletes or teams choke under pressure when you know how much time and effort they have invested in their sport. This is especially evident during competitions like the Olympic Games: a situation where an athlete has to wait for four years before they can have a second chance to medal in their sport. The same is the case when athletes try to qualify for the Olympics and they miss out by a small margin. Performance breakdowns occur, of course, in other competitions as well. However, we need to be cautious in considering what leads to performance excellence and what leads to performance breakdowns. There might be just minor differences or just random events that determine whether it becomes success or failure. We also need to be careful how we define success or failure. In addition, knowledge of the performance outcome also colors our interpretation of the performance.

There seem to be some common issues that prevent athletes from attaining performance excellence, and I would like to quote the explorer, Roald Amundsen who said that: "Victory awaits he who has prepared himself. They call it luck. Defeat is a certainty for he who has neglected to take the necessary measures in time. They call that bad luck." As mentioned earlier, a strong belief is important for performance excellence and so is having a positive response outcome expectation (PROE). One basic source of producing such beliefs is excellent preparation accomplished over time. Strong belief is a consequence of knowing that you have had the best preparation possible, the best physical conditioning, the best equipment, the best mental preparation, the best restitution, and the best rehabilitation if injury has interrupted your preparations. The ability (and creativity) to be able to cope with a range of different situations will enhance the chance for performance excellence versus a performance breakdown. I have always postulated that 80% of the mental training is conducted during the physical workout, meaning that the way you approach your daily training will determine how you will deal with the competition. Hence, the daily input into the athlete's life becomes the most important factor in order to prevent breakdowns.

But an athlete's belief in oneself is fragile. Although the common belief is that elite athletes have strong self-confidence and high beliefs about themselves and their abilities, my experience is that this is not always the case. One bad training session or a comment from the coach that may be wrongly interpreted can easily affect an athlete's self-efficacy for the upcoming event. To illustrate, I recall one cross–country skier unusually quiet and difficult to get eye-contact with during a conversation the day before an important competition. I normally let the athletes contact me if they need to talk before major competitions, but this time I felt it was time to be more proactive, and I asked how he was doing. At first he said, "Oh just fine," but when he realized that I had sensed that something was going on he took a big sigh and said that he was very concerned because his last training session before we arrived in Italy had been very poor and he had been way back behind the rest of his teammates on an interval session. I acknowledged that this could be a concern but then asked how the rest of the week prior to this session had been. He lit up and smiled and said that it had gone very well, in fact, much better than previous seasons. Just as he said it he continued to smile and said partly to me and partly to himself: "Of course, how stupid of me to be so short-sighted!!" And this is often the case; the athletes place too much emphasis on one simple training session, competition or match and forget all the hard work they have invested ahead of this incident. High efficacy beliefs must never be taken for granted, and well established athletes with an impressive list of achievements need as much reassurance as the new kid on the block. Performance breakdowns often occur because the athletes tend to forget how competent they really are.

Following this line of reasoning, we also need to consider the athlete's ability to be focused during competitions. A number of theories try to explain why athletes lose focus or choke when they were expected to do well. In my view, one explanation seems to be especially relevant and that is what I term "information overload." This may be more significant in team sports, although I strongly believe that it is relevant in individual sports, too. Coaches want to prepare their players as well as possible and, thus, provide them with information about the other team's tactical and technical skills, strengths, and weaknesses. Video analyses of both teams' performance is being studied, and there is a fine line between presenting important and vital information to the players and overloading them with too much detail and knowledge (so much that it in fact overloads the players). I believe this has been an underestimated theme in the sport psychology literature, and some coaches also find it hard to comprehend that information can harm their players' performance. An additional challenge when it comes to teams is that there are huge individual variations also within the team. Thus, there will be some players who want a lot of information while others prefer to trust that they will solve the challenges as they occur during the game. When working with teams, I often find myself dealing with these kinds of issues both when talking with coaches and players, especially during championships. If we want players and teams to stay focused here and now we need to carefully consider the amount and type of info they should be presented before games. One important job for the coaching staff will be to filter the information provided by the video analyst so that it boils down to one or two main issues the players need to be concerned about.

Aside from being very well prepared and able to be attuned to the challenges that are present, there is one main component that may "rock the boat" and that is the coach-athlete relationship. Although it is difficult to quantify how important this relationship is for successful versus unsuccessful performances, it seems to play an essential role when you talk with athletes. Coaches have a tremendous power, which they may or may not be aware of. Their ability to get to know their athletes, to understand their needs and way of thinking is vital. Therefore, I find it important to try and facilitate this communication so that both the coach and athlete can appreciate each other's differences and perspectives. At first, I thought that this was more important for female athletes than for their male counterparts. However, now, I will argue, it is less of a gender issue but it is more related to individual needs. But even for the athlete who is not so concerned with having a close relationship with their coach, it is still important that the coach understands, appreciates, and respects this importance of how they relate to their athletes. Further, it is the coach's responsibility to make sure there is a mutual understanding of whether the expectations are met or not. Otherwise, the coach can easily be the most damaging source of stress for the athlete, regardless of how ironic this may sound.

CONSULTING PROCESS

Because my doctoral dissertation focused on the relationship between motivation and coping with stress among Norwegian Olympic and Paralympic athletes and the fact that the Winter Olympic Games was held at Lillehammer in 1994, I soon got involved with consulting elite athletes. In addition, I held numerous lectures on mental training and sport psychology during this time. I found it very inspiring to have these talks, and it also helped me to clarify my own philosophy and approach since I had to present my arguments in a convincing way. I often used examples from my experiences with expeditions and extreme outdoor life in my talks and it seemed to be well received by the athletes. In 1995, I was asked to be in charge of developing a Female Athlete Project 2000, of which a mental training program was a major part. The reason was that although Norway did very well in the Winter Olympic Games in 1994, it was primarily the male athletes who earned the medals. This made a kick start on my applied career at a time when sport psychology was not a mainstream professional service to national teams. In the fall of 1995, I was invited by the Norwegian female soccer team to work as a sport psychologist. This was already a successful team, but they wanted to develop further and had decided that they could improve their mental skills.

At the present time, nearly two decades later, the role of sport psychology in Norwegian elite sport is quite different. From being a rarity, it is now more usual than not that national teams hire sport psychology consultants. In 2002, I was appointed head of sport psychology services at the Norwegian Olympic Training Center and we have built up a group of five consultants who serve the different teams. Three of the consultants have PhDs in sport psychology, one is a clinical psychologist and one is a psychiatrist. I have deliberately tried to build a group with diverse backgrounds so that we can meet different demands. At the beginning of my career, I mainly worked with performance enhancement issues. This continues to define my main bulk of work also today, but because I received a specialized training in cognitive therapy a few years ago, I also attend to clinical issues, especially anxiety disorders (i.e., social anxiety and also panic disorders). My work is mainly organized in two ways: either as a clinician at the Olympic Center or as a contract consultant with teams. In the latter case, I travel extensively with those teams.

UNIQUE FEATURES

There are two aspects of human nature that have always fascinated me: why people are motivated to achieve extraordinary outcomes and how they cope with adversity. It was the great explorers who I feel were the first ultimate achievers in our modern times, and in whose lives I was looking for answers to these two questions. Without the security net that we have today, they wandered into the unknown, not quite fearless, but very motivated and very well prepared. A combination of extreme high physical preparation and a mental toughness that we just occasionally see today was needed in order to achieve what they had set out to do.

Grounding my existence in nature is essential to me. Without the daily contact with the forest, the mountains, the hills or the lakes, I lose touch with myself and my ability to be a proficient consultant and more importantly, a well functioning human being. What now is known as mindfulness, I view my connection with nature as being just that: a mindful way of being. With all our senses present, walking into nature provides you with a natural environment for being aware, and thus, for being present here and now. This awareness is important also when you perform at the highest level. In June 2000, the Norwegian female soccer team had invited their strongest opponent, the USA team, to Tromsø, a city in the northern parts of Norway, to play a training match as part of the preparations for the upcoming Olympic Games in Sydney later that year. On match day, we took the Norwegian team to one of the high mountains close to downtown Tromsø. It was one of those clear, bright days where you could watch all the spectacular mountains and islands surrounding Tromsø, and the ocean kissing the skies far west. Sitting close together absorbing the scenery, we all touched the mountain with our hands and I read the poem "Look to the North" by the Norwegian poet Rolf Jacobsen. The poem is about looking north and to dare to face challenges. The atmosphere was magic.

Combining cultural traditions, poetry and nature to enhance team spirit and self belief is something I find works very well and also illustrates how everything is integrated. Historical examples can also make excellent points and I often use them when I conduct workshops. There is an educational aspect of this, and I also believe that the athletes (and coaches) can be inspired by learning what their ancestors accomplished. I also invite other "modern" explorers, both men and women, who tell their stories. One reason why this seems to work well in Norway is probably due to our strong traditions in polar expeditions.

When an athlete enters my office at the Olympic Training Center, they are often met by my two dogs, Nuna and Nivi. Actually, the dogs are so used to visitors that they merely open their eyes when someone enters the room, but just the fact that there are two very relaxed dogs in the room seems to have a calming effect on the athletes. It also provides a unique entry point for the rapport with the athlete, especially if this is their first meeting with a sport psychologist.

I have been fortunate to work with some outstanding coaches throughout my career and I have learned so much from all of them. One of the most exciting exercises to conduct with coaches is to figure out how to best integrate mental skill training into the daily training program. Coaches often design practices from a physical, technical, and tactical point of view while I want them to consider the mental aspect as well. How can a soccer player practice awareness during a technical drill, for example? How will this particular exercise influence this player's self-confidence? How should we design this drill in order to test the athletes' ability to cope with uncertainty? How does the coach make sure that the message she wants to convey is understood the way it was meant to be understood? In other words, combining knowledge about the sport with psychological training is an approach I strongly believe in. I also find that the coaches highly appreciate these types of discussions and it helps them to design high quality training sessions. In return, it helps me to better understand the demands placed on the athletes and, thus, I am more able to provide valid recommendations.

CASE STUDY

In 2000, the Norwegian Olympic female soccer team won the Olympic gold medal: a remarkable achievement for a small nation with fewer than five million inhabitants and strong traditions in winter sports, but not in summer sports. Since the early days of women's soccer, Norway has maintained a strong position and is typically ranked in the top five in the world. Over time a belief that we can do well has been established and in the two years leading up to the 2000 Games this foundation was further strengthened, building a "Yes—we CAN do it!" culture.

Even after a 2-0 loss against the consistently top ranked US team in the opening match, the faith did not fade. After the game, head coach Per Mathias Høgmo and I sat down and worked through how we should handle the defeat after having experienced a run of strong results in the preparatory matches preceding the Olympics. Several approaches were discussed, but above all I emphasized that keeping calm and displaying complete faith in the team (no doubt and no fear) were of utmost importance. He did follow through with this plan when facing the press the next morning.

Strong faith or belief has to be developed over time in order to withstand challenges of all kinds. With the women's national soccer team, we had been working on this aspect throughout the entire year, ever since the 1999 World Cup in the US where the Norwegian team placed fourth. Identifying strengths and weaknesses, focusing on the player development more than on the outcome, and grounding it all in Norwegian traditions all contributed to the strong belief that the team later displayed during the Olympic Games. As one of the players expressed on the plane back home after the Games: "I felt totally invincible—nothing could stop us, nothing!"

Another example that captures some key elements of my consulting style is the work with the highly successful Norwegian female handball team who crowned a string of strong championship performances with an Olympic gold medal in the 2008 Games in Beijing. The players exhibited a belief so strong that it almost overwhelmed the team atmosphere from day one of the Olympics. The team had used "mental toughness" as a theme throughout the season leading up to the Olympics and especially worked on dealing with the expectations that had been built up back home. An Olympic gold medal was the only achievement that was missing for Head Coach Marit Breivik and the remarkable history of this team. Instead of seeing these expectations as threatening, we emphasized the positive aspects of being among the favorites and the privilege to be considered as one of the best teams in the world. This was a team with a history of success and it was therefore natural to talk about outcome goals. But when the Games commenced, the main focus was on our own strengths and possibilities and only a small percentage of time was spent on the opponents. This was a very deliberate approach because there can be a tendency among coaches to provide the players with too much information prior to important games. My main job during the games was therefore to function as a sounding board for the coaches and, at the same time, to have debriefs with the players in order for them to maintain their positive outcome expectancy.

I became involved with the soccer and handball teams for two and three years before the Olympic Games, respectively. A long-term involvement with a team before they enroll in a major championship is of great importance when it comes to a sport psychologist's possibility to make a positive contribution during the Games. When you are considered a natural part of the support team, the players will be confident in your role and also be familiar with your presence.

Recommended Readings

Amundsen, R. (1913). *The South Pole: An account of the Norwegian Antarctic expedition John Murray*. London.

Bandura, A. (1977). Self-efficacy: Toward a unifying theory of behavioral change. *Psychological Review, 84,* 191–215.

Ingstad, H. (1931/2007). *Pelsjegerliv.* [Trapper life] Oslo: Gyldendal

Krakauer, J. (1997). *Into thin air.* New York, NY: Villard.

McEnroe, J. (2003). *You cannot be serious.* New York, NY: Berkley Publishing Group.

Nansen, F. (1890). *The first crossing of Greenland* (H.M. Gepp, Trans.). London: Longmans, Green.

Nicholls, J. (1989). *The competitive ethos and democratic education.* Cambridge, MA: Harvard University Press.

Næss, A. (2005). *The selected works of Arne Naess.* Eds. Harold Glasser & Alan Drengson in cooperation with the author. Dordrecht: Springer. (Vols. 1–10).

Railo, W. (1990). *Best når det gjelder* [Best when it counts]. Universitetsforlaget, Oslo.

Turner, J. (1996). *Abstract wild.* Tucson, AZ: University of Arizona Press.

Ursin, H., & Erikson, H. R. (2004). The cognitive activation theory of stress. *Psychoneuroendocrinology, 29,* 567–592.

Wooden, J., & Jamison, S. (2004). *My personal best: Life lessons from an all-American journey.* Chicago, IL: McGraw-Hill Professional.

Wooden, J., & Jamison, S. (1997). *Wooden: A lifetime with observations and reflections.* Chicago, IL: McGraw-Hill Professional.

Wooden, J. (2003). *They call me coach.* Chicago, IL: McGraw-Hill Professional.

Commentary on Recommended Readings

The first book I read was written by the Norwegian professor in pedagogy, Willy Railo, and was called *Best When It Counts!* ("Best når det gjelder"). This was a classic in Scandinavia in the eighties and nineties and new editions are still being printed. This is a toolbox book where a plethora of different techniques are presented, but no theoretical foundation or explanation is offered. On the master course in sport psychology (where we were only three students) we read all the classic articles from stress research (Mc-Grath) and also the work on achievement motivation by McClelland and later also John Nicholls' books and articles, where especially his 1989 book *The Competitive Ethos and Democratic Education*, has been read over and over again. Bandura's 1977 article[3] "Self-efficacy: Toward a unifying theory of behavioral change" became a key reading for me where the importance of linking theory and applied work became evident to me.

In addition to the professional books on psychology and sport psychology, the books by Beck (both Aaron and Judith) and Wells have been important from general psychology and, biographies written by former athletes and coaches have been of great inspiration. For example John McEnroe's book *You Cannot be Serious* (2003) provided me with an insight into a sport personality characterized by strong emotions and a turbulent life. And the thoughts and philosophy of basketball coach John Wooden have also been helpful in order to see how mental practice can be a natural part of an ordinary training session.

However, most important for my own development and motivation throughout my whole life has been the plethora of expedition literature, ranging from the early classics written by Roald Amundsen, Fridtjof Nansen, Ernst Shackelton and Robert F. Scott to the more modern explorers such as Helge Ingstad, Børge Ousland, Liv Arnesen, Marit Holm, Reinhold Messner[4] and also the recent books by Jon Krakauer. *Into Thin Air* by Jon Krakauer is for example an excellent account of how things can turn out very bad when one does not stick to the plan in critical circumstances[5]. Another excellent book, although in a very different genre, is *Abstract Wild* by Jack Turner. The second time I read it, this thin book but rich in content and depth, was when I together with my friend Marit Holm skied across Svalbard, Spitsbergen in 2000, with our two Greenland huskies Zapman and Tundra. Turner questions the way we try to organize whatever is left of the world's wilderness and is very critical to many of the solutions that are put forth. Reading this while skiing through Norway's last real wilderness, where polar bears outnumber human beings, made a strong impression and reminded me that we need to be extremely thoughtful about how we take care of our immediate surroundings. And this brings me to the final person I would like to pay tribute to and that is the founder of deep-ecology, the late philosopher, Arne Næss. His philosophy can in essence be said to have self-realization at its core for every being, whether human, animal or plant: Everybody has an equal right to live and to flourish. He was an eager mountaineer and spent a lot of time up in the mountains both in Norway and abroad. He also advocated having a pluralistic approach when it came to use of methods to study different questions. It was originally applied to science and research methods, but it is also applicable to the applied world as well.

Summing up, my career has been a mix of coincidences, inner drive, a fortune in meeting extraordinary people at important times in my educational development, and the love of nature has been a main cord throughout my life and continues to be so.

Endnotes

1. Although PROE might very well be compared with Bandura's concept of self-efficacy, the two concepts are not identical. For a detailed discussion see Ursin, H., & Eriksen, H. R. (2004). The cognitive activation theory of stress. *Psychoneuroendocrinology, 29,* 567–592.

2. Although Norwegians would never call it meditation when they go for their long walks in the forest or in the mountains—it is just an element of their lifestyle that they have done for years.

3. Bandura, A. (1977). Self-efficacy: Toward a unifying theory of behavioral change. *Psychological Review, 84,* 191–215.

4. Helge Ingstad was a traveler, trapper, and writer ("Pelsjegerliv" [Trapper Life]; published in English as "The Land of Feast and Famine" (Knopf, 1933)). Børge Ousland went unsupported and solo to the North Pole. Live Arnesen was the first woman who went unsupported and solo to the South Pole. Marit Holm traversed Alaska on foot together with Lars Monsen. Reinhold Messner is a well know climber and polar trekker (i.e., climbed Mt Everest without Oxygen supply).

5. "Into thin air" is Jon Krakauer's personal account of the disaster that happened on Mt. Everest in May 1996 where eight people died.

12

Dr. Ken Ravizza

PROFESSOR, CALIFORNIA STATE UNIVERSITY, FULLERTON

Dr. Kenneth Ravizza is a professor at California State University at Fullerton in the Department of Kinesiology and Health Science. He has served as a sport psychology consultant for the US Olympic Field Hockey, Water Polo, Baseball, Softball, and Volleyball teams. He spent 27 years consulting with Major League Baseball teams (Los Angeles Angels, Los Angeles Dodgers, and Tampa Bay Rays). In addition, he has consulted with 40 universities in the area of "Coaching Effectiveness." He has had the privilege to learn from many coaches and athletes and his effectiveness is evidenced by his continuous work with teams. He has conducted numerous workshops and given presentations nationally and internationally. He is a co-author of *Heads-Up Baseball* and one of the authors of the *Consultant's Guide to Excellence*. Ken enjoys playing in his garden to keep a sense of balance in his life.

AUTOBIOGRAPHICAL SKETCH

I grew up in a suburban neighborhood in Connecticut near a playground with numerous athletic fields. I have two older brothers with whom I played sandlot sports; I was always competing, trying to keep up, and trying to fit in with the older kids. This ability to fit in and observe became critical in my work in sport psychology consulting. I played football, basketball, and ran track in high school. My dream graduating from high school was to be a college football coach. I went to Springfield College, majored in physical education and minored in United States History and played football. I went to college during the 1960s so it was a wild, crazy, soul searching, and exciting period in history. I took a lot of physical activity and coaching classes but it was a very strict and rigid program. My junior year, I started to rebel against the structured physical education approach that Springfield offered at that time. When I graduated, I knew the mechanical and technical aspects of sport, but I didn't know "why" sport participation was so powerful and could have such a great impact on a person's life. This desire to know why people played motivated me to go to the University of Southern California and do my PhD in sport philosophy with an emphasis on existential philosophy/phenomenology.

Growing up in New England and then living in Los Angeles was like moving to another world. I was exposed to different values, cultures, and sexual orientations; it was a wonderful, eye-opening experience and it helped me learn to see and respect how unique we are as human beings. This experience directly and indirectly prepared me for working with teams and associations throughout the world. I also gained a wealth of insight on the sport experience from taking classes in sociology and sociology of sport. I learned to observe sport teams as sub-cultures and this aided me immensely in figuring out the context of the situation I was working in. For example, team vs. individual sports, contact vs. non-contact sports, objective vs. subjective sports, and ball-centered vs. performance sports. This information and perspective is critical in modifying my approach, program, and skills to meet the unique needs of that group. As a graduate student, I was a teaching assistant in the physical education classes and I taught classes in basketball, racquetball, and conditioning. I took selected courses in the Psychology Department because at that time there was not a field of applied sport psychology, but I was fascinated with a new field in psychology called Humanistic Psychology that had its foundational roots in existential philosophy. At this time the human potential movement in California was very popular and for three years I attended seminars and workshops in the Los Angeles area. My motivation was to know myself: encounter and self-exploration groups, massage, and Rolfing courses were all part of my self-exploration.

As a graduate student at the University of Southern California, I had headaches almost every day in the late afternoon. In a graduate class, a friend saw me with an aspirin bottle. She told me she was going to a Hatha

Yoga class and invited me to go with her. At the beginning of the class, I sat by my yoga mat and set my aspirin bottle up, just in case I got a headache. When the teacher saw it, she asked me, "Are you setting yourself up for a headache?" I did not understand what she meant by that comment. During the first exercise I was lying on my back, eyes closed, and was asked to raise my arms towards the ceiling. But I was asked to feel my arms as they slowly moved through space. As I was doing this, I could feel tears in my eyes. What the tears represented was the realization at that moment, that at age 22 I had never experienced my body. As an athlete, I used my body as an object to show people that I was good and that I was okay. This simple experience heightened my awareness of my body and myself. After this class, I found myself much more aware of my body and was constantly stretching it. At first, it was like I was cursed with awareness, but from that point on, there were fewer headaches. This experience and the human potential movement helped me to explore myself, to get better, grow, and develop.

My first full-time academic position was at the State University College of New York at Brockport. We had 35 faculty members in the physical education department; 20 of us were under 35 years old. We were young, fresh, and energetic PhDs teaching, exchanging ideas, and conducting research in four core areas: psychology, philosophy, sociology, and physiology of sport and human movement. The phenomenological and existential aspects of sport were the focus of the Human Movement program that I was part of. The curriculum was based on learning about oneself in human movement, learning about others, and learning about the movement form. The major conviction was to study an athlete's movement experience and the knowledge that developed from that "lived" movement experience. The approach was unique because it was studying the human movement experience and not just applying concepts and theories from other disciplines to human movement, for example, psychological theories as they relate to sport performance. When I taught basketball class, we would play and then we would discuss what we learned from our experience. This focus on awareness and self-reflection is basically the foundation of my work today. My job is to help athletes become aware and facilitate a consciousness and/or mindfulness of their experience, because this perspective will aid in empowering the athlete to make the adjustments needed to perform at a more effective level. I have always walked the thin line between awareness and conscious thought (which can lead to paralysis by analysis).

After four years at Brockport, I took a position at Cal State Fullerton, which was a smaller department of 12 people. The university had Division 1 Athletics and the athletic department was housed in the same building as our department. This provided me an opportunity to observe and learn from elite coaches and athletes. I would go to the gym and watch the gymnastics team work out. One particular day the gymnasts were really having a problem on the balance beam. So in the midst of it, the coach turned to me and said, "Ken you do relaxation, don't you? So, do something." I had the girls lie down on the floor and took them through some relaxation and imagery. They got up on the beam and there was no performance change whatsoever. So my first adventure into sport psychology had no impact on performance, but the next day coach asked if I would start working with the team. He said the girls loved what I was *trying* to do. This experience formed the foundation of my consulting experience by teaching me that there are no easy solutions and that mental skills must be practiced and developed like physical skills (Ravizza, 1982; Ravizza & Rotella, 1982).

THEORY OF PERFORMANCE EXCELLENCE

My work has been influenced by my experience doing and teaching Hatha Yoga (Ravizza, 1983). For example, going into a stretch, doing the stretch, and coming out of the stretch has influenced my development of pre- and post-performance routines, going into performance and coming out of performance.

In Hatha Yoga the "Ha" in Sanskrit represents the sun, or active force, and "tha" represents the moon, or passive force. In addition, the word Yoga basically means the union of the mental, the physical, the emotional, and the spiritual domains (Ravizza, 1982). The mental is the concentration and awareness focused on what you're doing. The physical is the asana, posture, or movement the person is engaged in. The emotional is revealed in the person's feelings and sensations as they engage in the movement. The spiritual is reflected in the breath, which connects the mind, body, and emotions. These four aspects of Hatha Yoga are also present in all sport performance. The biomechanics and physiological aspects of performance comprise the physical and technical aspects of performance. Athletes must be mentally prepared to think clearly, know the strategic aspects of performance, make a commitment to their plan, and maintain awareness. The emotional component of performance is reflected in the intensity level and ability to regulate one's self. The breath is a key way to monitor emotions in sport; athletes must be in control of themselves before they can control their performance. A simple way to check in and regain self-control is to take a slow steady breath at some point before performance execution. This sounds simple, but it is so difficult to do when adversity strikes. The sense of purpose an athlete feels to participate in their sport is the "spiritual" part of performance. Even at the elite levels, athletes have a love-hate relationship with their sport. Understanding why they chose to compete and having a sense of purpose can help them handle the negative or difficult times that come with high-level performance.

In 1977, I published my first article based on my PhD research, "A Study of the Peak Experience in Sport" (Ravizza, 1977a, 1977b). I was the first to conduct systematic research on this exciting issue and at the time the only previous research was Maslow's work on Peak-Experience, but he did not address sport specifically. After this study, I was into the "zone" and the accompanying characteristics: total involvement, present focus, relaxed concentration, and clarity of thought. And for the next 25 years I wanted to get everyone into the "zone." However, when I was working with the coaches, many of the coaches were saying to me, "Ken, this type of experience does not happen that often. We need to claw, we need to grind, we need to compete and stop worrying about how we feel." It wasn't until an AASP (Association for Applied Sport Psychology) meeting in 2002 when I gave a formal presentation on my years of research on peak experience that I was extremely critical and basically stated that flow and peak experience were overrated (Ravizza, 2002). Instead, I started to address concepts like "comfortable being uncomfortable," "compensate and adjust," and develop methods to help athletes segment and/or "take one thing at a time." I became fascinated with methods to help athletes deal with adversity by taking one thing at a time as they perform. I synthesized the information gained from my years of observing and listening to athletes and coaches, and many hours of discussions with fellow sport psychology professionals to develop a systematic three-step approach to take one thing at a time: self-control, plan, and trust. I developed the "Rs" (recognize, release, regroup, refocus, ready, respond) as a method to implement this three-step approach and to put the principles of my initial research on peak-experience into practical application (Ravizza, 2001; Tilman, Ravizza, & Statler, 2004).

The foundation of the "Rs" process is *responsibility*. The athlete must be responsible and be accountable for his or her actions. One must learn to control what can be controlled and be in control of one's self before controlling one's performance. The athlete must learn that self-control leads to body control, which contributes to skill control. I have found that for many athletes, the breath is a good indicator of whether or not one is in control. If you can breathe, you give yourself an opportunity to perform with a clarity, calmness, and proper focus (Ravizza & Hanson, 1995). This sounds so simple, but it is so difficult when it is needed most.

As mentioned, the Rs involve three steps: self-control, plan, and trust. One gains *self-control* by recognizing where one is mentally and emotionally and having knowledge of where one needs to be. Transitioning to the *plan* phase is to refocus on the task at hand and make a commitment to what you are doing at that moment. The final phase is to *trust* your ability and training to execute your performance. These three components provide a framework and tools to help the athlete manage the moment and be prepared to be effective when the pressure is on. Thus, the athlete must have a task-relevant cue to focus on. For example, as a tennis player you are selecting your type of serve and you are selecting your location. Once players are committed to the plan, they must check in and see if they are "ready" to trust the execution. The most effective technique to know you are "ready" is that once again you can take a slow steady breath. It is at this point you can "respond," or just trust oneself.

The first "R" is to *recognize* what is happening and determine where you are mentally and emotionally and where you need to be (Ravizza, 1977c; Ravizza, 1991). If athletes can learn and become more aware of where they are with their mindset, and make the adjustments to where they need to be, they can learn to perform at a more consistent level because they will have a "mental skill to go to" when adversity shows itself. Athletes must become aware of their particular indicators that they are losing control so that they can make the adjustments that are required. I often discuss that athletic performance is like driving a car; when you come to a signal light, you have to check in and see the signal light. If the light is green then go, with minimum thought and conscious effort. However, if the light is yellow you either speed up or stop; and most of us speed up. This is the reason why the game appears to speed up. When the light is red the driver must stop. I teach athletes to increase awareness of their signal lights. If the athletes have yellow or red lights, then they have to release the distraction or emotion. I have discovered many athletes lack awareness of themselves and the situation. Heightening their awareness is so powerful. For example, an aware softball player who swings and misses will step out of the box and squeeze the bat to release the last pitch. I use the symbol of a toilet to "flush it" and the mission is now to get to the next pitch. Once you release, the next step is to regroup. This involves taking a slow deep breath and pulling your head and chest up. Lengthen your spine and allow your shoulders to drop. Regroup is where you change your body alignment to a more confident stance. And sometimes, you have to "fake it 'til you make it" because in competition you can't give non-verbal cues that you are struggling. Another tool that can be used to help the athlete regroup is the use of a focal point or visual trigger that reminds her that she is prepared and ready to perform. Some baseball players choose something in the outfield to remind them to get their head up, chest out, and take a deep breath (Ravizza & Hanson, 1995).

The next "R" is *refocus*: What is your plan, what are you trying to do? What do you need to do right now? Athletes have to have a task-relevant cue to focus on and must commit to it. Once athletes are clear what they are trying to do and commit to it, they must move to the fifth "R": be certain that they are *ready*. One way to check if you are ready is to breathe. The final "R" is to *respond*. This is where the athletes must simply trust themselves and perform.

The Rs is the method that I have developed, adjusted, and refined over the years to help athletes learn to take one thing at a time and develop skills to more effectively manage the moments of competition. It is one thing to say "be in the moment," and this is a method to give athletes a resource to do just that. Confidence to me is being prepared to win the next pitch, the next play, the next possession. I want the athletes I work with to use the "Rs" and/or their personal variation as a method to cope with adversity. Peak performance is not about being perfect, being in the zone, or letting it happen; it is about grinding, compensating and adjusting, and learning how to handle adversity. If you are not feeling great and you only have 70%, use 100% of that 70% and do battle. Confidence is knowing that you have put in the preparation to get it done with your 70%. When an athlete is in the zone he or she does not have to worry about anything it is just happening effortlessly.

THEORY OF PERFORMANCE BREAKDOWNS

An athlete's greatest strength is his or her greatest weakness. The athlete who is very competitive sometimes gets over-aroused. They are intense and perform with passion, but sometimes this inhibits performance. They have to learn to control this intensity level and channel their energy effectively. This also relates to perfectionism, which is a double-edged sword because it motivates the athlete to work hard but it can be a negative because you constantly have the inner-critic judging your performance. I often attempt to work with humor to regulate the perfectionism, trying to get the athlete to step back and laugh at it. I ask questions like "Are you that bad that you have to feel 'great' to perform well?" This serves to short circuit the whole perfectionistic thought process.

Another challenge is that the athlete can use the mental skills or do the physical actions of a routine, but there is no meaning in it. It is the difference between my experience "raising the arms" in the yoga class and really "feeling the arms" in that class. Practice can become so repetitive that a pitcher loses touch with what he is doing and just goes through the motions. There is no awareness. How can you know what's not working and what to correct if there is no awareness and meaning behind the action? This goes back to the basics of my approach that deals with one's self-knowledge and bringing a purpose to movement, to execution of the skill.

Being obsessed with outcomes is yet another challenge. The entire world of sport is about achieving the outcome in competition. The paradox is that it is not about the outcomes; instead, it is about the process. As a result, much of my work deals with how to translate the result into an accumulation of task-relevant process cues one has control of and what one can do in the heat of the competitive struggle. This focus on "behaviors that count" in sport while pursuing the outcome ties into "controlling what you have control of." Thinking about the referees and the rationale for their judgments is simply a waste of energy. This is another challenge and deals with the lack of ability to segment and let things go. Athletes carry "stuff." This was my idea with the "Rs"—to provide the athlete with a systematic technique to let go of "carrying stuff."

CONSULTING PROCESS

The consulting process includes collaboration with the coach, the players, the athletic trainer, the administration, and the strength and conditioning professionals. Everyone has an important role to play and everyone is valuable. I don't go in as the authority and convey that I have the magic answer that is going to make them a champion. We must collaborate to develop an effective program. I always want to get everyone on board, but I have learned that some people just aren't going to embrace my method or approach. I want everyone to be involved and it frustrates me when they are not (Ravizza, 2001).

The other feature of my consulting style is my careful examination of the context of the situation in which I will be working. Context, I believe, is the biggest and most important concept in the consulting process. During the assessment phase, it is important to figure out the context of how you're going to deliver your services and determine if you even want to work with this group in the first place. When I was young, I would work with anyone that would have me. That was great and I needed to do that and I learned a lot by doing that. Today, I'm much more selective about who I choose to work with, because I want to take the Mental Game to its full potential.

It is critical to gain entry by building relationships and earning the trust and respect of the coaches and athletes (Ravizza, 1988). It includes figuring out who are the "gate keepers" in the organization. If you have a big ego or issues surrounding your sense of self-importance, you are going to upset people and eventually you will get crushed. You have to go slowly and figure things out. I have been shocked at times by the power structure of some sport organizations. For example, athletic trainers are the gate keepers for a lot of teams. They are the ones taking care of, protecting, and looking out for members of the team. I have seen many consultants unable to gain entry because they are oblivious to the subtle "turf battles" that exist.

You have to understand the environment you're in, how the environment functions, and what your role in it is. For example, going into a major college football team, the coach asked me to talk to his coaching staff first and explain my approach and have them determine if they wanted to use my services. He recognized that it was critical to get a "buy in" at all levels. After this initial interaction with the coaching staff, the head coach had me leave the room so the staff could discuss my involvement and get a decision on whether the coaching staff thought this would be of benefit. After acceptance at this level, I needed to get the players to value the program potential. I talked to the team with the coach observing my presentation. After this step, I left the room again, and the coach talked to the players and got their input. The lesson here is clear: You can't force the Mental Game on athletes and coaches. You will be "checked out" by the players and coaching staff and that is part of the consulting process. And just like the coaches and athletes you work with, as a sport psychology consultant, you must perform when the pressure is on.

When I speak with a team, I try to do it at the beginning of practice when they are fresh. I'm also not going to do it at the end of practice when they are tired. I'm not talking about one or five sessions; most of my work occurs over the course of the season. It is important that the mental training becomes not only a regular part of the training but also an important and valued element of overall preparation. One cannot expect an athlete to connect with you when tired, hungry, or frustrated with how practice went for them.

The final phase of the consulting process is the evaluation of your service. I think this is an area of sport psychology that needs advancement. In psychology and education, I have found people are more familiar with being honest, open, and direct with the people they work with compared to the coaching environment. You may not receive direct verbal feedback from coaches. The first and most important evaluation is that you are invited back for the next season. Also, ongoing feedback is very subtle: The rate that phone calls are returned is an indicator of how you are progressing as a consultant. Some coaches will call back within an hour and some not at all. If you get to hear from a coach quickly, it sends a message that you are valued.

Finally, what enhances my consulting process is having a support group of peers who give me feedback and constructive criticism. I have gained so much from my support group. At Cal State Fullerton, I keep in touch with former coaches, athletes, and students about how they are using the mental skills throughout their lives. Many claim they use the skills more now than they ever did as an athlete. I also have a group of colleagues with whom I share ideas and to whom I make referrals. I can't emphasize enough how critical this has been in my work, because at times you are all alone in your role. I organized two "think tanks" where about 40 coaches, athletes, and sport psychology consultants met in Redondo Beach, California, to share ideas and insights in a completely supportive environment (Poczwardowski & Lauer, 2006).

UNIQUE FEATURES

My perspective has always been grounded in existential philosophy, which emphasizes accountability and responsibility. The athlete makes choices and he or she is responsible for these choices. That is their freedom. I have athletes reflect on their experience. I value the athletes' experience and what they can learn from it. If she comes up with the solution then she will take ownership of it. For example, if I'm working with a pitcher and I ask, "So how did that performance go?" and she replies, "Things sped up on me a little, I think I need to take it one pitch at a time," then I go with that, because it's coming from her and she has just communicated a productive level of awareness, responsibility, and knowledge of what to do mentally to get back on track. I am going to follow the athlete's lead until I am convinced it is not effective.

Another important feature of my style is gaining entry (Halliwell, Orlick, Ravizza, & Rotella, 1999; Ravizza, 1988). Gaining entry is how one goes about setting oneself up to get in there and assess the situation. Very often there are no definite answers. To get a feel on how to proceed with a person and a given context, you need to assess where the person is at and what the best strategy is to move them to where they want to go. A lot of times you do not end up at the desired outcome, but you move them along the continuum from where they started to where they need to be. Awareness is critical in terms of this development and/or assessment.

This is not only for the athlete but also for me. The majority of this knowledge is gained by observation. As Yogi Berra stated, "If you want to see, you have to watch." Observing the athlete in his or her "lived experience" is essential. Being with coaches and letting the environment "show itself to you" is critical. A question I ask coaches at practice is "What are you seeing as you watch performance?" The challenge is that this approach takes a lot of time, energy, and commitment, but isn't that true for anything? You have to spend hours and hours doing this. After working with any team or athlete I record the lessons and insights that I have gained. Learning from coaches and athletes is critical.

Another feature of my professional style and identity is that I am an educator. I provide information, I give athletes and coaches skills to use that information, and then I support them in developing and refining the skills. I think one of my greatest strengths is to get that coach who is resistant to see that he or she is already doing a lot of these things we talk about in applied sport psychology. What I do is provide a structure for coaches to see the relationship between so many of the techniques that they implement.

All of the techniques we use with the athletes, we have to use for ourselves in the consulting process. We have to take one thing at a time, we have to compensate and adjust, and we have to deal with rejection.

As mentioned earlier, integrating the mental skills into task-relevant performance cues is also a unique feature of my style. When I gave my book to baseball coaches they often told me it was not a sport psychology book, but it was a baseball book (*Heads-Up Baseball*, Ravizza & Hanson, 1995). It wasn't mental skills, but instead it was looking at the sport experience and relating the mental skills to performance-related cues. In my early years, I conducted mental skills training one hour per week. Then the team would go out to practice and that's the last they would hear about it until the following week. It is a different experience when they hear the mental skills vocabulary being implemented by the coaching staff in practice on a daily basis and it becomes part of how they play, prepare, and perform, and it is much more effective. For example, how does one release? I talk about "flushing it," but the coach might say "let it go." You have to use their vocabulary because that is what the athlete will hear on a daily basis. Another place you see the integration of mental skills is at the professional level when the players use the vocabulary when media interviews them.

You have to practice the mental skills just like you practice the physical skills. At times, I have athletes practice making errors so they can establish contingency plans to get it back together. I remember working with a men's gymnastics team in preparation for National Championships where they performed for 20 minutes and then sat in another gym for 20 minutes and then went back out and had to perform. What I would do is simulate that in practice; if a coach is willing to give you that time, then that is fantastic. You are integrating it into their world. With Olympic teams, the vast majority of my work is at practice.

A major shift in my sport psychology consulting career was when I first started; I was thinking big competitions and getting people ready for nationals. Today, 98% of my energy is focused on today's meeting and today's practice. This is where we are "working it." That is where we can really make a difference. Get teams to be more deliberate and have more quality practice. You will not be getting in the way of what coaches are trying to do if you talk about making practice more effective. At the college level, due to NCAA guidelines restricting the number of hours the athletes spend on practice, my job is to educate the coaches on the specific methods to enhance the quality of training.

These are some of the insights and changes I have made in my approach. I know that I will always be learning as I continue my work in applied sport psychology and the day I stop getting better will be the day I retire.

CASE STUDY

One of the graduate students I mentored in our sport psychology program at California State University, Fullerton was a marathon swimmer training to swim the 21-mile Catalina Channel, between Catalina Island and San Pedro, California. Her sport is unique because it is a continuous sport with limited external cues in the environment and lasts for an extremely long period of time. A marathon swimmer may expect to swim continuously for anywhere between 8 and 15 hours, with a 30-second break to drink fluids and eat every 30 minutes, where they must stay in the water without touching the boat or kayak following them. This is all done without a wetsuit and at least part of the swim typically occurs at night. In this case, starting a Catalina crossing begins at midnight. Like most athletes, this swimmer struggled at times during training and competition and had a hard time letting go of "stuff." Although she was familiar with the "Rs," from having gone through the program, and was fairly good at "recognizing" when she had stuff going on, she had difficulties "releasing." We had many discussions throughout her training and time in the program about how to adapt the Rs to fit her sport so she could use them more effectively.

For her, taking responsibility and recognizing was not the issue. She was aware that while training, she would experience fear from the perceived, although not always realistic, threat of wildlife. Additionally, she was aware of when she was experiencing anger (from rough conditions at sea or being passed by another swimmer), pain (she dealt with a shoulder injury), and frustration (when her support crew made a mistake or when a segment of a swim was taking much longer than expected). The difficulties she had lay in utilizing the Rs after that, and her personal struggle of feeling that as a student of sport psychology she should not be having such difficulties.

To address the guilt she felt for not being able to effectively deal with her emotions in her sport, I reminded her that what she was doing is difficult and no one does the mental game perfectly. I administered a test I do with all perfectionists: the Ken Ravizza Bathtub Test. I instructed her to fill her bathtub with one inch of water and to stand on the surface of the water. If she touched porcelain, she was not perfect, and no longer needed to expect herself to be.

To help her more effectively deal with adversity, we discussed several ways she could "release" while swimming continuously (stopping was typically not an option) and she experimented in training and found what worked for her. When she became aware that one of the previously mentioned adversities was affecting her, she would count down from five beginning with the next stroke. During those five strokes, she would allow herself to fully experience that negative emotion and feel like a victim. Once she got down to zero, she knew it was time to let that emotion go.

To prevent that emotion from resurfacing, as it likely would if the process ended there, she then moved on to the next R: "refocus." For her, focusing on her arms was important: she would make sure she could clearly see her arms and hands below her and listen to the rhythm of the sounds they made as they hit the water. If she could do this, then she had let the previous emotion go and regrouped. Next, she "refocused" on what was important. For her, this was almost always analyzing and correcting her stroke technique. She would continue to watch her hands and listen to the rhythmic sounds of her stroke, but she was also aware of any potential inefficiencies in her stroke and constantly refocused on removing them.

Because she was already doing the thing she needed to be doing, the final two Rs, "ready" and "respond," were modified. For her, "ready" represented a time for her to check in with her breathing. When swimming continuously, one cannot stop and take a lengthy "trusting breath," but one can be aware of how they are breathing. She would again notice the rhythmic sounds of her stroke and breath to make sure her breaths were not shallow, were well timed, and that she was fully and continuously exhaling when her face was in the water (holding the breath while swimming was not uncommon for her, and this always produced muscle tension, especially in the shoulders). Finally, rather than "respond," she "reaffirmed" her plan. This involved trusting her preparation and re-committing to her plan, knowing she was in full control of herself and her performance.

Recommended Readings

Camus, A. (1955). *The myth of Sisyphus.* New York, NY: Vintage Books.

Carroll, P. (2010). *Win forever.* New York, NY: Portfolio.

Davis, M., Robbins-Eshelman, E., & McKay, M. (2008). *The relaxation and stress reduction workbook.* Berkeley, CA: New Harbinger Press.

Frankel, V. (1984). *Man's search for meaning.* New York, NY: Touchstone Books.

Herrigel, E. (1989). *Zen in the art of archery.* New York, NY: Vintage Books.

Metheny, E. (1968). *Movement and meaning.* New York, NY: McGraw-Hill.

References

Halliwell, W., Orlick, T., Ravizza, K., & Rotella, R. (1999). *Consultant's guide to excellence.* Quebec: O'Keefe Publications.

Poczwardowski, A., & Lauer, L. (2006). The process of the Redondo Beach sport psychology consulting think tank. *The Sport Psychologist, 20,* 74–93.

Ravizza, K. (1977a). The potential of the sport experience. In D. Allen & B. Fahey (Eds.), *Being human in sport* (pp. 61–72). Philadelphia, PA: Lea & Febiger.

Ravizza, K. (1977b). Peak experiences in sport. *Journal of Humanistic Psychology, 17*(4), 35–40.

Ravizza, K. (1977c). The body unaware. In D. Allen & B. Fahey (Eds.), *Being human in sport* (pp. 99–113). Philadelphia, PA: Lea & Febiger.

Ravizza, K. (1982). Concentration: Its relationship to gymnastics and Hatha yoga. *International Gymnast Supplement, 8,* 8–10.

Ravizza, K. (1984). Concentration skills for gymnastics performance. In L. E. Unestahl (Ed.), *Mental preparation for gymnastics performance* (pp. 113–121). Sweden: Veje Forlag.

Ravizza, K. (1988). Gaining entry with athletic personnel for season-long consulting. *The Sport Psychologist, 2,* 243–254.

Ravizza, K. (2001). Reflections and insights from the field on performance enhancement consultation. In G. Tenenbaum (Ed.), *The practice of sport psychology* (pp. 197–215). Morgantown, WV: Fitness Information Technology.

Ravizza, K. (2002). The spiritual path to excellence. Selected presentation, *AAASP Annual Meeting*. Tucson, Arizona.

Ravizza, K., & Hanson, T. (1995). *Heads-up baseball*. Indianapolis, IN: Masters Press.

Ravizza, K., & Osborne, T. (1991). Nebraska's 3R's: One play at a time pre-performance routines and performance enhancement for college football. *The Sport Psychologist, 5*, 256–265.

Ravizza, K., & Rotella, R. (1982). Cognitive somatic-behavioral interventions in gymnastics. In W. Sime & L. Zaichkowsky (Eds.), *Stress management in sport* (pp. 25–35). Washington D.C.: AAHPERD.

Ravizza, K., & Statler, T. (2003). Lessons learned in sport psychology consulting. In T. Morris (Ed.), *Sport and exercise psychology: International perspectives* (pp. 57–65). Morgantown, WV: Fitness Information Technology.

Tilman, S. T., Ravizza, K., & Statler, T. (January–April, 2011). Clear your mind to clear the way: Managing the moment. *Engineer*, 46–49.

13

Dr. Jim Taylor

PRIVATE PRACTICE, SAN FRANCISCO, CA

Dr. Jim Taylor has worked with professional, world-class, junior-elite, and age-group athletes in many sports for over 27 years. A former internationally ranked alpine ski racer, Jim is a 2nd degree black belt and certified instructor in karate, a certified tennis coach, a marathon runner, and an Ironman triathlete. Jim is the author or lead editor of 14 books, including *Prime Sport: Triumph of the Athlete's Mind*, *The Triathlete's Guide to Mental Training*, and *Applying Sport Psychology: Four Perspectives*; has published over 750 articles in popular and professional publications; and has given more than 1,000 workshops and presentations throughout North and South America, Europe, and the Middle East. He also blogs on the psychology of sport for psychology today.com and huffingtonpost.com. To learn more, visit www.drjim taylor.com.

AUTOBIOGRAPHICAL SKETCH

There's a cliché that people get into the field of psychology to figure themselves out. Well, that adage certainly applies to me. As a teenager, I aspired to be the best ski racer in the world. Yet, despite achieving a top-40 national ranking, I had the reputation of being a "mind job" or "head case," meaning my head always got in the way of my skiing. I lacked confidence and got really nervous before races. I was very inconsistent in my races, falling or not finishing far too many times to achieve my goals. The results and rankings that I did have were achieved almost despite myself.

One summer I took a college class related to sport psychology that introduced me to many of the techniques that I use with athletes in my consulting practice (e.g., goal setting, self-talk, relaxation and focusing exercises, mental imagery). For the final project that required students to apply mental imagery to an area of our lives on which we wanted to improve, I chose to focus on my ski racing. Through the conclusion of the class and into the fall and the next race season, I imagined myself skiing in races the way I wanted to. Over the ensuing weeks and months, my imagery improved dramatically, evolving from being unable to even finish a race course in my head (an indication that I had a fundamental lack of confidence in my ability as a ski racer) to being able to ski fast, confidently, aggressively, and consistently. That following season was a breakthrough for me. My ranking rose to the top 20 in the nation, I finished 75 percent of my races, and I finished in the top 5 of all but one slalom race all season. But, more important than the results, I had a quantum change in my psychology. Before races, I was relaxed and focused, and when I stood in the starting gate, I not only knew I was going to finish, but I knew I was going to win. Of course, I didn't win every run, but I believed that I could.

A year later, when I arrived at Middlebury College in Vermont, I took an introductory to psychology course taught by Dr. Marc Reiss, the professor who would become my mentor and advisor. As the course progressed, I felt a profound connection with psychology and, by the end of the semester, I knew that I had found my calling. I wanted to study psychology and pursue a career in sport psychology. During these years, I continued to compete collegiately and internationally as a ski racer and I continued to apply the sport psychology lessons I learned from that summer course to my ski racing and other aspects of my life. Back then, almost 30 years ago, there were no clearly defined career paths that exist today. I wrote several sport psychologists I had read about and all recommended that I get a PhD in psychology; so that's the road I took.

After graduating from Middlebury, I was accepted into the doctoral program at the University of Colorado, Boulder. During my four years there, I conducted a variety of sport psychology research projects that were later published in peer-reviewed journals and began to develop my consulting skills by working with athletic teams at C.U. In 1985, I received my PhD in social/personality psychology with a minor in clinical psychology and set out to establish a career in applied sport psychology.

Without any guidance or clear path, I followed my instincts as I set my career in motion. Over the next two years, I returned to Middlebury to teach a psychology class and taught tennis to pay the bills. I reached out to my network in ski racing and began to give free talks to junior race programs in New England. Seeing the need to build my credibility in sports beyond ski racing, I became certified as a professional tennis instructor by the United States Professional Tennis Association. I also started writing articles for small sports publications. A slow trickle of athlete clients soon began.

After two years of laying this foundation—and struggling to make ends meet—I accepted a full-time faculty position in the School of Psychology at Nova University in Fort Lauderdale, Florida. For the next five years, I lived the life of a typical academic—teaching classes in Nova's doctoral programs in clinical psychology, conducting sport psychology related research, and expanding my consulting practice nationally, mostly in skiing and tennis. I also made my first foray beyond sports into work with ballet dancers and other performing artists. I was fortunate during this period to develop several strong mentoring relationships with incredibly capable clinical psychologists and to gain more clinical training. Both of these experiences helped me deepen my understanding of the complexity of people and expand my theories of what makes athletes and people tick.

After five years at Nova, I felt it was time to move on and pursue my passion for applied sport psychology consulting full time. I moved to Colorado where I continued to grow my practice, expand my speaking nationally and internationally, and write my first books. During my time in Colorado, I established my first long-term consulting clients, which provided me with much-needed financial security. I also began to expand my practice beyond sports performance to include business consulting, work with injured athletes, training of medical professionals (e.g., surgeons, nurses, physical therapists), and parent education.

After seven years living a small-town life (with lots of traveling) in a Colorado mountain town, I felt the pull toward a big city where I could better leverage my skills and reach a larger audience. So, in 1999, I moved to San Francisco, California where my practice grew considerably to include more work in the business world, expansion into more sports (particularly the endurance sports of running and triathlon), more international speaking opportunities, and book writing.

During these years of building my practice, I also stayed active in competitive sports. After ending my ski racing career in my final year of graduate school, I trained for and earned a 2nd degree black belt and became a certified instructor in karate, played competitive tennis, ran marathons, and competed in triathlons, including two Ironman competitions. These activities held several benefits for me. I stayed healthy and active, and acted as a role model for my clients. I used myself as a "test subject" for the theories and techniques that I applied to my clients. I used my ongoing athletic participation as a source of credibility with which I could attract clients. And I was able to gain access to new sports because of my diverse sports experience.

After more than 27 years, 14 books, countless clients and workshops, many ups, downs and adventures, having begun my career with no clear roadmap to follow but just trusting my passions and instincts, I feel like a living testament to Mark Twain's well-known recommendation, "Find something you love to do and you'll never work a day in your life."

THEORY OF PERFORMANCE EXCELLENCE

My own theory of performance excellence has become the foundation on which every aspect of my professional work rests, including how I assess, interpret, and conceptualize clients, the type of relationship I establish with clients, as well as the course of intervention I choose to take. This theory is also the basis for all of my writing and speaking. My theory has not evolved from courses, lectures, or books, but rather through my own personal and professional experiences. I believe that our personal theories are expressions of our individual personalities and a direct reflection of our development as people, in addition to our professional experiences. I further believe that our personal theories can only come from getting "hip deep" in life, grappling with our own individual psyches and from helping others wrestle with their own.

My considerable involvement in writing and speaking also played a key role in the formulation of my theory of performance excellence. I actually found a reciprocal relationship between the evolution of my theory and my writing and speaking. In one direction, I learned that you don't really know a subject unless you can express it coherently either in spoken or written form. The development of a defined structure, detailed process, and an articulated vocabulary unique to my theory (e.g., Prime Performance) enabled me to convey my theory in a clear, practical, and compelling way. In turn, my speaking and writing were incredibly creative experiences in which I would generate new ideas from which my theory continuously evolved and grew.

Role of the Mind

When athletes compete in their sport, they will, in fact, be competing in two competitions. The obvious competition is the one that occurs against the opponent. The more important competition, though, is the mental game that athletes play inside their head against themselves. Here is a simple reality: If athletes don't win the mental game, they won't win the competitive game. Contrary to what athletes may think, at whatever level in which they are competing, the technical and physical aspects of their sport don't usually determine the winner. Athletes who compete at the same level are very similar technically and physically. For example, is Luke Donald better technically than Rory McIlroy? Is Novak Djokovic stronger than Rafael Nadal? In both cases, the answer is no. So, on any given day, what separates one from the other? The answer lies in who wins the mental game.

Whenever I talk to athletes, I ask them what aspect of their sport seems to have the greatest impact on how they perform. Almost unanimously they say the mental part. I then ask how much time they devote to their mental preparation and their answer is almost always little or no time. Despite its obvious importance, the mental side of sport is often neglected, at least until a problem arises. The mistake athletes make is that they don't treat their mental game the way they treat the physical and technical aspects of their sport. Athletes don't wait to get injured before they do physical conditioning. They don't develop a technical flaw before they work on their technique. Rather, athletes do physical and technical training to prevent problems from arising. They should approach the mental game in the same way. Athletes seem to have the impression that sport psychology can produce miraculous results in a short time. But I am certainly not a magician. Athletes don't expect increases in strength by lifting weights a few times or an improvement in technique by working on it for a few hours. The only way to improve any area, whether physical, technical, or mental, is through commitment, hard work, and patience. But if athletes make the same commitment to their mental training as they do to their physical and technical training, sport psychology can play a key role in helping athletes achieve their goals.

My Phrase for Performance Excellence

My theory continued to take shape with the phrase and definition of the performance goal toward which I want athletes with whom I work to strive. One of the most popular phrases in sport psychology is "peak performance." Athletes typically think of peak performance as performing their best and being at the top of their game. When I came out of graduate school, peak performance was what I wanted athletes to achieve. But as I became more experienced as a consultant and a writer, I began to appreciate the power of words and how important it is that the words I use are highly descriptive of what I want to communicate. I decided that peak performance was not descriptive of what I wanted my athletes to achieve. I saw several problems with peak performance:

- A peak is very small, so you can't stay there long.
- Once the peak is reached, there's only one way to go—down!—and, as with most peaks, the drop is usually precipitous.
- The peak can be poorly timed, with athletes reaching their peak too early or too late, missing an opportunity for success.

I needed a phrase that accurately described what I wanted athletes to achieve. I struggled for several years, unable to find such a phrase until one day I had one of those rare meetings of readiness and luck. Walking through the meat section of a supermarket I saw a piece of beef with a sticker that read "Prime Cut." I had an "aha!" experience. I looked up "prime" in the dictionary. It was defined as "of the highest quality or value." I had finally found the phrase, *prime performance.*

I define *prime performance* as performing at a consistently high level under the most challenging conditions. There are two essential words in this definition—first, "consistently." I'm not interested if athletes can have one or two great performances and then some poor ones; that is not enough to be truly successful. I want athletes to be able to train and compete at a high level day in and day out, each week and month, all season long. This means performing with minimal ups and downs instead of the large swings in performance that are so common among athletes. The second essential word is "challenging." I'm not impressed if athletes can perform well under ideal conditions against an easy opponent when they are on top of their game. Anyone can do that. What makes the great athletes great is their ability to perform their best under the worst possible conditions, against a tough opponent when they're not on their game.

My theory of prime performance becomes further articulated with my understanding that the role of the mind in athletic performance actually has two parts, the athlete-as-performer and the athlete-as-person. Another way to look at this role is that of a facilitating side and an interfering side (the latter to be discussed in the next section). The facilitating part of the mind is the one that aims to maximize the psychological "muscles" that most impact performance.

Prime Performance Pyramid

A key part of my theory of athletic performance has involved identifying what I consider to be the most important psychological factors that impact performance and offering athletes the information and tools they need to fully develop those factors. My framework for understanding these factors is what I call the Prime Performance Pyramid.

The Prime Performance Pyramid (see Figure 13.1) provides both a structure and a process for identifying and developing the key contributors to individual and team sports performance. The Prime Performance Pyramid is composed of five psychological factors that most directly impact athletic performance. My goal with athletes with whom I work is to help them to understand their relationship with each of these factors and develop strategies and a plan of action for alleviating their psychological weaknesses and building on their psychological strengths.

The Prime Performance Pyramid is ordered in a purposeful and logical manner. Its order is based on the sequence in which the factors impact sports performance. The first two factors (motivation and confidence) prepare athletes for competition, while the next three (intensity, focus, and emotions) directly impact their training and competitive performance.

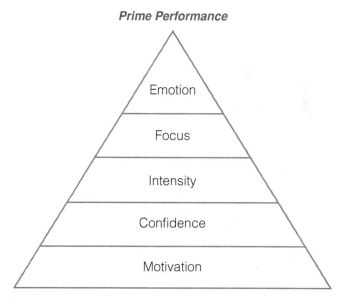

Figure 13.1. Prime Performance.

MOTIVATION. At the foundation of the Prime Performance Pyramid lies motivation, because without athletes' determination and drive to take action in pursuit of their goals, all efforts would stop and any other contributors to performance, whether physical, technical, equipment, or team, would be moot. Motivation ensures that athletes do everything they can to be totally prepared to achieve their goals. Essential to developing motivation is athletes' understanding of what motivates them and how they can continue to work hard in the face of fatigue, pain, setbacks, and frustration.

CONFIDENCE. Confidence is so important to athletic performance because athletes might have all the ability in the world to achieve their goals, but if they don't have confidence in that ability, they won't use that ability. Many athletes defeat themselves even before the competition begins with doubts and negative self-talk. Like all mental skills, confidence is a skill that develops with practice. A deep faith in their capabilities comes from total preparation, exposure to adversity, support from others, a toolbox of mental skills, training and competitive success, and positive thinking skills.

INTENSITY. Intensity may be the most important contributor to sports performance once the competition begins. It's so important because all of the motivation, confidence, focus, and emotions in the world won't help athletes if their bodies are not physiologically capable of doing what they need to for them to perform their best. Intensity involves the amount of physiological activation athletes feel before and during training and competition and lies on a continuum between sleep (very low intensity) and terror (very high intensity). Somewhere between those two extremes athletes perform their best, and my challenge with athletes is to help them find the ideal level of intensity that works best for each of them in their sport.

FOCUS. Focus involves the ability to concentrate on those things that facilitate performance, shift focus when the demands of the training or competitive situation change, and avoid distractions that are ever present in the athletic arena. The ability to focus effectively is especially important in technically complex sports or those that last a long time, and when there are considerable expectations and pressure.

EMOTIONS. Sports can evoke a wide range of emotions, from inspiration, pride, exhilaration, and satisfaction, to fear, frustration, anger, and despair. Emotions lie at the top of the Prime Performance Pyramid because I have found that they are the ultimate determinant of athletes' ability to achieve prime performance, namely, to perform at a consistently high level under the most challenging conditions. Emotions also contribute significantly to athletes' abilities as team members and leaders. Most powerfully, emotional mastery—for example, the ability to overcome frustration, relieve anger, and stay motivated in the face of disappointment—gives athletes the power to use emotions as tools to facilitate individual and team performance rather than weapons that hurt them and others.

THEORY OF PERFORMANCE BREAKDOWNS

My theory of performance breakdowns is composed of two parts. The first part involves the *athlete-as-performer* and deficits in the five psychological areas that I described above in the Prime Performance Pyramid. The focus of this notion of athlete-as-performer is on athletes' thoughts, emotions, and behavior in the sports arena. Athletes may find some success by developing some of the five factors fully or by developing all of the factors to some degree. But for athletes to achieve prime performance and fully realize their goals, the five factors must be developed to their greatest extent. Any weaknesses in motivation, confidence, intensity, focus, or emotions will inevitably lead to, at best, less than maximum performance and, at worst, breakdowns in performance in important competitions. For example, less than high motivation will result in a lack of preparation due to insufficient repetition or poor quality in training. Lower confidence will result in negative thinking (which hurts the other four psychological factors) and the unwillingness to take the necessary risks ("leave it all on the field") to achieve competitive success. Poor intensity control will mean that athletes lack the ideal level of physiological activation that is necessary for their bodies to perform at their highest levels. Poor focus will involve athletes' inability to focus on the relevant cues necessary for maximum performance and block out the inevitable distractions that are a part of all sport training and competition. Finally, the absence of emotional mastery will mean that athletes will be at the mercy of their emotional reactions and vulnerable to emotions, such as frustration, anger, and despair, that will hurt performance.

I can't understate the importance of helping athletes fill their "mental toolboxes" with useful tools they can take out to both develop the five psychological factors of the Prime Performance Pyramid, thus preventing performance breakdowns, and use when they experience breakdowns in training and competitions to recover from them quickly. I use the metaphor of a flat tire while driving: If a flat occurs and drivers don't have a spare tire, jack, and tire iron (or a membership in a roadside assistance program), they will be stuck on the side of the road and unable to progress toward their destination. If they have the necessary tools to change the flat tire, they may be slowed a bit on their journey, but they will have the means to get themselves on their way as quickly as possible. The same holds true for athletes and their mental toolbox.

Breakdowns in training and competitions are an inevitable and, yes, valuable part of the pursuit of athletic goals. Whether in the form of obstacles, setbacks, failures, or plateaus, how these "bumps in the road" impact athletes depends on their capabilities to "fix" the breakdowns. If athletes lack the necessary tools, then breakdowns will have a debilitating effect on them. However, if athletes have the relevant tools to "repair" the breakdowns, several essential benefits accrue. First, athletes will receive a boost in their confidence because they will see that they have the means to surmount these frequent challenges. Second, athletes will not be prone to shy away from them. Third, a fully stocked mental toolbox will allow athletes to respond positively to a wider range of psychological, physical, technical, and tactical breakdowns. Fourth, athletes will gain a competitive advantage because most athletes against whom they compete will likely not have such a mental toolbox at their disposal. Finally, the mental toolbox will have the broad benefit of strengthening and maintaining all five of the psychological factors described in the Prime Performance Pyramid.

The second part of my theory of performance breakdowns focuses on the *athlete-as-person*, in which who the athlete is as a person impacts their ability to perform in the field of competition. I believe that there is no true distinction between who athletes are on and off the field. In other words, when athletes walk into the sports arena, they don't leave their "personness" outside. Instead, that personness has an immense influence on who they are as athletes and their ability to perform their best and achieve their goals. In fact, I believe that whatever strengths or weaknesses they may have as athletes, in terms of the five Prime Performance Pyramid factors, are eclipsed by their strengths and weaknesses as people. As such, everything that I do in my work with athletes is, directly or indirectly, about performance enhancement. This aspect of my work, unlike my traditional mental skills training efforts that facilitate performance, involves identifying off-field issues that interfere with performance and removing those psychological obstacles, thus freeing the athlete-as-person from inhibitions that prevent them from fully realizing themselves as the athlete-as-performer in the competitive arena.

Let me state that I don't practice clinical psychology: I don't do psychotherapy, diagnose psychiatric disorders, or treat psychopathology. What I do in my practice is consult, coach, and counsel on issues related to life and development. Issues that I find relevant in my exploration with athletes in their roles as athlete-as-person include habitual negativity, perfectionism, and fear of failure. It has been my experience that if athletes have significant obstacles in these areas, then many or all of the strengths they may possess as athletes in the five Prime Performance Pyramid factors will be negated by these roadblocks. Additionally, this over-riding of their athlete-as-performer by their athlete-as-person will result in their being incapable of performing to their fullest ability or, though they may achieve substantial success, they are nonetheless unhappy and disconnected from their achievements.

Further, it is usually safe to assume with the young athletes with whom I work that if they have problems, those problems likely originate with their parents. As the author of three parenting books unrelated to sports, I have the knowledge base and skill sets that allow me to explore whether the parents are playing a facilitating or interfering role in their children's sports lives. If I find that parents are a detrimental influence on either their young athletes' sports efforts or healthy development, I work separately with the parents to help them understand that influence and guide them in becoming more positive forces in their children's athletic and personal lives.

CONSULTING PROCESS

I gain my clientele through three primary avenues. First, through my many high-level athletic pursuits (e.g., ski racing, karate, tennis, running, and triathlon); I have a large network of contacts in a number of sports through which my name is disseminated. For example, because of my many years of competitive experience and professional involvement in ski racing, many ski racers in the US seek me out when they are looking for a sport psychology consultant.

Second, I actively pursue speaking and writing opportunities, which gives me exposure to large audiences. For example, I give talks, many at no cost, to all sorts of athletic organizations, junior training programs and youth sports leagues. These audiences usually generate individual clients. I also have my four-book *Prime Sport* series of mental training books (general sports, tennis, golf, and ski racing). I have written articles for all manner of sports publication, from local to national, as well as publish a bi-monthly e-newsletter, *Prime Sport Alert!* Additionally, I have leveraged social media, including creating a professionally designed website (a must for any consultant), blogging on sport issues for a number of prominent websites such as Facebook, Twitter, and YouTube (on which I post video versions of my e-newsletter), to draw traffic to me. I'm constantly amazed at how many people find me with a simple Internet search.

Third, the best way to get clients is by doing quality work. I've been fortunate to have many new clients referred to me by the word of mouth of past clients.

Consulting Style

My consulting style, which evolved iteratively as an expression of my personality and personal and professional experiences, is grounded in my theories of performance excellence and performance breakdowns I described above. At the heart of my relationship with athletes is their trust and comfort with me. My style is direct, no-nonsense, and goal oriented, yet also caring and supportive, with a large dose of levity to lighten what is often a heavy load that athletes carry. The recipe for establishing productive relationships comes from my professional and athletic credibility, appropriate boundaries, and, a dash of humanity. Also, very importantly, the athletes with whom I work understand immediately that I am their ally and advocate in pursuit of their sports and life goals, and that I am available to them at any time.

Consulting Approach

I follow two paths of intervention in my consulting work with athletes that mirror my athlete-as-performer/athlete-as-person model. The first path, which focuses on the athlete-as-performer, emphasizes the development of the five psychological areas in my Prime Performance Pyramid through the teaching and use of traditional performance-enhancement strategies—for example, goal setting, positive-thinking skills, intensity-control techniques, focusing techniques, mental imagery, and routines. This mental training occurs in two settings. First, I introduce these concepts to athletes in an office setting in which I educate the athletes as to their meaning and value to sports performance, assess their relationship to the five factors, and choose the best forms of intervention to develop these areas. Second, and most powerfully, I then work with the athletes in their actual training setting (e.g., court, course, hill, field) and show them how to use the mental skills while they are actually performing their sport. I have found that this in vivo experience with mental training enables them to ask questions, experiment, get feedback from me, and see the direct connection between doing the mental skills, being more mentally prepared, and, most importantly, performing best. If they see that connection between doing mental training and seeing improvement, I know there will be continued buy in. My goal on this path is to strengthen the five Prime Performance Pyramid factors so that athletes can gain the most benefit from their training and be maximally prepared to perform their best in competition.

The ability of athletes to fully develop these five factors, through the use of relevant mental skills, will determine their psychological readiness and their capacity to fully harness their physical, technical, and tactical skills, perform at their highest level, and achieve their competitive goals. My work with athletes-as-performers focuses on educating them about these five contributors to performance, providing them a "toolbox" of essential mental skills for strengthening these areas, and ingraining those skills through repetition so that they can be used in competition to enhance performance.

A well-stocked mental toolbox provides athletes with tools to strengthen or respond to breakdowns in the five Prime Performance Pyramid areas. Motivation tools that I use include goal setting, focusing on the long-term goal when short-term feedback (e.g., breakdowns, fatigue, pain) is demotivating, pushing through what I call "The Grind" (that period in training when it is no longer fun), having a training partner, focusing on athletes' greatest competitor, motivational cues and images, support from others, and, most importantly, having a clear and justifiable reason to work hard toward their goals.

Confidence tools that I teach athletes consist of quality preparation, developing the mental toolbox, exposure to adversity, support from others, experiencing small successes, focusing on what athletes can control, accepting that mistakes and failure will occur, and positive self-talk.

Psych-down tools to reduce intensity I have found effective include deep breathing, muscle relaxation, calming self-talk and keywords, slowing the pace of the competition, maintaining a process focus, relaxing music, and smiling. Psych-up tools to increase intensity include intense breathing, physical activation, high-energy self-talk and keywords, high-energy body language, and fire-up music.

Focusing tools I use with athletes include training and competitive focus and distraction analyses (helps athletes identify what they need to focus on and what may distract them), controlling the eyes, focusing on what they can control, the four Ps (positive, process, present, and progress), and focus keywords.

Emotional mastery tools consist of understanding of athletes' "hot buttons" (situations and issues that cause strong emotional reactions), emotion analysis (identify emotion, cause of emotion, assess value or harm of emotion, and options for expressing emotions), and frustration and anger training. Other "tools" used to develop emotional mastery will be described in the following section of my chapter.

Perhaps the two most powerful mental tools available to athletes that impact athletes-as-performers psychologically are mental imagery and routines. I think of mental imagery as weight training for the mind because it offers broad-based benefits in which it can strengthen all five of the Prime Performance Pyramid factors through rehearsal of positive thoughts, emotions, and behavior in training and competition. Routines are equally valuable because they ensure total preparation, create consistency of mind and body, and enable athletes to see and feel the maximum expression of the five key psychological contributors to performance.

The second path, related to the athlete-as-person, explores any obstacles that may have been put into place that prevent athletes from performing their best—for example, as noted above, habitual negativity, perfectionism, and fear of failure. As I noted above, I consult, coach, and counsel them in ways that help them understand why these obstacles interfere with their athletic efforts, how they developed, and provide insights and tools to remove the obstacles and allow the athletes to continue on the path toward their goals. This work occurs generally in an office setting, but I have also been able to be productive in exploring these issues in a sports setting. For example, I have found that athletes can be very receptive to deeper exploration while, for example, riding a chairlift skiing or out on a run or bike ride. I believe that this openness occurs because athletes are in a setting in which they are comfortable and confident, and they feel less pressure to "figure things out." I also want to note that if I recognize that these obstacles are grounded in clinical issues, I will make the appropriate referral and may or may not continue to work with the athlete in areas in which I have competence, depending on how those issues impact the pursuit of the athlete's goals.

UNIQUE FEATURES

I don't really know what other consultants do, so it's difficult for me to judge what is unique and what is not in the way I work. However, I can highlight some of the features of my practice that are quite different from the usual in-the-office consultation approach.

Though having been an accomplished athlete isn't necessary to be an effective consultant (a perusal of the leading consultants supports this observation), my high-level athletic experience in a number of sports provides me with an unusual opportunity to connect and communicate with athletes

(Warning: Don't participate in a sport with a client unless you are compe-tent, otherwise you'll lose credibility). Being able to engage in their sport along with my athlete-clients allows me to get to know and work with them in ways that can't be done in an office setting. I can see in action their moti-vation, self-talk, intensity level, focus styles, and emotional reactions. I can also observe their training and competitive habits and routines.

My in-depth, comprehensive, and usually long-term work with athletes ena-bles me to do things with athletes that aren't often possible for consultants who work in an office setting on an hourly basis. For example, I immerse my-self in their world, enabling me to conduct extensive assessments of the ath-letes that include subjective and objective evaluations, in vivo observation during training and competition, and interviewing of coaches and parents. Of particular value is my ability to be a "fly on the wall" in athletes' lives and both gain valuable information and be able to intervene as life happens.

My strong experiential foundation in the sports sciences enables me to consider non-psychological causes of performance breakdowns. For exam-ple, I always examine whether there are physical, technical, or equipment causes of athletes' performance problems before I consider psychological causes of the breakdowns. In fact, I typically ask for a complete assessment of areas that may be relevant to performance problems (e.g., illness, injury, nutrition, technical flaws, equipment problems, learning challenges). Be-cause of the depth of my work with athletes, I often collaborate with their coaches, biomechanists, fitness trainers, and nutritionists, developing a ho-listic body of information for us each to use that isn't typically available and working together with experts in other fields, enabling all of us to create an integrated program for athlete preparation.

CASE STUDY

Jamie (fictitious name) was a 15-year-old world-ranked junior tennis player who was referred to me by one of the USTA National Team coaches. Jamie had risen quickly in the rankings and was considered one of the future stars of US tennis. She had recently hit a bad patch where she was having emo-tional "meltdowns" during matches and losing in the early rounds of inter-national tournaments in which she was expected to advance deep into the draw. There had also been talk about Jamie turning pro within the next year (with potentially hundreds of thousands of sponsorship dollars on the line), so there was an urgency to get her back on track.

We arranged that I would spend three days a month with Jamie at the tennis academy in Florida where she trained and to have regular telephone contact with her during the rest of the month. During my first visit, it became clear that Jamie was one very unhappy girl who seemed to have the weight of the world on her shoulders. As we worked together over the first few months of what became a productive, satisfying, and, ultimately, successful relationship of more than three years, three areas of concern became evident. First, Jamie had progressed quickly on immense natural talent and an unsurpassed drive to be the best. And her successes came early and often. But she had little self-awareness or insight into what enabled her to play her best. Second, Jamie was a perfectionist with a profound fear of failure and habitual negativity that, up to that point, had served her well by driving her to be perfect and avoid failure. But as the stakes rose and the pressures grew, those assets had become liabilities that resulted in a loss of motivation to work hard, a plummeting of her confidence, and emotional threat that expressed itself in on-court temper tantrums. Third, Jamie's father, Karl, was an over-involved, angry, and demanding taskmaster if ever I saw one, who had raised her with the dream, his dream, that she would be a professional tennis player.

My work with Jamie focused on those three areas. We spent many hours on the court with Jamie practicing with her coach where I showed her how to incorporate mental skills into her game. We worked on retraining her negativity with positive self-talk and body language, relaxation techniques, better managing her focus to avoid over thinking, learning how to master her frustration (which was the first emotion that led to her emotional breakdowns), and developing between-point and changeover routines.

Jamie and I also talked for hours on end about her pained internal life. We explored her negativity, perfectionism, and fear of failure, helping to identify where they came from, how they made her feel, and, importantly, changes she could make to the way she thought and felt about herself. It became clear that these perceptions and emotions came directly from her father, who was punitive when she played poorly, but not complimentary when she played well. Jamie was, she admitted, in a constant state of fear of her father's reactions. Plus, not unexpectedly, she wasn't having any fun playing tennis either. To Jamie's credit, she was incredibly motivated to change and we were able to develop a trusting, deep, yet also somewhat playful relationship in which we dealt with some tough issues, but she was also able to laugh at herself when necessary.

I also spent a lot of time with Karl. He was a bully of a man who used his aggressiveness to become very successful financially, but who was decidedly poor at relationships. Karl was not prone to introspection or admitting that he was the cause of his daughter's problems, but he loved Jamie more than life itself (though he didn't know how to express it) and, deep down, wanted what was best for her. Karl was also accustomed to bullying people into submission and not used to others confronting him, which I did. Though he later told me that he almost slugged me on a number of occasions for standing up to him, he developed a begrudging trust in me, partly because he respected my willingness to not be cowed by him and partly because he saw how committed I was to helping Jamie (the fact that she was playing better was another factor that allowed our relationship to continue). I set some ground rules about his involvement with her tennis. For example, he could only attend her practice in the mornings, he wasn't allowed on court during practice, and he couldn't talk to either Jamie or her coach during practice. I wanted the tennis court to be "sacred ground" where she felt safe rather than a threatening environment where she felt scared. I also referred him to a psychiatrist who immediately diagnosed him as clinically depressed and prescribed psychotherapy and depressants, which made an immediate difference.

As Karl gave Jamie more ownership of her tennis, her motivation began to return, she was having more fun on court, her emotional over-reactions declined in intensity and frequency, and she began to play outstanding tennis again. Everyone around Jamie noticed that she no longer seemed to be living under a dark cloud and was happier and enjoying herself more.

We concluded our professional relationship after more than three years and I followed Jamie from a distance as she turned pro and began to climb steadily up the rankings. We stayed in touch by email and phone for the first year after our formal work ended to periodically discuss new challenges, insights, and changes that were occurring. I then didn't hear from Jamie for several months, when out of the blue, I got a call from her telling me that she quit tennis. I was, of course, surprised by her decision because of the success that she had been having. When I asked Jamie why, she said, "How can I be truly successful and happy at something that I hate so much." That made sense to me; tennis had been her father's dream, not hers. I subsequently got a call from her father pleading with me to convince Jamie to change her mind. For professional and ethical reasons, I didn't. Instead, I assured him that this decision was the right one for her. In time, Karl accepted her choice because he saw how much happier she was with tennis no longer in her life.

Over the decade since my work with Jamie, we have stayed in touch with some regularity. After she left tennis, she enrolled in and graduated with honors from a top state university, was accepted into and graduated from an Ivy League medical school, and is now finishing her residency. From a struggling and unhappy 15-year-old tennis player, a happy and successful 27-year-old woman has emerged. Sounds like a victory to me.

References & Recommended Readings

Taylor, J. (2000). *Prime ski racing: Triumph of the racer's mind*. New York, NY: iUniverse.

Taylor, J. (2000). *Prime tennis: Triumph of the mental game*. New York, NY: iUniverse.

Taylor, J. (2001). *Prime sport: Triumph of the athlete mind*. New York, NY: iUniverse.

Taylor, J. (2001). *Prime golf: Triumph of the mental game*. New York, NY: iUniverse.

Taylor, J. (2002). *Positive pushing: How to raise a successful and happy child*. New York: Hyperion.

Taylor, J. (2005). *Your children are under attack: How to protect your kids from American popular culture*. Chicago, IL: SourceBooks.

Taylor, J. (2011). *Your children are listening: 9 messages they need to hear from you*. New York, NY: The Experiment.

Taylor, J., & Schneider, T. (2005). *The triathlete's guide to mental training*. Boulder, CO: VeloPress.

Taylor, J., & Taylor, C. (1995). *Psychology of dance*. Champaign, IL: Human Kinetics.

Taylor, J., & Taylor, S. (1997). *Psychological approaches to sports injury rehabilitation*. Gaithersburg, MD: Aspen Publishing.

Taylor, J., & Wilson, G. (Eds.) (2005). *Applying sport psychology: From researcher and consultant to coach and athlete*. Champaign, IL: Human Kinetics.

Taylor, J., Stone, K., Mullin, M., Ellenbecker, T., & Walgenbach, A. (2003). *Comprehensive sports injury management: From initial exam to return to sport*. Austin, TX: Pro-Ed.

14

Dr. Ralph A. Vernacchia

PROFESSOR EMERITUS, WESTERN WASHINGTON UNIVERSITY

Ralph Vernacchia, PhD, is a professor emeritus at Western Washington University where he directed the undergraduate and graduate sport psychology programs. He is the founder and former director of WWU's Center for Performance Excellence. He has presented extensively on a variety of sport psychology topics throughout the nation and co-authored or authored four sport psychology textbooks including *Coaching Mental Excellence*, *Inner Strength*, and *The Psychology of High-Performance Track and Field*. He is a fellow and certified consultant of the Association of Applied Sport Psychology (AASP). Dr. Vernacchia served as a sport psychology consultant to the Western Washington University Athletic Department and is a former chair of the Sport Psychology Academy of the American Alliance for Health, Physical Education, Recreation and Dance (AAHPERD). He has traveled internationally as a sport psychology consultant with several USA track and field teams, including the 2000 USA Olympic Track and Field Team that competed in Sydney, Australia. He has been inducted into the Western Washington University Athletic Hall-of-Fame and the National Association for Physical Education (NASPE) and Sport Hall-of-Fame.

AUTOBIOGRAPHICAL SKETCH

From the time I was a child, I loved to play and to be physically active; and it is this enduring passion for sport that has served to form and fuel the core of my beliefs about the value, values, and importance of sport and sport psychology in the lives of sport participants and leaders. Certainly my educational experiences have strongly influenced my view of sport psychology as well. As a high school cross country and track and field athlete, I read what I consider to this day to be the best sport psychology book ever written, *The Four Minute Mile* by Roger Bannister (1955). In college I majored in physical education and continued to participate in cross country and track and field. My studies in physical education were fascinating and introduced me to the intriguing world of human movement and performance. I enjoyed learning about the scientific foundations of athletic performance, particularly the psychological aspects of human performance that were embedded in physiology of exercise, motor learning, and coaching theory courses.

I enjoyed being a student of physical education and sport and entered graduate school to pursue a master's degree in physical education. In addition to my graduate studies, I served as a graduate assistant, taught physical education activity classes, and served as an assistant cross country and track and field coach. It was 1967 and sport psychology was not a standalone sport science, but I selected the psychology of athletic performance as my graduate thesis research project. Although I enjoyed the research aspect of my graduate studies, I never viewed research as an end in itself, but as a means to an end, that is, to understand, predict, and influence effective human performance.

While pursuing a doctoral degree in physical education in 1971 at the University of Utah, I continued serving as a teaching assistant and assistant cross country and track and field coach. Coaching was an excellent laboratory for the ideas about the psychology of athletic performance that I thought about every day. Most importantly, I was fortunate to be mentored into the profession of sport psychology by my advisor, Keith Henschen. It was also at this time that I made a conscious decision to continue coaching in order to field test the theories and concepts of the rapidly emerging field of sport psychology. Upon the completion of my doctoral studies, I accepted a position as an assistant professor of physical education (teaching courses in motor learning and the psychosocial aspects of sport) and head men's cross country and track and field coach at Western Washington State College (now Western Washington University). This was my dream job.

I retired from coaching in 1987 to focus on leading our undergraduate and graduate sport psychology programs. Twenty-two years of coaching experience and eight years of athletic participation have enabled me to not only live the reality, magic, drama, and glory of sport but also to truly understand what I refer to as the "breathing mechanism" of sport. These athletic and coaching experiences have been invaluable in helping me relate to and effectively serve the coaches, athletes, parents, and administrators of sport.

Since 1987 I have served as a performance consultant to our athletic department and have had the opportunity to serve and interact with student-athletes and coaches on a daily basis. In 2000 I also founded the Western Washington University Center for Performance Excellence, which has served to provide educational performance psychology programs that focus on quality of life and the healthy pursuit of personal excellence.

Apart from my professional pathway and educational background and training in sport psychology, there have been three major events that have influenced my perspective and practice of sport psychology. The first of these events was my affiliation with USA Track and Field Sport Psychology in 1982. Known as The Athletic Congress or TAC at the time, the sport psychology program was under the direction and leadership of Rick McGuire. Over the years, I was fortunate to serve in various leadership roles and as a performance consultant to numerous track and field athletes and coaches. In addition I was able to travel as a performance consultant with several USA international track and field teams, including the 2000 USA Olympic Team. My experiences with USA Track and Field have been instrumental in formulating my views of performance psychology for elite athletes and coaches.

The second of these events was the "Utopia" sport psychology group. This professional network was established in the late 1980s and was composed of many very prominent applied sport psychology professionals and coaches. Together we discussed, shared and lived the new frontier of applied sport psychology that emerged in 1986 with the formation of the Association for the Advancement of Applied Sport Psychology (AAASP).

Lastly, in 1990, while on sabbatical leave, I was able to pursue post doctoral studies in applied sport psychology at the University of Virginia (UVA). At the time, UVA was the clear cut educational leader in the field of applied sport psychology. I was fortunate to be mentored by Bob Rotella, attending several of his classes and interacting with him on a daily basis. Our conversations regarding the principles and practice of applied sport psychology were and have been invaluable in my professional development.

Toward a Philosophy of Sport Psychology

The afore-mentioned educational and professional experiences from 1963–1990 enabled me to solidify my philosophy of sport psychology. Hopefully this philosophy will shed light on the framework for performance excellence that I will present later in this chapter. Essentially, my philosophy of sport psychology has been greatly influenced by my professional preparation as a physical educator. For this reason my perspective and approach to the theory and practice of sport psychology is essentially a blend of several physical education sub-disciplines—namely, pedagogy, motor learning, and the psychosocial aspects of sport and physical activity. The following foundational belief statements represent my view of sport psychology:

Sport psychology is about sport. My academic training and experiential background in physical education and athletics have provided me with the ability to understand the "breathing mechanism" of sport. In its most basic form, sport psychology is about sport. The primary function of the sport psychology professional is to make sense of the sport experience to coaches and athletes so that they can develop, improve and realize their talents, as well as their personal dreams and goals.

Sport psychology is about education. Through my interactions with athletes and coaches I strive to help them keep sport in perspective by creating awareness and understanding of the culture, politics, and mentality of sport.

> *My educational mission is to help athletes understand and make sense of the achievement oriented world of sport, and to help them acquire the mental skills and attributes necessary to succeed in such a world.*

Sport psychology is about service. Throughout my career in sport psychology I have attempted to be an invisible but available educational resource for coaches, athletes, and clients. I have always respected the fact that the world of sport belongs to coaches and athletes and I continually strive to work in concert with them to enhance athletic performance.

Sport psychology is about ethics. It is very easy for sport psychology professionals to be swept away by the instrumental concerns and trappings of sport. Protecting the sanctity of sport is a tremendous challenge and responsibility for all sport educators. Keeping the value and values of sport in perspective for athletes and coaches by enhancing their moral reasoning and ethical decision-making abilities can contribute to the character-building, as well as the confidence-building nature of sport psychology.

Sport psychology is about life skills. Over the years, I have enjoyed bringing sport psychology to athletes, coaches, and university students because of the concomitant impact it has upon their personal lives, professional and/or academic performance. Many of the principles of sport psychology that we promote for use in sport are, in fact, very effective life skills.

Sport psychology is about mentoring. I am very aware of my personal responsibility to "give back" to sport psychology. For this reason, I have particularly enjoyed my work with undergraduate and graduate sport psychology students at our university. It is a real joy to be a part of the passion they have for sport and exercise psychology and to mentor them into our profession.

THEORY OF PERFORMANCE EXCELLENCE

My perspective regarding performance excellence is a traditional one in the sense that I regard performance excellence and peak performance as one in the same. To this end I have developed a framework for peak performance that I have titled "Inner Strength." I believe that such a framework has helped me operationalize my thoughts, beliefs and practices regarding the psychology of athletic performance.

Foundational Beliefs

Before describing and defining the components of the Inner Strength framework for peak performance, it is best to take a step back and review some of the guiding principles that serve as foundational beliefs for this framework. These principles are:

GOOD SCIENCE MAKES GOOD SENSE. Our challenge as applied sport psychology professionals is to present the principles of performance psychology to our clients in a way that resonates within them and in a way that makes sense to them. When consulting with clients, I frequently ask the question "Does that make sense to you?"

THE IMPORTANCE OF CRYSTAL CLEAR THINKING. In line with more traditional approaches to sport psychology, I believe that our thoughts are very powerful and influence the outcomes of our actions or behaviors—thought precedes action. I have come to learn that most, if not all of us, see things crystal clear once the performance is over. The most effective performers see things crystal clear and make effective performance decisions before performing and when they are in the middle of performing.

KEEP YOUR EYE ON THE BALL. Successful people think about and see what they want to have happen; unsuccessful people think about and see what they don't want to have happen. Distractions abound in the world of sport performance, but the key is to focus on what you would like to do and how you are going to do it. Furthermore, I develop the mental toughness of my clients by encouraging them to anticipate and prepare for effective responses to the obstacles, challenges, and distractions that accompany athletic performance.

FOCUS ON THE PROCESS OF SELF-IMPROVEMENT. Maintaining a clear and present focus by pursuing process goals is a trademark of effective athletic performers. In order to focus on the process of performing, athletes must attend to a challenge/mastery orientation that will motivate them to strive for self-improvement, self-fulfillment, and the pure enjoyment of athletic performance that result from meeting and mastering the challenges of athletic competition.

GIVE YOUR BEST EVERY DAY. I firmly believe that performance excellence is achieved through the consistent application of one's mental, emotional, physical and spiritual skills in challenging settings and situations.

BELIEF PRECEDES PERFORMANCE. Belief is at the core of an athlete's confidence. The quality of each athlete's performance is determined by their ability and commitment to believe in themselves, their preparation, their style, their strategies, techniques and skills, their coaches and teammates, and most of all, their ability to consistently be at their best in every performance situation.

RESILIENCY. I attempt to help athletes "walk through" the challenges of adversity. When reviewing past critical performances with clients I encourage them to take it one step at a time, talk about it, and review it in terms of what they will do next time in similar competitive situations.

ENERGY MANAGEMENT AND DISTRIBUTION. Based on ancient Greek philosophy, I believe there are four energy systems that athletes utilize to fuel their performances: physical, mental, emotional, and spiritual. The degree to which athletes are able to access and apply each of these energy systems in concert as they face performance challenges in large part determines their performance effectiveness.

QUALITY OF LIFE. In the course of my interactions with and observation of persons who wish to achieve personal excellence in their lives, I have found that happiness is at the core of quality of life issues. The healthy pursuit of personal and performance excellence is essential for achieving true success and happiness in sport, life and the workplace.

A Framework for Performance Excellence

It is important to note here that the peak performance framework (Figure 14.1) that I have termed *Inner Strength* took years of professional experience to develop, culminating in the publication of the 2003 text, *Inner Strength: The Mental Dynamics of Athletic Performance.* At the time of this publication, I had accumulated 36 years of teaching and consulting experience with coaches, athletes, parents and administrators from youth sport to Olympic and professional levels. This framework, or pyramid for peak performance, was reflective of a coming of age for me as a sport psychology professional and solidified a performance perspective of sport psychology that I had been formulating over the years.

CHARACTER, PASSION, AND ATTITUDE. The interactions of these three "intangibles" of peak performers are, to many performers, elusive at best. However, their mastery is integral to achieving true success in sport and life.

The pursuit of athletic excellence with integrity is a concept that forms the character base of the pyramid of peak performance. I once asked a very famous and successful coach what he thought was the one attribute that distinguished world class athletes; he stated without hesitation, "character." His answer rang true for me and I was sure it would for others as well. As a consultant, I strive to promote, develop, and encourage good sportsmanship as well as sound moral reasoning and ethical decision making skills and abilities of sport participants and leaders. As a sport psychology professional

Figure 14.1. Inner Strength.

I believe that fair play is the moral cornerstone of sport, and a prime dictate for all those who "play the game" to honor and respect their sport.

It takes great character to overcome adversity that accompanies athletic and life endeavors. There are many tests of personal integrity and honesty embedded in the athletic world of competition and performance. Other axioms regarding character that ring true are "adversity reveals character" and "character is defined by what we do when no one is looking." One of my foundational belief statements that I share with students and clients is "Winning is important, but it's not the only thing—character counts."

Passion is the enduring love of sport. From a motivational perspective it can be stated that when it comes to attaining athletic success, many athletes have the dream but no longer have the drive. While love of sport is a prime prerequisite for successful athletic participation, passion is what keeps athletes going in the face of challenge and adversity throughout the ebb and flow of their careers.

Athletic participation focused on achievement requires tremendous investments of passion and emotion. Passionate persons, particularly coaches and athletes, often deplete the emotional fuel they direct toward effective athletic performances as they experience the paradox of passion, that is, "the endeavor that excites you the most, exhausts you the most."

This paradox of passion often leads coaches and athletes to become overly passionate or obsessive regarding their athletic endeavors and careers. Overly passionate coaches and athletes sabotage their performances by overworking, overtraining, and burning out. There is a fine line between the passion and poison of athletic participation, training, and performance. As an educator and consultant it is my job to help clients realize the importance of leading a balanced lifestyle and engaging in daily self-care activities (e.g., proper nutrition, rest and recovery, environmental influences, quality training).

Attitude is the mind-set that an athlete adopts and implements in each and every practice and performance situation. Attitude is everything, and highly effective athletic performers bring their attitude to practice or the athletic arena—they don't just "show up" and then try to figure out what their attitude is going to be as situations arise during practice or competition. Having a "great" attitude about athletic performance requires a childlike perspective, that is, a return mentally to the time when an athlete participated in sport for fun, enjoyment, and pleasure. As children we all possessed the inherent abilities to succeed at sport; we had great imaginations, could focus seemingly forever on sport, and thought that we could take our chosen sport to the highest levels.

Over the years many athletes' attitudes regarding their sport and their performances can become jaded and worn. Oftentimes a renewed attitude of optimism and confidence is needed to provide the energy necessary to achieve and thrive in the athletic performance setting. Attitude can make or break an athlete, and in some cases, predetermine the level of athletic and personal success or failure. Attitude is the precursor of success; bringing a "great" attitude to practice and the competitive situations sets the tone for quality efforts in the athletic arena.

It is these three attributes of effective athletic performers—character, passion and attitude—which triangulate the physical, mental and spiritual skills necessary to achieve athletic excellence.

QUALITY PRACTICE. Sports are physical. Athletic performance is predicated on the ability of athletes to execute their physical skills on a consistent basis in challenging situations. I am mindful of the relationship of motor learning principles to athletic performance. Motor skill acquisition and performance are integral to athletic success and I firmly believe that we play like we practice. Furthermore, I have come to understand that learning, which we do in practice, is an invisible process—we really don't find out what athletes have learned in practice until they perform.

Simply "going through the motions" in daily practice sessions will not result in the effective execution of athletic skills or overall performance in athletic contests. In reality I have found that many athletes spend their time at practice perfecting their mistakes. In effect, they become tired and fatigued, practice their mistakes, and create bad habits. Coaches and athletes can design and engage in *quality* practice sessions that are both efficient and effective in facilitating motor skill acquisition, development and refinement. Quality practice allows athletes to build their confidence by providing mental and physical opportunities to master the conditioning, motor skills, and performance demands of their sport.

To ensure more effective performances and to strengthen the practice-performance connection and transition for athletes, here are four principles or elements of quality practice to consider:

1. **Practice with a purpose.** Focusing on self-improvement can link into the motivational process necessary to affect future performance outcomes. Essentially, athletes must ask themselves on a daily basis, "What can I do today in practice to make myself a better athlete, a better performer?" To this end I encourage athletes to set clear daily goals for practice and review them just prior to the practice session. This type of focus pre-

pares athletes to "be in the moment" during practice and during performances and is a learned attribute of effective athletic performers.

2. **The importance of feedback.** Feedback, or information about practice and performance outcomes, is a critical factor in determining the effectiveness of quality practice. Information sources sought by athletes regarding the process and product of their performances can come from both internal (self-regulation) and external (coaches, sport scientists, technology, etc.) sources.

3. **The importance of 'feedforward.'** While providing athletes with feedback that will help them evaluate and refine their physical skills, *feedforward* can mentally prepare athletes to maximize their practice and performance efforts. The use of various mental training and rehearsal techniques such as simulation training and visualization or mental imagery can complement and enrich physical practice and promote a performance mindset that can respond effectively to the emotional challenge of performing on demand in stressful situations.

4. **Quality rest.** Quality practice or training requires quality rest. Rest and recovery are essential to the development and realization of athletic talent. The sports world is littered with over-motivated, over-trained, under-recovered under-performers. Rest or restoration provides athletes with the opportunity to reenergize and rejuvenate themselves following demanding practice and performance efforts. Sleep, for example, is often overlooked as an integral part of a quality training program. Changes in sleep patterns due to jet lag, emotional stress, lifestyle demands, or injury, for example, can have a negative impact on athletic performance. Quality practice can be realized through the use of periodized training programs that provide a post-season recovery phase for athletes, as well as rest and recovery periods within seasonal training phases to meet the physical and emotional demands of training.

THE 4 CS OF HIGH-PERFORMANCE SPORT. I refer to the mental skills of concentration, confidence, composure and commitment as the 4 Cs of high-performance sport. Each of these skills is composed of various subsets of mental and emotional skills. Sport psychology professionals should be able to teach the mental skills that appear in Figure 14.2 to their clients and also provide follow-up assessment of the ability of clients to utilize these skills in performance settings and situations. Mastery of these skills will also aid in countering the effects of performance breakdowns that athletes may experience.

THEORY OF PERFORMANCE BREAKDOWNS

Performance breakdowns can be assessed and addressed in relation to the mental skill matrix that is presented in Figure 14.2. I have identified the prominent performance breakdowns related to the 4 Cs of high-performance sport that I have observed in work with performers in sport, life and in various professions (Figure 14.3). A perspective regarding each of these performance challenges or obstacles is presented throughout the remainder of this section. It should be noted that several performance breakdowns are related to more than one of the 4 Cs, as they are multifaceted in their implications for disrupting performance behaviors, process and outcome.

BELIEF. The majority of performance breakdowns for athletes are related to issues of confidence and belief. As stated earlier, I believe that belief precedes performance. Athletes must learn to make a conscious effort to voluntarily choose to exert their free will or to free up their willpower so that they

CONCENTRATION	CONFIDENCE	COMPOSURE	COMMITMENT
Mental routines	Belief	Relaxation training	Constructive evaluation
Mental toughness	Self-talk	Breathing	Patience
Concentration drills	Visualization	Emotional rehearsal	Lifestyle management
Attuning	Performance mindset	Arousal control	Courage
Distraction control	Attitude	Emotion management	Persistence and perseverance
Trust	Affirmations	Simulation training	Spirituality
Refocusing		Process orientation	Trust
Alertness		Stress management	Belief
Use and types of feedback		Social support	

Figure 14.2. Mental skills and the 4 Cs of high-performance sport.

CONCENTRATION	CONFIDENCE	COMPOSURE	COMMITMENT
Endwatching	Lacking Belief	Endwatching	Doubt
Distractions	Ego orientation	Shallow breathing	Impatience
Overthinking	Doubt	Poor emotion management and distribution	Lacking quality of life
Spill-over effects			Lacking belief
Doubt			Destructive evaluation
			Poor lifestyle management

Figure 14.3. **Performance breakdowns and the 4 Cs of high-performance sport.**

choose confidence, trust and ultimately belief over fear, doubt, worry, and hesitation. Self-doubt can creep into pre-performance thinking and derail the performance intentions of any athlete. I believe that the most important mental skills to use as performances approach are positive self talk (affirmations) and thought stoppage and replacement techniques. These two techniques basically help athletes to hit their mental and emotional reset buttons in order to restore themselves to a confident and trusting mindset; a mindset of belief. Other mental skills that are key to developing confidence and belief are positive visualization and adherence to goal setting and attainment strategies and techniques.

OVER THINKING. Athletes must learn to be mentally active and physically passive prior to performing, and physically active and mentally passive when performing. Thinking and performing at the same time doesn't work. Thinking and then performing does. Simplified thinking works best. The use of routines and cues help athletes organize and simplify their thinking prior to performing, thus creating a smooth transition between conscious thought and unconscious performance. Sport performance is physical and in the final analysis, "execution is the solution" to effective athletic performances.

TRUST. Automatic execution of sport skills is the difference between the practice mindset and the performance or trusting mindset that typifies high-performance athletes. The practice mindset is critical, analytical, and mechanical and lacks flow as athletes use feedback and instruction to think through the execution of sport skills. The performance mindset is character-ized by the letting go of conscious expectations regarding performance out-comes. "Trust as a mental performance skill involves freeing oneself of ex-pectations, fears, or other conscious activity and maintaining a clear and present focus necessary to attend to higher aspects of sports competition, such as cue utilization and strategy" (Moore & Stevenson, 1994, p. 3).

DISTRACTIONS. Effective athletic performance is not about focusing; it's all about an athlete's ability to re-focus. Athletes who learn to respond effec-tively to prominent distracters in their lives, particularly as competitive per-formances approach, have the best chance to maintain their focus and con-centration on the task at hand. A clear and present focus is often blurred by a fractured focus and wandering mind. Athletes can maintain, retain, and recapture their attentional focus through the use of mental toughness train-ing, attuning, and mental routines.

Anticipation and preparation are the keys to mental toughness, and ath-letes must mentally prepare to expect the unexpected. Mental toughness training simply encourages athletes to develop a mental, emotional, and physical contingency plan for performance settings and situations. Attuning or focusing strategies allow athletes to "get in sync" with the physical, men-tal and emotional components of an athletic performance as they become "game ready" to perform.

Mental routines, when blended with physical performance routines, aid the performer in maintaining their focus with a quiet, clear, confident mind. Each of these skills fall into the category of mental preparation, and most of-ten we find that athletes lack the mental preparation and skills to respond effectively in the face of the inherent distractions that are embedded in the athletic environment.

ENDWATCHING. Maintaining a clear and present focus, free from distractions, is a universal challenge for performers at all levels. Over the years I have found that focusing on performance outcomes rather than the performance process is often the greatest roadblock to achieving athletic and personal ex-cellence. I refer to this performance breakdown as endwatching. Recogniz-ing that their process is their product is an important first step in the proc-ess of adhering to a process. I have found that helping individuals focus on the process of effective performance, rather than the excess mental and emo-tional baggage that accompanies winning, works best for my clients. Being in the moment and focused on the task at hand provides a sense of control for performers. In essence, I work with athletes to identify the performance goals and behaviors that will lead to an effective performance.

SPILL-OVER EFFECTS. Without life skills training and education, real life challenges, problems and distractions can "spill over" into athletic performance. I believe that athletes are concerned and focused on intended greatness and then life gets in the way. Learning to respond effectively to both the predictability and unpredictability of lifestyle demands is a learned attribute of effective athletic performers.

EMOTION MANAGEMENT AND DISTRIBUTION. An athlete's management and distribution of their emotional resources and energy is essential for achieving performance excellences. Ken Ravizza puts it best when he states, "athletes must learn to be comfortable in uncomfortable situations." Emotional energy and the principle of use it or lose it go hand in hand in fueling effective performances. Composure is a learned attribute of highly effective athletic performers, and mental training techniques such as arousal control training, attuning, and relaxation training are essential to emotionally prepare athletes for competitive efforts.

I often remind athletes that their emotional challenge in sport is to play with emotion but not be emotional. Athletic performance is an edgy undertaking in terms of emotional involvement. Understanding and managing the passion and poison of athletic performance efforts enables athletes to play "on the edge" while delivering inspired performances. Lastly, the advice of Terry Orlick is well taken when it comes to emotion management prior to performance: "Make a conscious choice to choose positive emotion, but don't expect constant elation."

EGO-ORIENTATION AND CONSTRUCTIVE EVALUATION. Tender-minded athletes are ego driven and unable to utilize performance feedback, particularly constructive evaluation, effectively. Ego-centered athletes interpret performance results self-referentially. I often explain to athletes of this mindset that the feedback they are receiving from coaches, for example, is not about them as a person, it is about their performance. Performance feedback is all about error detection and correction and not about who you are as a person. In this way constructive evaluation becomes task oriented and ultimately ego enhancing rather than ego threatening. Gloria Balague says it best: "Sport is what you do, it is not who you are."

CONSULTING PROCESS

My consulting process is to: (1) identify and assess the performance issue(s); (2) provide education or a process of normalizing the athletes' thinking regarding their performance concerns (cognitive intervention); (3) provide mental training strategies for athletes to use that will help them manage the performance issues (education phase); (4) develop a performance plan (cognitive-behavioral intervention); and (5) to meet with the athlete after the performance (follow-up performance evaluation).

I have retained the low-tech approach to the practice of sport psychology that I was introduced to and practiced at the beginning of my career. The social skill of relationship building and maintenance is at the core of my consulting interactions with clients. It is my contention that communication and social skills are at the heart of effective consulting practices. For this reason, I would classify my consulting approach to working with clients as primarily one of conversational sport psychology.

There are three keys to the practice of conversational sport psychology: listen, listen, and listen. Effective consulting occurs when we gain an empathic understanding of how our clients view their world because this is their reality. Keeping it real is at the core of conversational sport psychology. Listening helps us to understand client issues and concerns; listening more helps us to understand the real issues our clients bring to us.

In order to have conversations with athletes, for example, regarding their performances, one needs to follow their performances and if at all possible, attend their practices and games, in addition to making presentations in team meetings or in private office consultations. Social support goes a long way in building credibility with clients, teams, coaches, and athletes. I avoid using athletes as research subjects, use psychometric testing and questionnaires sparingly, and treat the practitioner-client relationship as a sacred and special educational experience and opportunity for both parties.

My conversations with clients take place in a variety of places: in the gym, in the hallway, in the classroom, on the athletic field, at practice, in the training room, on the bus to an event, and, of course, in my office or in their office. Most of these conversations serve to build a social and "communication bridge" with my clients so they regard me as approachable and someone who cares about them and their world both on and off the athletic field. I have always believed that if someone catches you doing sport psychology you're really not very good at it. I believe that sport psychology consulting is a natural process approach phenomena and that is the approach I have chosen to take in my work.

The consulting process I favor is transformational in nature. The process is relationship based which serves to strengthen communication, trust, and self-awareness. It is directed toward helping clients identify and understand their own foundational core values regarding sport and encouraging them to take ownership of the value and values of their relationship with sport. I find that most athletes are in the driver's seat when it comes to their careers and performance; I encourage them to actually get behind the wheel and take control of their destiny. A quote I often use is, "great things don't happen by chance, they happen by design; so be the architect of your destiny."

One of the important aspects of successful consulting is accountability. It is not so much what we do with clients during our consulting sessions that counts; it is really about what our clients do between each session or time that we meet. For this reason, and to assess the commitment level of a client, I give them homework that we can review and evaluate when we do meet. This could be keeping a performance journal or diary, utilizing a daily planner, or reviewing goals that they set for practice sessions and games.

When working with clients I ask myself four questions: (1) "Who's the client?" (2) "What's the issue?" (3) "What's the real issue?" and (4) "How do I resolve or address the issue(s)?" (Vernacchia, 1998). Of these four key questions, "Who's the client?" has been the most challenging one to address and answer, primarily because of its ethical underpinnings and its political and economic ramifications. Just as there are the issues and the "real" issues to address in consulting so too are there clients and "real" clients. While we may be hired as consultants by a sport organization or team, it is the athletes who are our real clients. Sometimes walking the political tightrope regarding consulting issues such as confidentiality can have a direct effect on whether we are retained, or for that matter, even hired in the first place.

UNIQUE FEATURES

I was educated and trained as a teacher, and my education-related skills, namely communication and social skills, combined with professional competencies have formed the foundation of my consulting style. It is important to realize that there is not a right way or a wrong way to consult; there are different ways. As consultants we must find the way that works best for us—the way that is reflective of our personalities and our philosophy of consulting. The overarching theme for my career has been, "Work hard, play fair, and always give your best every day!" In addition my consulting theme has been, "Be professional, be honest, and be yourself!"

These themes help me focus and refocus on my role and function as a person and professional. At the most basic level I view my role and function as a sport psychology professional to know people and to know sport and help clients learn and master the physical, mental, emotional, and spiritual skills and behaviors that will meet their needs as sport participants.

Most performance consultants know the science and mechanics of mental skills training, and in my mind, the best or most effective consultants have learned and mastered the art of applied sport, exercise, and performance consulting. The artistic side of consulting is developed over time as consultants build a diverse experiential consulting background. In order to gain this experience, it becomes an educational necessity to give away our services particularly at the start of our careers. At least that is the way I learned to do sport psychology consulting. This is why sport psychology students serve internships under the supervision of a professional in the field of sport and exercise psychology.

I also believe that learning the art of any profession is facilitated and made possible by mentoring. Learning the "intangibles" of sport, exercise, and performance consulting is passed on to us by faculty advisors, teachers, coaches, colleagues, and ultimately by the clients that we serve. Throughout my career I have been fortunate to have great mentors, many of whom I have mentioned previously in this chapter.

The focal point of my consulting has been to instill confidence in the clients that I serve. In addition to providing clients with the basic confidence-building mental skills, I have endeavored to help athletes believe and trust in themselves, their talent and their preparation at all times, particularly as athletic performers.

CASE STUDY: Female Junior National Distance Runner

The following case study of composure and concentration typifies the approach I take toward performance consulting. While we would like to have a great deal of time to work with our clients, I have found that the reality of performance consulting provides us with very limited amounts of time. In many cases we are challenged to provide a "band-aid" approach to consulting as evidenced in the case study presented here.

INTRODUCTION. Janice was a very talented 17-year-old high school senior middle distance runner. She was a member of the USA World Track and Field Championships Team. I was traveling with this team and provided sport psychology services for the team. Janice asked to see me regarding her ability to concentrate during races. She was specifically having a difficult time coping with the pain and discomfort she was experiencing during the course of her races.

She felt she could have performed better in her recent races but the "period of fatigue" she anticipated and experienced before and during her races

(1) created self-doubt regarding the race outcome, and (2) affected her ability to maintain her racing pace and "stay in the race." She was attempting to qualify the next day for the world championships in the 3,000 meters, a distance she had not run competitively for the last four years. She had already qualified for the team in the 1,500 meters and therefore felt the upcoming race was a "no pressure" situation.

EDUCATION AND BEHAVIORAL PHASE. The evening before her qualifying race we spoke at length about her perceptions and feelings regarding her racing ability and effectiveness. She needed to recognize the fact that fatigue is an integral part of her sport and that she must understand the "ebb and flow" of athletic competition. She would need to accept the fact that she must endure the difficult and challenging aspects of athletic performance in order to achieve effective and consistent performances. I reassured her that this process was under her control and challenged her with the following statement: "Do you train to train or do you train to race?"

I encouraged her to trust in her preparation and had her talk about her accomplishments and athletic talents in an effort to reinforce her feelings of competency. It was important to help her identify her skills as a middle distance runner in order to help her positively reaffirm her athletic talents as well as to have her reflect on her past successful racing experiences. I suggested that Janice establish, in writing, a flexible race plan which incorporated

- the lap or pace times she needed to reach her overall qualifying time of 9:35;
- physical skills she could incorporate into her race plan to help her effectively deal with the discomfort/fatigue she would experience during the race (e.g., pumping her arms vigorously in order to regain her desired tempo); and
- cue words which triggered the use of specific racing strategies and physical skills (i.e., "tempo," relax and flow," "lift and sprint," "control"). These cue words were to be used during the actual race.

I asked Janice to review her race plan with her coach prior to the race.

PERFORMANCE PHASE. Janice achieved her goal (9:30) by running 9:28 the following day. She was very excited and felt in control throughout the entire race. She continued to work closely with her coach to implement strategies to ensure her performance effectiveness and went on to qualify for the 3,000 meter final at the world championships, improving her personal best to 9:25.

References and Recommended Readings

Balague, G. (1999). Understanding identity, value, and meaning when working with elite athletes. *The Sport Psychologist*, *13*, 89–98.

Bannister, R. (1955). *The four minute mile*. New York, NY: Dodd, Mead & Company.

Gordin, R., & Reardon, J. (1995). Achieving the zone: The study of flow in sport. In K. P. Henschen & W. F. Straub (Eds.), *Sport psychology: An analysis of athlete behavior* (3rd ed.) (pp. 223–230). Longmeadow, MA: Mouvement Publications.

Moore, W. E., & Stevenson, J. R. (1991). Understanding trust in the performance of complex automatic sport skills. *The Sport Psychologist*, *5*, 281–289.

Moore, W. E., & Stevenson, J. R. (1994). Training for trust in sport skills. *The Sport Psychologist*, *8*, 1–12.

Ogilvie, B. C., & Tutko, T. A. (1966). *Problem athletes and how to handle them*. London: Pelham.

Orlick, T. (1996). The wheel of excellence. *Journal of Performance Education*, *1*, 3–18.

Orlick, T. (1998). *Embracing your potential*. Champaign, IL: Human Kinetics.

Orlick, T. (2007). *In pursuit of excellence: How to win in sport and life through mental training* (4th ed.). Champaign, IL: Human Kinetics.

Orlick, T., & Partington, J. (1988). Mental links to excellence. *The Sport Psychologist*, *2*, 105–130.

Reardon, J. (1992). The three c's of success: Concentration, composure, confidence are the key. *American Athletics*, *4*(3), 48–50.

Reardon, J., & Gordin, R. (1992). Psychological skill development leading to a peak performance "flow state." *Track and Field Quarterly*, *92*(1), 22–25.

Syre, J., & Connolly, C. (1987). *Sporting body, sporting mind: An athlete's guide to mental training*. Englewood Cliffs, NJ: Prentice Hall.

Thompson, M. A., Vernacchia, R. A., & Moore, W. E. (Eds.) (1998). *Case studies in applied sport psychology: An educational approach*. Dubuque, IA: Kendall-Hunt.

Veit-Hartley, S. (2005). Spirituality and athletic excellence. In R. A. Vernacchia & T. A. Statler (Eds.), *The psychology of high-performance sport*. Mountain View, CA: Track and Field News.

Vernacchia, R. A. (1998). Use of the casebook in applied sport psychology. In M. A. Thompson, R. A. Vernacchia, & W. E. Moore (Eds.), *Case studies in applied sport psychology: An educational approach*. Dubuque, IA: Kendall-Hunt.

Vernacchia, R. A. (2003). *Inner strength: The mental dynamics of athletic performance*. Palo Alto, CA: Warde.

Vernacchia, R. A. (2005). Working with individual team sports: The psychology of track and field. In R. Lidor & K. P. Henschen, *The psychology of team sports* (pp. 235–263). Morgantown, WV: Fitness Information Technology.

Vernacchia, R. A., McGuire, R. T., & Cook, D. L. (1996). *Coaching mental excellence: It does matter whether you win or lose*. Portola Valley, CA: Warde.

15

Dr. Dave Yukelson

PENN STATE UNIVERSITY

Dr. Dave Yukelson is the director of sport psychology services for the Penn State University Athletic Department. In his 25th year at Penn State, Dave provides counseling and support to coaches and athletes in the areas of motivation and goal setting, mental training techniques for managing peak performance under pressure, leadership and team cohesion, stress management and interpersonal skill development, and issues pertaining to personal growth and development of student-athletes. Dr. Yukelson is a past-president and fellow in the Association of Applied Sport Psychology (AASP). He has published numerous articles in professional refereed journals, and is a frequent invited speaker at various national and international conferences. Dr. Yukelson has traveled internationally as team sport psychologist for USA Track and Field with various national and junior national teams. He also serves on the advisory board for USA Football, and is an associate consultant with Lane4 management group, a leading global high performance development company based in England with a unique heritage in elite sport and business performance. Dr. Yukelson obtained a BA degree in 1976 from the University of California at San Diego (social psychology); MS degree in 1979 from Florida State University (movement science with specialization in motor learning and sport psychology), and a PhD in 1982 from the University of North Texas (higher education with specialization in sport psychology). A native of Los Angeles, CA, Dave and his wife Marla have been married 37 years, and have three children: Adam, Joshua, and Drew. In addition to spending quality time with family and friends, his hobbies and interests include traveling, biking, relaxing at the beach, playing racquetball and golf.

AUTOBIOGRAPHICAL SKETCH

The past 25 years, I have served as the director of sport psychology services in the Morgan Academic Support Center for Student-Athletes at Penn State University where I provide counseling and mental training services for all 31 teams and support staff in the athletic department. Interested in performance excellence as it applies to sport and life, I work a lot with coaches, athletes, and teams on developing individualized strategies to enhance concentration, belief, consistency, and meaningful purpose. Life as a Division I coach or athlete brings with it multiple demands and pressures, emotional highs and lows, situational and interpersonal stressors that can undermine one's confidence, focus, demeanor, and/or persona. As such, I provide counseling and support in the areas of motivation and commitment, persistence and mental toughness, stress management and responsible decision making, mental skills training for managing peak performance under pressure, leadership and team cohesion, and intra/interpersonal skill development. In terms of the latter, I offer support and assistance to those individuals having difficulty balancing multiple demands and stress successfully, making the transition and adjustment from high school to college smoothly, navigating interpersonal relationships effectively, or coping with the trials and tribulations of being injured.

My interest in sport psychology began as a young baseball and basketball fan growing up in Los Angeles, California reflecting on questions such as why do certain athletes not perform well under pressure?; what was it about Walter Alston and John Wooden that made them such great coaches and leaders?; and why did those UCLA basketball dynasties have so much difficulty winning on the road in hostile gyms like the Pitt in Eugene, Oregon? The seeds were planted early on; I attended LA Valley College in 1971 and my first psychology course was taught by an instructor named Steve Saltzman, who introduced me to three instrumental books that to this day have influenced my counseling style: Abraham Maslow's *Toward a Psychology of*

Being (e.g., hierarchy of needs), Carl Rogers' *On Becoming a Person* (e.g., empathy and listening), and *Siddhartha* by Hermann Hesse (e.g., self-exploration and self-awareness). Interested in social psychology, I transferred to UC San Diego and did an honors project on social facilitation theory, investigating the influence of crowd size on the performance of professional basketball teams. After taking a year off from school and seeking the counsel of Tara Scanlon at UCLA, I decided to pursue my master's degree at Florida State University under the direction of Bob Singer in the Department of Movement Science. My educational interests at Florida State were deeply rooted in social psychological theory and cognitive motivational strategies (e.g., social learning, self-determination, information processing, group processes, self-efficacy, and attributions in sport). Seeking applied experiences, I introduced myself to head baseball coach Woody Woodward, who gave me an opportunity to work as a graduate assistant for two years with the nationally ranked Seminoles. Being "in the trenches" and learning what it is truly like to be part of a Division I intercollegiate athletic program proved to be an invaluable educational experience that to this day has had a profound influence on what I do now at Penn State.

I continued my graduate education at the University of North Texas, where I pursued a PhD under the direction of Bob Weinberg. My doctoral dissertation was on group cohesion in basketball teams and while studying at North Texas, I was influenced by professor emeritus Dr. Merle Bonney, who was an early pioneer in organizational psychology and taught me a lot about transformational leadership, interpersonal communication, and group processes. Upon graduation in 1982, I was hired as a visiting assistant professor at the University of Houston, where I taught graduate and undergraduate courses in the Department of Physical Education and worked with a variety of teams in the athletic department. Scrambling to find full time employment the following year, my eclectic experiences and training in sport psychology and exercise science served me well. I learned how to market my services to coaches, athletes, and athletic administrators, and through networking, became a department manager in a hospital based sports medicine center while continuing to teach courses and consult with teams at the University of Houston and Rice University. Five years later, a full time position opened up in the Penn State Athletic Department and the rest is history. In addition to my formal education in social psychology of sport and unique career path, I am indebted to the multitude of athletes and coaches I have been fortunate enough to be around and learn from, as well as professional mentors and colleagues such as Ken Ravizza, Bob Weinberg, Ralph Vernacchia, and Gloria Balague, who have influenced my philosophy and approach to the practice of sport and performance psychology and have been trusted confidants along the way.

THEORY OF PERFORMANCE EXCELLENCE

Only one more point needed for the Penn State Women's Volleyball Team to win an unprecedented fourth consecutive national championship in a row. The team suffered through growth pains at the beginning of the year. It was not easy replacing the productivity of three All-Americans from last year's championship team; nine new freshmen were learning the system, there were new roles to fill and the chemistry early on could be characterized as inconsistent at best. A stickler for accountability, quality practices, and attention to detail, Coach Rose demanded excellence and that the girls come to practice every day with the intent of getting better. The performance and synergy of the team improved over the course of conference play, and by the time the NCAA tournament came around, they were burning on all cylinders, playing with a collective confidence and determined focus every point and every game. It is match point; our freshmen middle blocker reads and reacts to a ball coming from across the net: block, kill, "Point Penn State." The match is over and pandemonium prevails, a jubilant celebration spills over to the court and somewhere in the middle of the mayhem are three seniors who won a national championship each of the four years they competed; they experienced a "Four Peat!"

To achieve consistent performance at the highest levels requires commitment, focus, belief, and perseverance. In my experiences, individuals and teams that are successful are driven by the desire to be successful. They commit themselves to excellence, work hard to improve their skills, believe in what they are trying to accomplish, and are passionate about what they do.

With that said, I believe performance excellence starts at the beginning of the year when a coach outlines the vision and goals an individual or team is striving to accomplish for the season and creates the training environment and team culture conducive to achieving these goals. From this, athletes internalize the day-to-day commitment, work ethic, accountability, and focus required to make that vision a reality. Penn State volleyball coach Russ Rose has won five national championships in his career and points to the importance of quality training and individual and mutual accountability when he states, "If you are going to build a championship team, it starts with commitment and work ethic, teammates holding each other accountable, pushing one another in practice every day to get better. It is a mindset that gets transmitted from seniors to freshmen; in order to be good you have to train like a champion." He goes on to say, "Practice prepares you for what you are going to deal with in games. As a coach, you have to set up drills that are physically challenging and emotionally demanding. It is that type of preparation that builds mental toughness and allows athletes to find a comfort zone and compete well under pressure." Whether the ultimate goal is playing for a national championship or competing for a spot on the travel team, the conditions that lead up to performance excellence start months in advance and are a culmination of motivation, preparation, quality training, and the focus and willpower to stay on track.

If I were to succinctly summarize what performance excellence looks like, I would say there is a certain rhythm, cadence, energy level, and connected focus that are unique to each individual and sport. Sustainability, consistency, trust, and composure are also important considerations. When I watch athletes perform well, their body language and competitive demeanor exudes confidence and true belief; they bring enthusiasm and positive emotional energy to their performance; they compete with a clear and free mind, totally focused and engaged in the moment, doing whatever it takes to get the job done. For instance, the shooting guard in basketball wants the ball with the game on the line, creates a little separation from the defender, confidently pulls up and swishes the game winning basket; the outside hitter in volleyball embraces the opportunity to close out a match, instinctively reads the defense across the net, explodes to the ball, point, match Penn State; the 4 × 400 meter anchor runner has that grit of determination and fire in her eye, her mind and body in perfect rhythm and harmony, and she wills her way into the home stretch securing another Big Ten Championship for the team. In each of the aforementioned scenarios, the athlete is self-aware and attuned to what they need from themselves in order to perform well; confident, energized, focused, composed, expecting the best, competing like a champion.

The literature is replete with citations addressing the efficacy of self-awareness, self-regulation, concentration, and resiliency in sport (Csikszentimihalyi, 1990; Jackson, Thomas, Marsh, & Smethurst, 2001; Jones, Hanton, & Connaughton, 2002; Nideffer, 1976; Orlick, 2008; Ravizza & Hanson, 1995; Vernacchia, 2003). Years ago, the late cognitive behavioral psychologist Michael Mahoney worked as an intern at the US Olympic Training Center and subsequently produced a collection of writings and tapes discussing the role of concentration, self-regulation, and attentional focusing in sport (referenced in Yukelson, 1989). According to Mahoney, to concentrate means to center, to become totally absorbed and connected with what one is doing, free from any irrelevant internal and external distractions, tuned in to only those cues most relevant to performing effectively at peak. Being in the moment and sustaining focus is a huge part of performance excellence. When an athlete is fully focused, he or she competes with a free mind, totally absorbed and immersed in the "doing," free of any worry, doubt, fear, or distracting thoughts. These features are consistent with the writings of Orlick (2008), who notes that best performances occur when athletes are totally connected or riveted to their performance, often to the point of performing on autopilot, letting their bodies lead without conscious interference.

From a practical perspective, two important considerations regarding concentration and attentional focus are teaching athletes what to focus on and how to sustain intensity of focus for the entire duration of an event. Former Penn State basketball coach Ed DeChellis constantly implores his players to bring focus, energy, and effort for 40 minutes each game. Focus is tied to preparation, game plans, role execution, and instinctive decision-making. Through scouting, film analysis, mental preparation, and quality practices, each player internalizes what his offensive and defensive responsibilities are for each game and visualizes appropriate responses (e.g., tenacious defense and rebounding, crisp cutting and passing, effective use of ball screens, confident shooting). In terms of sustaining concentration and focus, Coach DeChellis talks about valuing each possession, embracing the physicality of the game, being mentally and emotionally ready to do battle, bringing energy and enthusiasm to the court yet staying composed and in control. From a mental training standpoint, the key is for each athlete to know what their core confidence is all about, and to bring a connected focus and toughness into competition on a consistent basis.

Consequently, performance excellence really is a byproduct of motivation, positive emotional energy, belief, and focus. It starts with an athlete's motivation and work ethic, the internalized drive, desire, commitment, and willpower to improve and want to be better. Positive emotional energy is the arousal and adrenaline that fuels performance excellence. It is the passion and enthusiasm that percolates inside, it is the mojo (rhythm and cadence) that allows an athlete to trust and perform instinctively without conscious interference, and yes it needs to be channeled, monitored, and regulated throughout competition. Being confident and having steadfast belief in one's ability to persevere and stay focused is also an important consideration. Confidence comes in knowing you are prepared; training the mind to think confidently and adapt well under pressure is intimately linked to resiliency, perseverance, and mental toughness. Being able to sustain concentration, confidence, belief, and composure for the duration of competition is what mental toughness is all about.

I do believe there are differences between confidence and belief. Whereas confidence can fluctuate game to game and even moment to moment based on situational factors and opponents' ability, belief is a more enduring volitional mindset linked to a "can-do, will-do, never-give-up" attitude no matter what the situation. I have spoken with many athletes who go into a mental fog prior to major competitions who lack confidence and worry about what the opponent is going to do to them (e.g., pre-competition anxiety). I point out that "it is OK to be nervous but don't lose sight of the hours of preparation, the belief and faith in yourself to rise to the challenge and get the job done. As a result, focus on your game plan and those things within your immediate control (e.g., competing with intensity, effort, belief, and trust)."

There is one more component of performance excellence that has not been addressed: feeling good about oneself. Life as a Division I intercollegiate student-athlete (or coach) brings with it multiple demands, stressors, pressures, and distractions that if not managed properly can impact an individual's confidence, focus, and self-esteem. Trying to find and maintain balance academically, athletically, personally, and socially is not an easy undertaking, particularly if you are an 18-year-old student-athlete leaving behind familiar environments and having to adapt independently to the nuances of college life on your own. Consequently, I spend a lot of time counseling student-athletes on various stress management and interpersonal issues that impact their persona and self-confidence both in and out of sport. Whether it is team drama or an acute interpersonal situation that has spiraled out of control, they cannot allow the situation or stress to interfere with staying focused and performing effectively at practice or in a competition. Hence, I am there as a sounding board to help them navigate life's lessons, move forward, and make responsible decisions/choices for themselves.

THEORY OF PERFORMANCE BREAKDOWNS

At Penn State, I find the most common issues that prevent student-athletes from attaining performance excellence are self-imposed barriers that arise from fear, worry, and self-doubt. Intercollegiate athletes are high-achieving competitors. They come to college with high aspirations and dreams, work hard to improve, and are often perfectionists who expect nothing but the best from themselves. The same motive that drives them to be successful, competitiveness and the need to achieve, can also turn against them when they try too hard, become self-critical, or are overly concerned about letting coaches, teammates, or themselves down. Similarly, many athletes get caught up in the debilitating effects of "stinking thinking" prior to or during big competitions where their mind gets cluttered with worry and "what ifs" or consumed by the negative consequences of messing up. Sometimes they think too much, and other times they simply are not focused or thinking correctly where they become passive, cautious, hesitant, indecisive, and not trusting. Hence, interventions are geared toward empowering athletes with self-control strategies that facilitate positive thoughts, positive emotions, and confident actions.

Recognizing intercollegiate student-athletes have other needs and responsibilities, I can point to a number of other psychosocial issues that interfere with performance excellence. Team variables such as role uncertainty, poor leadership and internal team dysfunction, perception that the coach does not believe in the athlete, and egocentric selfishness as opposed to collective selflessness can all be a detriment to performance excellence. Similarly, off the field distractions such as relationship issues, excessive partying, lack of commitment to team norms, and poor discipline can be a problem, as are poor time management skills and failure to effectively navigate life's daily stressors. Some athletes get so caught up in the repercussions of winning and losing that they have difficulty adjusting to other aspects of their existence. To help them find balance, one of my favorite Yukelidian nuggets is "Athletics is what you do; it does not define who you are." When you walk onto the athletic field, give it everything you have, but once it's over, hit the switch and focus on what you need to do to transition to other aspects of your life.

CONSULTING PROCESS

At Penn State University, I am responsible for coordinating sport psychology services for over 800 student-athletes and 31 different athletic teams and coaching staff. I work closely with various athletic administrators, sport medicine doctors, athletic trainers, academic counselors, psychologists at the university health center, and a sports nutritionist. I have been at Penn State for 25 years so I have pretty much established my role within the athletic department and have a good working relationship with most of the coaches and teams (not all). In the beginning, I spent a lot of time building bridges, networking, getting to know coaches and athletes, and educating them on the types of services I provide. I spend a lot of time listening, observing, asking questions, and collaborating. With regard to gaining entry, I strive to find out as much as I can about the person I am dealing with and the psychosocial contexts that exist within each athlete, coach, and team.

Likewise, I try to attend as many practices as possible because it is important to be visible, available, and accessible. One of the advantages of full time employment in the athletic department is familiarity and history with each team. I understand the context and culture of each team, what the coaches' goals, expectations, and philosophies are, and the developmental growth cycles individuals and teams go through from freshmen through senior matriculation.

To me, the most satisfying aspect of my job is the quality of relationships that are established with coaches and athletes. Everyone has their own counseling style; personally, I strive to be authentic, caring, genuine, nonjudgmental, real (transparent), effective, and respectful. When counseling student-athletes, I adopt a holistic developmental approach based on individual needs and concerns. For instance, freshmen have their own adjustment issues they typically go through: being in a new environment, struggling to fit in, missing friends and family back home, academic overload, adjusting to new coaches, teammates, roommates, and the increased intensity of practices and athleticism at this level. Regardless of what year they are in school, athletes often complain about not having enough time for themselves; how difficult it is to find and maintain balance academically, athletically, personally and socially; wanting to develop meaningful relationships outside of sport but can't; morning practices and conditioning workouts; and the 12-month commitment to sport. Other common issues athletes talk with me about include stress and time management, maladaptive perfectionism, interpersonal relationships and communication issues, leadership and team issues, injury management and the frustration of numerous hours spent in rehab. The demands and pressures are relentless. The key is having someone to talk with, someone who understands their culture and will help them sort through perceived stressors and setbacks, someone who will be an advocate in helping them make responsible choices and decisions. Likewise, coaches need an outlet as well. Hence, I spend a lot of time talking with coaches about team issues, performance issues, team leadership issues, the mental side of coaching, and the stress of coaching. Oftentimes, I think the greatest service I provide coaches is simply being a trusted confidant and sounding board while helping them keep things in proper perspective.

In terms of the art of consulting, over the years collaborating with coaches, athletes, mentors, and fellow sport psychologists, I have developed a variety of "tools in the toolbox" to help individuals and teams become more attuned and aware of things that impact their concentration, confidence, consistency, and mindfulness while competing in sport. When I have a first meeting with an athlete to discuss their mental game, I often have them reflect on what it is like when performing with confidence. What does it feel like and what does it look like? Going a step further, I have them articulate what it means to be fully focused and totally absorbed in "doing the doing." Although a bit avant-garde, this type of questioning often evokes rich descriptive responses. As noted before, when an athlete or team is fully engaged in what they are doing, there is a certain rhythm, cadence, and persona transmitted that is unique to them and is characteristic of performance excellence. Likewise, it is important to know what it is like when they are stinking up the place and not performing well. What is the context of the situation like? What causes them to lose focus and perform tight? What are they thinking? What is happening internally and externally to not trust themselves? Usually, the responses revolve around pressing, trying too hard, over thinking/analyzing, being indecisive, self-critical, and a fear of messing up.

In preparing for competition, the athlete and I will then work on developing a mental plan that highlights their core confidence and the desired focus they want to carry with them into the competitive arena (e.g., mental, emotional, technical, and tactical readiness to perform). In terms of self-awareness, self-regulation, and composure skills, we develop a mental plan to "check in and move forward." Based on many conversations I have had with my good friend and colleague Ken Ravizza regarding the "Rs" (Ravizza & Hanson, 1995), "check in" refers to attuning to oneself and the environment the athlete competes in (e.g., What is happening inside? Where are you at? What needs to be done to click on the focus and get the job done?). "Move forward" means just that; get to the next point, play, sequence, period, and so on. If not performing well, it could also be a signal to let go and refocus, to keep believing, persisting, adapting, to stay connected with your performance and be mentally tough. At the intercollegiate level, this self-regulation technique has excellent application for student-athletes in and out of sport, for it helps them focus on things within their immediate control. On the field, it enhances confidence, consistency, composure and attentional focus; off the field it serves as an excellent stress management tool for handling multiple demands and interpersonal stressors effectively.

Similarly, in order to offset the potential debilitating effects of competitive anxiety, I often have athletes develop and visualize playing with confidence, toughness, and a fun competitive persona under pressure. One of my favorites is "Bringing the Nasty." This is not intended to be X-Rated or unsportsmanlike; rather, it is a symbol that connotes a confident, mentally tough athlete that loves to compete and embraces the situation at hand. Under pressure, many athletes succumb to thinking too much or worrying about messing up rather than seizing the moment, choosing to think confidently, and stepping up and having a peak performance when it matters most. For a tennis player, "bring the nasty" could be a last minute reminder affirming "serve tough, be aggressive, play today's match on my terms;" a closer in baseball "work the count, my nasty slider is going to make the hitter's knees buckle;" wrestler "keep looking to score, seven minutes of intensity;" gymnast preparing for floor routine "show time, let's get after it." I can't tell you how many athletes come up to me at practice or before competitions saying "Yuke, I am going to bring the nasty tonight." Some even use it before taking a test. I simply laugh at the enduring characteristic this simple metaphor has produced. It's an efficacy expectation affirming an "I can, I will, nothing is going to stop me today" kind of thing. Hence, the metaphor serves as a positive reminder to stay focused, have fun, and compete with a confident, trusting, playful attitude.

An important part of mental training is teaching athletes how to adapt skills and strategies to meet the demands of the competitive situation, particularly self-control and composure skills. Composure is a huge part of competitive athletics and is linked to emotional self-control and mental toughness. Athletes need to be attuned to situations that cause them to lose focus and develop appropriate coping strategies that will enable them to respond well under pressure. I worked with one of our tennis players for four years on concentration and composure skills. Early on, he had a tendency to get tight and cautious on big points. Highly self-critical and easily frustrated, he would have difficulty letting go of mistakes and the constant berating of himself affected his concentration and confidence. We worked on relaxation, routines, visualization, and focusing strategies to gain control over his emotions and self-talk under pressure. He developed energizing cues and focal points as a means to reframe stinking thinking into task-relevant actions (e.g., good rhythm and movement, quick to the ball, solid crisp shots, win the next point). Being one of the top players on the team, it was also important for him to have back-up plans in case he did not have his "A" game on a particular day. Recognizing the importance of making on-the-court adjustments and fighting through adversity, he notes that "when you are having a rough day and things are not going well during a match, you can't give in to negativity or emotional frustration; you need to stay focused, level headed and mentally tough to pull yourself through. That is where mental training really helped: believing, fighting, focusing, staying composed, getting to the next point/game."

Referring back to our Penn State volleyball team, early in the year following a hard fought loss, a very talented freshman burdened with enormous expectations sought my advice on how to sustain the intensity of her concentration without allowing negative self-defeating thoughts to enter her mind (e.g., "Why am I not . . . , I can't get my game together . . . , Uh oh, another shank"). We worked on challenging her fears and frustrations and had a good talk about embracing pressure rather than having to be perfect. Oftentimes, when an athlete's internal dialogue has gone awry and their perceptual stress filter gets clogged with negativity and stinking thinking, they get stuck in what I call "mental goo." Whether it is over thinking or worrying about the consequences of failing, athletes have to learn how to "clear the mechanism" so to speak in order to compete with a free and clear mind. Drawing on the work of Albert Ellis and the Louisiana BP oil disaster a few years ago, I often bring out a picture of a pelican whose wings are saturated in gooey oil; all it wants to do is fly and catch fish but can't because of the sticky goo. Athletes respond well to this metaphor and recognize they are the ones that control their thoughts and emotional reactions to the way they perform. With regard to the volleyball player, we first worked on strategies to become attuned and aware of situations that caused her to lose focus (check in), then specific interventions to let go and move forward. In particular, relaxation and breathing techniques to control the autonomic side of competitive anxiety (slow things down, get back into rhythm), routines and focal points to improve concentration (e.g., adjust kneepad, step into imaginary circle of excellence, ready, read, and react), and refocusing strategies to let go of frustration and keep the mind clear and focused (playful self-talk such as "oh, you shouldn't have done that" after getting blocked). She really responded well to the intervention and we came back to this template over the course of the season, particularly the area of attributions and playful self-talk, for it reminded her of the attitude and demeanor she used to carry with her when she was the "go to" player in high school and club ball after making a mistake: fearless, trusting, and unstoppable.

From a team perspective, coaches are very much interested in learning techniques to enhance team focus and team mental toughness. That is, the coaches want me to work on sustaining positive emotional energy and the intensity of their focus for an entire competitive contest. A technique I have used with success in basketball to accomplish this goal is something called "segmented focusing." Grounded in research from the areas of goal setting and performance profiling (Butler & Hardy, 1995), leadership and team building (Yukelson, 1997), visualization and goal planning (Murphy, 1996; Taylor, Pham, Rivkin, & Armor, 1998; Vealey & Greenleaf, 2010), and team mental toughness (Jones, 2010), the idea in basketball is to get athletes to harness the intensity of their focus in four-minute segments, with the goal to win as many segments as possible—ideally all 10 segments in the game. The concept brings together collaborative goal planning, internalization of game strategy, role execution and synergistic team functioning, energy and emotion management, concentration focusing skills, and composure skills for handling shifts in momentum.

UNIQUE FEATURES

There are unique factors that make consulting full time in an intercollegiate athletic environment different than other sport psychology positions. First, there is one of me and 31 teams to work with. The thought of that is overwhelming but through good organizational skills and ongoing communication, coaches and athletes know where and how to find me. During the summer and early fall, I touch base with coaches to find out what their needs and concerns are for the upcoming year. At one of the first team meetings of the year, coaches will bring me in to meet the freshmen, reintroduce my services (mental training, stress management, leadership and team functioning, interpersonal communication), review things that worked well last year and areas I can be of service this year. These team meetings are very important for establishing credibility, connecting with the athletes, opening lines of communication, and clarifying where my office is and how to get in contact. As things have evolved over the years, I currently stay in close contact with coaches and athletes via e-mail correspondence, text messaging, and social networking sites such as Facebook. Although good for communication, I will not counsel athletes using any of the aforementioned devices.

Issues that impact the delivery of services include fall/winter/spring overload (only so much of me to go around), dealing with various personalities (every team and coaching staff is different), dealing with multiple demands (sport psychologists have to find balance as well), standing my ground in a politically sensitive environment (sport psychologists should never compromise their own integrity and sometimes it is best not to work with a particular coach or team), and losing and its impact on coaches and team culture (losing oftentimes causes this sport psychologist to walk on egg shells).

When the opportunity presents itself, a unique feature about my job that has helped me gain acceptance and establish credibility with coaches and athletes is traveling with teams. I learn so much about team dynamics, team culture, individual personalities, and how people react in unfamiliar surroundings and different situations. Likewise, athletes and coaches learn a lot about the sport psychologist's ability to adapt interpersonally and bond with a team on the road, particularly in informal settings such as bus rides, team meals, or simply just hanging out. There is an art to fitting in and connecting with team personnel, being fluid and nonintrusive, finding the teachable moment to intervene when appropriate in a timely manner without overstepping unspoken boundaries. Similarly, there is something special about being there on the road with a team at competition venues, sharing and experiencing the emotional highs and lows together, bonding together as a family. Thus, being part of the travel party increases awareness and builds credibility, loyalty, acceptance, and trust for future interactions.

In summary, building effective relationships and earning the respect and trust of intercollegiate coaches and athletes is essential for me to do a good job. Being visible, accessible, approachable, and adaptable are keys to being successful in college settings, and so is consistency and perceived loyalty. If you can't fit in or are unable to intervene in a practical and timely manner, coaches will not ask you back and athletes will stop coming in.

CASE STUDY

Brad is a sixth year senior at Penn State (medical redshirt and NCAA exemption) on the wrestling team whose goal has always been to be an All-American and NCAA National Champion. Throughout his career, physical injuries and mental setbacks have held him back. A hard worker and person of great character and moral integrity, in major competitions, Brad has a tendency to get in his own way (e.g., tries too hard, thinks too much, narrowing of attentional focus and inflexible on mat decision making under pressure). In collaboration with the coaching staff, we worked extensively on goal setting and confidence building with corresponding action plans for achievement (physical, mental, technical, and tactical goals, performance and process goals such as increasing percentage of take downs per match, and techniques to improve finishing shots, riding opponents, and getting off bottom). We developed mental plans for training and competition that included relaxation and visualization techniques, pre-match preparatory routines, energizing cues and focusing strategies that enabled him to sustain the intensity of his concentration and mental toughness for the entire match or duration of a tournament. We also worked on coping imagery techniques in case things did not go the way he wanted during a match and he needed something to come back to in order to regain control.

Based on self-efficacy theory (Bandura, 1977) and performance profiling (Butler & Hardy, 1995), Brad and I would talk about what it takes to be a champion and reasons why he should be successful. There are a variety of factors that go into building an athlete's confidence, so I had Brad develop a belief wall with foundational bricks identifying what his core confidence is all about. Affirmations he came up with as to why he should be successful included his incredible work ethic and passion for wrestling, his love of competition and belief he is one of the top wrestlers in the country, he trains with one of the best coaching staffs in the country and gains confidence in knowing he is prepared. From this we would develop a script of excellence that would form the basis for his visualization. His script included his pre-performance routine and vivid energizing cues affirming the attitude and focus he wanted to carry with him onto the mat. In getting ready to wrestle, Brad would often enhance the vividness of his imagery by shadow wrestling (e.g., mentally rehearsing various moves while mimicking corresponding physical movements with his arms, hands, legs, and feet). He embraced the metaphor "Bring the Nasty," and it got him energized and into the right mental state of mind without having to think per se. He also liked the oil drenched pelican metaphor mentioned earlier and would often come up to me before a match and say "No goo tonight Yuke, I am bringing the nasty." Tactical cues he would use to get himself focused included "dominate from the get go, seven minutes of intensity, keep attacking and looking to score points, break him down physically, mentally, and emotionally to the point he will never want to wrestle me ever again."

Brad was very diligent and committed to the mental game. During the season, we would meet twice a week to discuss progress he was making with his mental skills training or simply chat about things going on in his life personally, socially, academically, or athletically. While on the road, we would stay in close contract via text messaging and cell phone conversations. Brad was very much attuned to what he needed from himself mentally and emotionally in order to perform well. Leading up to tournaments, our discussions typically centered on three mental training components: preparation, focus, and composure. Keeping things simple before a match, Brad wrestled best when he adopted a piss and vinegar attitude: wrestle hard, wrestle smart, get after it from the get go type of mentality. His focus was on dominating his opponent down, 420 seconds of intensity, and scoring as many points as possible. Composure was tied to adaptability and resolve, sustaining concentration, not allowing frustration to undermine his confidence or focus. "Check in and move forward" often became a center piece of our conversations, serving as a reminder for Brad to tune into what is happening internally, regulate and adjust energy and focus if needed, and keep working to score points. This thermostat analogy was effective for post-match attribution assessments as well; Brad was very good at drawing positive lessons from each competitive match and implementing appropriate adjustments in follow up matches. I firmly believe the time Brad put in working on visualization and coping imagery in particular was instrumental in helping him be composed and adjust under pressure. For instance, part of his script and visualization involved controlling the tempo of a match. If he found himself getting too quick or sloppy with technique, he implemented well-rehearsed refocusing plans to slow things down and "find his metronome" so to speak, regaining his tempo and focus. Similarly, Brad would have a tendency to shut down during a match and go into "brain lock" from time to time (e.g., mind gets locked into hitting one particular shot no matter what, afraid to make a mistake and wrestling not to lose). We worked on various mental rehearsal scenarios to broaden his attentional focus, work through lapses in concentration, increase aggressiveness, and be more creative with his decision making on the mat.

Brad has had to deal with a lot of adversity and setbacks in his intercollegiate athletic career. More than just a mental coach, I serve as a trusted confidant in helping Brad be resilient and keep things in proper perspective. His junior year at NCAA's, he lost to the number one seed in the tournament and in wrestle backs in a match that would have earned him All-American status lost a three point lead with less than a minute to go and was devastated. Determined to become an All-American, he started his senior year with vertigo, then tore his ACL and meniscus early in the season. Deciding to forgo surgery, he worked his way back into the line up to compete in the qualifying tournament for NCAA's. Limited in mobility but competing with heart and resolve, he came back the next morning from a devastating loss to tech fall an opponent and earn enough bonus points to help the team win a Big Ten Championship by one point. Everyone on the team was ecstatic and I was so proud of the way Brad handled himself. His mantra throughout his senior year was to keep believing and keep persisting; he did just that.

References

Bandura, A. (1977). Self-efficacy: Toward a unifying theory of behavioral change. *Psychological Review, 84*, 191–215.

Butler, R. J., & Hardy, L. (1992). The performance profile: Theory and application. *The Sport Psychologist, 6*, 253–264.

Csikszentimihalyi, M. (1990). *Flow: The psychology of optimal experience.* New York, NY: Harper and Row.

Jackson, S. A., Thomas, P. R., Marsh, H. W., & Smethurst, C. J. (2001). Relationships between flow, self-concept, psychological skills, and performance. *Journal of Applied Sport Psychology, 13*, 129–153.

Jones, G. (2010). *Thriving on pressure: Mental toughness for real leaders.* Westport, CT: Easton Studio Press.

Jones, G., Hanton, S., & Connaughton, D. (2002). What is this thing called mental toughness? An investigation of elite sport performers. *Journal of Applied Sport Psychology, 14,* 205–218.

Murphy, S. (1996). *The achievement zone.* New York, NY: G.P. Putnam

Nideffer, R. M. (1976). *The inner athlete.* New York, NY: Thomas Crowell.

Orlick, T. (2008). *In pursuit of excellence* (4th ed.). Champaign, IL: Human Kinetics.

Ravizza, K., & Hanson, T. (1995). *Heads up baseball: Playing the game one pitch at a time.* New York, NY: McGraw Hill.

Taylor, S. E., Pham, L. B., Rivkin, I. D., & Armor, D. A. (1998). Harnessing the imagination: Mental simulation, self-regulation, and coping. *American Psychologist, 53*(4), 429–439.

Vealey, R. S., & Greenleaf, C. A. (2010). Seeing is believing: Understanding and using imagery in sport. In Williams, J. (Ed.), *Applied sport psychology: Personal growth to peak performance* (4th ed.) (pp. 267–304).

Vernacchia, R. A. (2003). *Inner strength: The mental dynamics of athletic performance.* Palo Alto, CA: Warde.

Yukelson, D. (1997). Principles of effective team building interventions is sport: A direct services approach at Penn State University. *Journal of Applied Sport Psychology, 9,* 73–96.

Yukelson, D. (1989). Concentration: A key to performing effectively. *Sports Medicine Digest, 11*(3), 4.

Recommended Readings

Albaugh, G., & Bowker, M. (2006). Winning the battle within. Placerville, CA: Kele.

Collins, J. (2001). *Good to great: Why some companies make the leap . . . and others don't.* New York, NY: HarperCollins.

Coop, R. (1993). *Mind over golf: How to use your head to lower your score.* New York, NY: Wiley.

Dorfman, H. A., & Kuehl, K. *The mental game of baseball: A guide to peak performance* (2nd ed.). South Bend, IN: Diamond Connections.

Gallway, T. (1976). *Inner tennis: Playing the game.* New York, NY: Random House.

Hesse, H. (1981). *Siddhartha.* New York, NY: Bantam Books.

Krzyzewski, M. (2001). *Leading with the heart: Coach K's successful strategies for basketball, business, and life.* New York, NY: Warner Books, Inc.

Mack, G., & Casstevens, D. (2002). *Mind gym: An athlete's guide to inner excellence.* New York, NY: Contemporary Books.

Martens, R. (1975). *Social psychology and physical activity: Harper's series on scientific perspectives of physical education.* New York, NY: HarperCollins.

Martens, R. (2004). *Successful coaching.* Champaign, IL: Human Kinetics.

Maslow, A. (1998). *Toward a psychology of being* (3rd ed.). New York, NY: Wiley.

Nideffer, R. (1976). *The inner athlete: Mind plus muscle for winning.* New York, NY: Thomas Crowell Co.

Orlick, T. (2008). *In pursuit of excellence* (4th ed.). Champaign, IL: Human Kinetics.

Packer, B. (1999). *Why we win: Great American coaches offer their strategies for success in sports and life.* Chicago, IL: Masters.

Ravizza, K., & Hanson, T. (1995) *Heads up baseball.* New York, NY: McGraw-Hill.

Rogers, C. R. (1961). *On becoming a person: A therapist's view of psychotherapy.* London: Constable and Company.

Rotella, B. (1995). *Golf is not a game of perfect.* New York, NY: Simon & Schuster.

Vealey, R. S. (2005). *Coaching for the inner edge.* Champaign, IL: Human Kinetics.

Wooden, J. (2003). *They call me coach.* New York, NY: McGraw-Hill.

Afterword

Mark W. Aoyagi and Artur Poczwardowski

University of Denver

We offer this afterword as a chance to reflect on where we are at and what the future could be regarding the uniqueness as well as comprehensiveness and parsimony (Hall & Lindzey, 1957) of applied sport psychology theories. In sport and performance psychology, as a field, we have the privilege to distinguish our theoretical frameworks (i.e., building from the mainstream conceptual systems of personality used in psychotherapy) as especially well equipped to understand human behavior in performance settings. Aoyagi and Portenga (2010) defined performance as a "process of developing one's knowledge, skills, and abilities (KSAs) in a given performance domain and then recalling and demonstrating these KSAs during a discrete performance event" (p. 254). Further, performing KSAs depends, first, on the processes underlying their development and, second, processes allowing optimal expression of acquired and mastered KSAs. Consequently, personality theories and clinical systems form a foundation for understanding human behavior, but do not offer a comprehensive understanding of performance excellence capable of guiding practice in this endeavor. Even the best executed therapeutic approach attempting to remove the problems and barriers "does not directly improve people's ability to perform a desired skill, as it does not increase their KSAs in their performance domain" (p. 254). We think that the collective potential of the theories offered in the present book to fill the need for performance-specific frameworks (although, upon our editorial request, focusing on the athletic performance domain) is unquestionably promising.

We hope that the wealth and diversity of theories of performance excellence that the chapter authors managed to convey have been thought provoking. As one expects from theories, not only have the authors described the dynamics of performance excellence and performance breakdowns, but also explained the underlying mechanisms, which allows for predicting and modifying performance behavior. The 5 Rs, high performance blueprint, elements of Prime Performance, psychological mastery/performance loop, excelling in the Olympic environment, offensive and defensive mental skills, the HEART of athletic motivation, suCCCCCess, humanistic/whole person approach, sense of self, Wheel of Excellence, authentic identity, Inner Strength, characteristics of excellence, and bringing the nasty (to point out exemplary concepts from each chapter): The collective comprehensiveness of the presented theories seems to address the most frequently reported developmental and remedial performance issues. The authors' attempts to prioritize the performance behavior constructs to parsimoniously present their theories were evident through clearly outlined models, often accompanied by graphical representations. Linked to these explanations were the accounts of their unique consulting styles applied to the underlying theory of performance, which all culminated in illustrative case presentations. Finally, we as readers could trace the evolution of their theoretical frameworks and consulting styles back to their biographical facts. Together, the current content illustrates the science and art components of applied work as well as clearly points out the importance of the "you" (the consultant as the instrument of the sport psychology service delivery) in our profession (Poczwardowski, Sherman, & Henschen, 1998).

One might ask, "Where do we go from here?" It seems that perhaps at some point in the near future our field will be able to offer a few well delineated, comprehensive, and parsimonious theories of performance behavior that can be operationalized into testable hypotheses. This diversification in theoretical approaches to understanding humans in performance settings is needed for the maturation process of our field. We would hope that the theories presented in this book will inspire empirical research and additional practical insights validating the ecologically sound principles as presented by all the authors. Evidence-based practice is grounded in laboratory and applied studies and experiments as well as additionally informed by case studies and other practice-focused reports, and has been recently proclaimed as the current moment in the field of psychology and consulting (Brown, Pryzwansky, & Schulte, 2011). Importantly, evidence-based practice seems to be the necessary path for both distinguishing and advancing our field of sport and performance psychology.

We believe that the presented theories will add to advanced, applied courses in sport and performance psychology by providing clearly formulated guidelines for building the theoretical paradigm level in one's professional philosophy (Poczwardowski, Sherman, & Ravizza, 2004). This text can be considered as supplemental material to established and newly published textbooks on sport psychology theory and research as well as add to reading materials accompanying applied sport psychology courses. Instructors could capitalize on the widely accepted notion that sport psychology is science and art (e.g., Hays, 2009) and intellectually explore the chapters from this book as interesting illustrations of both, while simultaneously being enriched with personal background and unique professional style. Additionally, independent professionals might find some of the content inspiring in their own purposeful attempts to identify, refine, or enhance their own theoretical orientation to performance excellence.

Importantly, as a field we need new conceptualizations and further clarifications of the evolving theories with the necessary empirical and applied validation efforts. We as editors have been inspired to conceptualize a subsequent volume that would focus on yet another theory of human behavior in performance settings. While we hope that our readers will contribute to this collective task, we, too, plan on bringing together several emerging themes that underlie the ideas presented in this book into an overarching theory with an evident potential to describe, explain, predict, and modify human performance behavior.

References

Aoyagi, M. W., & Portenga, S. (2010). The role of positive ethics and virtues in the context of sport and performance psychology service delivery. *Professional Psychology: Research and Practice, 41*, 253–259.

Brown, D., Pryzwansky, W. B., & Schulte, A. C. (2011). *Psychological consultation and collaboration. Introduction to theory and practice* (7th ed.). Boston, MA: Pearson Education.

Hall, C. S., & Lindzey, G. (1957). *Theories of personality.* New York, NY: John Wiley & Sons.

Hays, K. F. (Ed.) (2009). *Performance psychology in action.* Washington, DC: American Psychological Association.

Poczwardowski, A., Sherman, C. P., & Henschen, K. P. (1998). A sport psychology service delivery heuristic: Building on theory and practice. *The Sport Psychologist, 12*, 191–207.

Poczwardowski, A., Sherman, C. P., & Ravizza, K. (2004). Professional philosophy in the sport psychology service delivery: Building on theory and practice. *The Sport Psychologist, 18*, 445–463.

Index

About the Editors

 Mark Aoyagi, PhD, is director of sport & performance psychology and an assistant professor at the University of Denver. Mark earned a PhD in counseling psychology with an emphasis in sport psychology from the University of Missouri in 2006 and was the sport psychology post doctoral fellow at the University of Southern California. Prior to that, he completed a bachelor's in exercise and sport science and a bachelor's in psychology from the University of Utah in 1999 and a master's in kinesiology, with a sport psychology emphasis, from Georgia Southern University in 2001. Mark is a recognized sport psychology consultant and has worked with several Division I athletic departments as well as professional and Olympic athletes. He is a licensed psychologist in the state of Colorado, a certified consultant, AASP (Association of Applied Sport Psychology) and is listed in the USOC Sport Psychology Registry. His areas of expertise include performance excellence, team effectiveness, and sport as a mechanism for personal growth and social change. Mark is active in several professional organizations including the American Psychological Association and the Association for Applied Sport Psychology; and has publications and national conference presentations on the topics of theory informing practice, team effectiveness, ethics, and training and supervision among others.

 Artur Poczwardowski, PhD, is an associate professor at the University of Denver. Artur received his PhD in exercise and sport science with specialization in psychosocial aspects of sport from the University of Utah, Salt Lake City in 1997, a master's in psychology from Gdansk University, Poland in 1991, and a master's in coaching and physical education from the University of Physical Education in Gdansk, Poland in 1989. Since 1991, Artur has consulted with athletes and teams from numerous sports (e.g., tennis, golf, hockey, judo, squash, team handball, soccer, track and field, diving, rowing, speed skating). He is a certified consultant, AASP (Association of Applied Sport Psychology) and is listed in the USOC Sport Psychology Registry. Artur has over 25 publications (in professional journals and as book chapters). He has delivered over 60

professional presentations on national and international levels and over 25 invited and educational lectures and workshops. His publications and professional presentations focus on sport psychology practice for performance enhancement and psychological well-being, coach-athlete relationships, and coping strategies in elite performers. He served as an associate editor for *The Sport Psychologist* (2004–2006) and currently serves on its editorial board. Artur and his wife, Kasia, live in Denver with their two children.